Contents

iv   *Contents*

Introduction

The area of special needs in education has changed fundamentally over the last decade and at the same time profound changes have been occurring in society. The view taken in this book is that neither children's problems nor teachers' responses to those problems can be isolated from these changes. Special needs has traditionally taken a segregated, isolated place in education. The approaches adopted to identify and treat special needs reinforced this position. But old approaches are being superseded by fresh perspectives on the difficulties children experience; existing practice is being examined and sometimes displaced by practices appropriate to the changes overtaking society. A set of new ideas is emerging and it is appropriate now that new thoughts are brought together and united by a theme.

This book marshals a range of methods for viewing children's needs in context. The aim throughout is to enable the reader to take a radically different view of need – one which sees need emerging out of situations rather than out of deficiencies in children. The ecological perspective under which these approaches are subsumed is attractive for a number of reasons: it is practical and recognises that the problems teachers often raise when faced with integration are real; it recognises the importance of the interaction between individuals and the contexts in which they operate, and it provides a meeting point for a number of approaches which have previously differed fundamentally on methodology.

With the move to take children who are experiencing difficulty from special schools and integrate them into ordinary schools it is becoming increasingly clear that the approach centred on the individual child, which has dominated our response to these children, is inappropriate. When presented with complex remedial programmes to be undertaken with a child who is experiencing difficulties in the mainstream, teachers are – justifiably – asking, 'What do I do with the other thirty?'. There is widespread awareness of this problem among teachers, educational psychologists and others concerned with special needs in education. Yet few attempts have been made to address the problem, perhaps because the alternatives to individual intervention take professionals into areas where they feel untrained and unconfident.

Part I of this book, *An ecological view* examines the context in which special needs are defined, at classroom, school and wider levels and suggests some strategies for effecting change in these contexts. Part II *The whole school* continues with some considerations for the planning for special needs and the development of the curriculum throughout the school. Part III, *The classroom* proceeds by examining the ways in which individual teachers may help to prevent children becoming 'special' through considering the involvement of 'special' personnel, grouping, the use of specialised teaching methods, the organisation of resources and the involvement of parents.

At no stage have we tried to steer to a 'party line' on the approaches we have brought together here. We have not taken a 'behavioural' or 'systems' stance or even a broader 'psychological' or 'sociological' perspective. In this sense it may be said that we have been eclectic. However, we hope that our selection of material has been rather more than eclectic. At its worst, 'eclectic' has come to mean a muddled rag-bag of techniques and methodologies which are employed simply because they work, with no consideration of *why* they work or of the wider ethical or moral issues raised in using them. Rather, our theme is that, as Bronfenbrenner (1979) has pointed out, children live in a variety of contexts, each one impinging upon the other. Any attempt to over-simplify the richness of the ways in which these contexts interplay is bound to have shortcomings. Bronfenbrenner proposed a complex 'ecological' model for helping to understand this diversity. It is this model which which has provided guidance for the way in which this volume has been organised.

References

Bronfenbrenner, U. (1979) *The Ecology of Human Development* Cambridge, Mass: Harvard University Press.

PART I
An ecological view:
the importance of context

Introduction

Major changes in special education are forcing a reappraisal of the methods and techniques with which we have become familiar. Increasingly, it is being realised that as integration proceeds, the focus of special eduation will have to shift: now more than ever we shall have to take account of the contexts within which children learn and behave.

The opening chapter of this first section argues that many of the traditions which have developed in the special sector have been unhelpful. Often they ignore the reality of school life and life in the 'outside world'. We trace the roots of the revolution in thinking about special needs and argue for a new perspective and different approaches which take account of these realities.

The second chapter looks at traditional assessment, with its emphasis on individual failure, taking it as an example of the traditions which have dominated special education. Assessment in its conventional form generates limiting expectations for identified children; by creating ability strata it encourages streaming, and even segregation. It is suggested that entirely different kinds of assessment are now needed.

Many of our recommendations depend on changes in the structures and routines of the school, so in her chapter Jane Weightman continues by offering a guide to working with the school as an organisation, advocating the use of clear goals and the development of a network of contacts to help achieve change. Geoff Trickey and Gordon Stobart continue the theme that change can be made to happen, by promoting the idea that teachers, far from being the passive recipients of educational policy, can actively effect change from the bottom up as participant researchers.

Our theme is the importance of context. Our aim in this section is to offer guidance on ways in which such context can be brought to the fore in explorations aimed at finding better ways of educating children who are experiencing difficulty.

1 Special needs: past, present and future

Anthony Feiler and Gary Thomas

Given the significance we are assigning to context, it would be inconsistent if our first chapter did not start with an attempt to understand the place of special education in the various contexts in which it has developed, and will develop. This chapter has three sections: the first looks at the nature of the new society into which today's schoolchildren will be moving, and contrasts this with the fundamentally different society in which special education was conceived; the second section examines the range of approaches which have emerged in the area over the last quarter of a century and traces a theme through them; the third section suggests some reasons for the fact that special needs often seems to turn into blind alleys and suggests an alternative way of proceeding.

Special education – geared for the future or stuck in the past?

SCHOOLS, CLASSROOMS AND SPECIAL NEEDS IN A CHANGING SOCIETY

In introducing the term 'post-industrial society' to the language, Daniel Bell furnished education with the kind of cliché of which it is so fond. The term became for many in education an excuse for doing nothing about the metamorphosis in society. It implied that the changes that were occurring were due to the remote, arcane workings of industry, and that the causes of change were the responsibility of people 'out there' – politicians, industrialists.

If this is the case, if teachers and others in education have insufficiently addressed deeper questions about the changing world into which schoolchildren are moving, it is not entirely their fault. There are enormous constraints on the ability of teachers to be creative or innovative in seeking solutions to the problems that confront the children in their charge. Politicians, the media and the public have clear expectations, often based on experiences of the society in which they were brought up rather than the one into which today's children will be moving; schools are underfunded and planning often appears to be piecemeal or politically opportunitistic. In such a climate – of coping and surviving – it is difficult to formulate projections for the next weeks and months, let alone the next 10 or 20 years.

Yet these constraints are not the only reasons for education's myopia. Education often appears to outsiders to be rather insular, satisfied with its own analyses and resentful of intrusion. Even if it were claimed that such a view is misconceived about general education, the same could not be claimed about that portion of education described as 'special'. Here, consideration of wider issues has so often been predicted on consideration of individual problems. This can no longer continue: with the determined efforts to improve in *ordinary* schools the education of low-achieving and disabled children, and with all the accompanying changes in expectation of these young people, comes a realisation that a range of hitherto neglected topics will need to be addressed.

With all this in mind we devote the next few pages to some views on the new world into which pupils of today are moving. Only a few observers appear to have had the prescience to predict an alternative to the depressing post-industrial landscape which is so often painted; here, we try to share their analysis and vision.

Economists such as Schumacher (1973), sociologists such as Touraine (1971) and futurologists such as Alvin Toffler (1980, 1985) have noted that the structure which underpins society is breaking down. They have observed the process whereby the units which comprise society are progressively becoming smaller. Schumacher's catch-phrase 'small is beautiful' has given the prelude to Toffler's sophisticated analysis of the breakdown of modern society. Toffler has spoken about the coming of a 'third wave' society in which the functions which were previously organised by large corporations and bureaucracies are becoming fragmented. Technology is rendering obsolete the economies of scale. Society is becoming more individual as technology confers upon its members the ability to communicate in ever more sophisticated ways. Working in smaller units, people will be more manoevrable, more sensitive, more adaptable in the face of rapid change. Increasingly, the qualities people will require in such a new society will be inventiveness, adaptability, creativity – in contrast to a narrow range of basic skills. There is a broad consensus about the nature of such changes: Clutterbuck and Hill (1981) in *The Remaking of Work*, Macrae (1984) in *2024 Report* and Handy (1984) in *The Future of Work* all predict a similar scenario.

Change, with its uncertainties and tensions, is accompanied by casualties. It is important, therefore, that special education, as the area of education that has traditionally dealt with the casualties of the mainstream, is absolutely clear about the nature of the new change. More importantly, though, this new change brings *opportunities* for education and special education. Recognition and understanding of its nature and of its context is essential for a sensitively articulated response. Let us look rather more closely at the dissolution of the systems which have until now characterised our society, and at the nature of the accelerating changes which are bring about that dissolution.

The coherence of industrial society has depended, over the last hundred years or so, on its success at bringing people together in large groups and then efficiently organising them. Organisational systems such as bureaucracy emerged to support this industrial edifice. As Illich (1973) has shown, school became an instrument in this process, catering for society's needs by efficiently corralling fairly large groups of children and training them in the behaviours and basic skills deemed necessary by society. In this position, school has adopted the prevailing organisational forms of society – such as bureaucracy – which are so limiting to creativity and personal autonomy. It is those very structures which hinder the efficacy of school as an educational instrument. Yet ironically it is neither attitudinal change nor political sensitivity which is bringing about the disestablishment of these structures in society and schools, but technology. To paraphrase Galbraith (1974): the enemy of the school is not ideology but the engineer.

The fact that these changes are occurring does not mean that they are perceived with sensitivity by society. And school, which is given its legitimation by society, is seen by the public in a time of rapid change not as an instrument for enabling and facilitating the new change but rather as a means for diminishing its undesirable side-effects: unemployment, alienation, anomie. There is the danger that, rather than making the best of the new changes, education might be seen to be continually following one or two steps behind them, engaging in a ritual dance with society, merely moving in the steps with which it and society are familiar.

The response school has to make to these changes will not be easy: the procedures, traditions, and architecture of today's schools still reflect the values of their nineteenth-century progenitors. Schools exist as authority-centred institutions in which structures are firmly established. They were relevant to the needs of an industrial society in which compliance and competence in the basic skills of literacy and numeracy were essential. Not only are such skills and such compliance now unnecessary; fostering them at the expense of more important goals will form a barrier to growth in a post-industrial society.

The changes about which Toffler and others have written demand a reappraisal of the structure of education and the ability of the education system appropriately to educate all of our children. Many of the processes which mark a reflection of the new change in society and schools also enable a radical reappraisal of the way in which children's problems within schools have been dealt with.

Increasing sophistication in information transfer, increasing appropriation by machines of sometimes highly skilled 'people functions' is accompanied by conspicuous disjunctions in society. But, as Buckminster Fuller (1970) saw, technological advance is making for a society which will be characterised eventually not by greater centralisation and greater similitude, but rather by increased personal autonomy and increased pluralism. Beyond the immediate symptoms of change (unemployment, unrest) Toffler also sees the possibility of a renaissance: a society in which the possibility of individualism and collective responsibility occurring simultaneously comes nearer.

As this process of loosening and reformulation occurs in society, how will its translation be felt in schools? Changes are already to be noted. In many schools there is a loosening of professional boundaries – parents are being invited into school to work with small groups of children. The natural base for work is not necessarily seen as the classroom; small groups of children work with parents in different areas – perhaps in the hall, perhaps in the corridors. The curriculum is less often seen as a set of strictly delineated subject areas. Formal class groupings are less common; dividing lines between professionals and non-professionals, between one subject area and another, between the pastoral and the academic sides of school life are more blurred.

So, paradoxically, the breakdown which characterises modern society perhaps enables many of the child-centred ideals which have been evolving since Rousseau, Montessori and Froebel to be realised. These have until now been conspicuously dissonant with the needs of an industrial, corporate society. But such child-centred ideals will increasingly be seen as consonant with the needs of a new society. The recognition by society of the fact that it will depend for its success more on individualism, creativity, cooperation of people in small groups and the ability of its members to communicate, than on the compliance and 'basic skills' of its members, should herald a new epoch in education. Toffler's analysis indicates that schools for a successful new society will have to become disestablished as many of the institutions, corporations and bureaucracies which have characterised our society for the last hundred years break down. If this is so, it may be a unique opportunity for reforming the practices of schooling.

Further disestablishment of society will be accompanied by an acceleration of such changes as previously clear-cut distinctions become less sharp. It is through renegotiations between the various participants in school life – teachers, children, parents – that the aims of a child-centred education might be realised. *Only* when the processes and institutions which surround education are seen to be working towards the fulfilment of child-centred aims will special needs truly have been met. Special needs at present exist because children do not fit into the tight structures which are currently found in schools. Positive discrimination for 'special' children, created with the best will in the world, only serves to shore up that system. The needs of special children are predicated on the needs of the larger system.

THE SPECIAL PLACE FOR SPECIAL EDUCATION NOW

Those of us working in education should surely aim to ease the passage of the positive benefits to be had in a new society. That section of education which has been given various labels over the years, but which has frequently had the prefix 'special', has a particular part to play. This is so for two reasons.

First, special education has often been associated with basic skills and it is these very skills which are at the front of society's demands on education. With its experience of teaching such 'basics' and with the evidence which can be adduced in favour of the need for motivation, encouragement and involvement, special education has a wealth of evidence to bring in rejecting the call for the traditional accompaniments to such basic education in the shape of discipline and formal work. The notion of basics is interesting to question and a couple of vignettes of current practice help in that questioning: first, recent studies of paired reading indicate that phenomenal progress in one of 'the basics' can be made in a short space of time if children simply are helped by their parents – complex instructional programmes provided in school are nowhere near as effective as such parental help; second, work by Paulo Freire (1972) in Latin America has shown that illiterate peasants can, with motivation, be taught basic competence in literacy over a period as short as six weeks. Perhaps what takes eleven years of compulsory education without motivation can be achieved in six weeks with motivation. The knowledge that basic skills can be taught with such facility, given certain fundamental and structural changes in the way that we conceive of education, must encourage us to look to alternative structures.

Second, special education, by the very nature of the problems it confronts, seeks imaginative and innovative responses and solutions. It is therefore frequently (but not always, see p 17) found in the vanguard of innovation and structural change. Paired reading experiments may again be used as examples of this kind of innovation. Another example is found in moves to whole-school approaches (eg Thomas and Jackson, 1986; see also Sewell's chapter in this volume, p 122 where remedial teachers have sought to break down the segregation that occurs in ordinary schools, by removing the divisive structures (pastoral/academic; remedial/mainstream) which exists in schools.

In its unique position, special education has a responsibility coherently to identify the real nature of the changes that are occurring and to develop ways of responding which will benefit *all* children. All children will be the responsibility of the staff previously designated as being in charge of special children as our view of what constitutes 'special' changes. The notion that a particular set of children are special, with identification and assessment procedures crystallising and fixing problems in this set of children, has created the 'static classroom'.

THE STATIC CLASSROOM

A number of forces limit the ability of teachers to move away from the static classroom. Those taking the initiative in attempts to make a more effective response to children's difficulties find that they face a number of constraints: as already noted, the public has traditional expectations of school from which it is difficult to break away. Schools are constrained by their architecture; the space within the classroom walls is still seen as the 'natural' place for children to work productively. Some teachers in secondary schools cling on to subject boundaries and find it difficult to move towards a process-centred curriculum; they are constrained by the existing classroom arrangements and by attitudes and expectations about the way in which children ought to behave in class; and they are constrained by a fibrous mass of assessment procedures which serve to reinforce existing ways of working.

Such factors repeatedly foster the impression that problems in school must occur as a result of a child's deficiencies. As long as the perceived locus of the problem remains distant from the child's interaction with the system within which he or she operates, very little is done to alter the situation for the child.

There are two constraints which are central to the difficulties which children often experience at school: segregation and assessment; and the sanctity of the teacher's territory in the classroom. Looking first at segregation and assessment, it is important to recognise that our views of the special problems which children experience in classrooms are constructed on a set of premises. Our current concern may be liberal and child centred; yet our thought is often bound by the organisational and physical parameters set for us by our predecessors. The idea that some children have special problems and therefore should be segregated—for their own benefit and for the benefit of others—is rooted in eugenics (the idea that human stock could be improved through selective breeding), in psychometrics, and in particular in the work of Cyril Burt. The notions that intelligence and attainment could be specifically measured and that there were certain levels of ability or potentials beyond which children could not progress gave us today's framework of segregated special education. Indeed, it was not so long ago that *all* children underwent selection for segregation at eleven. Although the layering of the education system is diminishing, and the picture appears to be steadily changing to a mixed ability system, the hidden agenda is still that of segregation. The process is nowhere more clearly seen than in the special needs area, where there has recently been only the most gradual breakdown of segregation. Even where children's special problems are catered for in the mainstream, the practices which have been at the backbone of provision for these children (such as withdrawal) mean that segregation still exists – but in a disguised form – on the mainstream school premises. Only in a few schools is segregation now disappearing entirely with remedial departments providing teaching support to teachers in the main body of the school and with mixed ability teaching throughout the school.

Although formal segregation is disappearing, the legacy of the psychometrics movement to education is a vast array of educational and psychological tests which purport to place children in scales of ability. Such tests reinforce the static classroom for a number of reasons:

a they give the idea that children can be effectively compared, thereby constructing, however informally, a hierarchy of ability in the class;

b they give rise to the idea that special problems are fixed in a certain set of children, and that it is therefore always those children who are going to have problems (in fact, a child who may have difficulty with one topic at one time may have no difficulty with another topic at another time);

c with their apparent 'scientificness' the tests have acquired a formal status in official procedures; teachers have lost confidence in their ability to make their own informal assessments of the way in which children are coping from one minute to the next with a particular topic. This reliance on tests for identification of problems further serves to desensitise teachers in their awareness of problems as they arise.

The problems of traditional assessment are now recognised, and as a result over the last fifteen years there has emerged to replace it a range of task-centred and criterion-referenced approaches. The problem with the task-centred approach is that, although it moves the problem away from the child to the teaching situation, the techniques thus derived still rely upon a heavy input of teacher to individual child work. While the locus has changed in terms of explanation, it has not changed in terms of amount of effort expected of the teacher. The move to task-centred approaches, while welcome, does little by itself to make the task of managing children's difficulties easier for the teacher.

Let us look next at the teacher's territory. True desegregation involves moving the people who have previously had responsibility for children who are experiencing difficulties – peripatetic teachers, ancillary helpers, welfare assistants – into the classroom to work alongside the classteacher. The evolution of the practices which teachers have developed over the last hundred years or so is geared almost exclusively to teachers working on their own with a class of some thirty children. The presence of an additional person therefore presents the teacher with a number of problems to do with negotiating effective working practices with the other person or people. Similar problems are engendered by the involvement of parents in the classroom. While the move is generally applauded, in practice parents are often relegated to the role of dogsbody. The problems raised by such moves are likely to be as great as the opportunities, yet a focus on the *child's* problems in the static classroom make the opportunities recede. Only through taking a radically different perspective – by concentrating on the way the classroom works – will it be possible to realise these opportunities.

The structures within which we provide education still prevent our making a flexible and effective response to children's needs. In the succeeding chapters of this book, ways of moving away from the static classroom are explored, in terms of adopting informal assessment and identification practices, giving identity and structure to the ways in which we re-establish grouping of pupils and working practices of adults in the classroom; and through concrete examples of the ways in which structures within the school can be altered in order to give meaning to the ideal of integration.

Before embarking on that task, we will examine the failure of some of the structures within which special provision is framed. The repeated message of this book is that the behaviour of individual children has to be seen in context. The corollary is that the behaviour of the adults who frame the structures within which these children live can be understood only through an analysis of the past context for special needs, an explication of the present context, and a prediction of the future. This chapter began with a prediction for the end of this century, and an analysis of the growth of special education from the turn of the last century; it proceeds by looking at the immediate past and the traditions and expectations which have provided the mould for current practice.

The last twenty years

THE FAILURE OF TRADITIONAL APPROACHES

During the past decade increasing concern has been voiced about many of the general approaches and specific techniques developed for the child with special needs. The manifestations of these approaches range from finely focused tests designed to identify a particular weakness in a child's cognitive skills, to well established, multi-disciplinary teams whose aim is to help families in difficulty. On the face of it these systems appear to share little common ground; diagnostic tests, child guidance services, and other services in special education – such as the remedial service, are not commonly grouped together under the same heading. Their instigators and proponents come from different professional backgrounds and often differ markedly in their views about the causes of problems and the goals of intervention. Nevertheless, one common factor links a large range of the traditional approaches in the special needs arena: their failure. Despite the dedication of individual workers, the planning, design and expense of certain assessment and intervention systems, in general they have all failed to achieve long-lasting improvements for children, their families or their teachers. An examination of some of these services and approaches will reveal that within each there is a common understanding (or misunderstanding) about the nature of the problems that children experience.

Child guidance services were developed in the 1940s and 1950s. They typically comprise a team of workers from different professional backgrounds. A child psychiatrist, social worker and educational psychologist would often be members of this group, and a teacher and psychotherapist might also be present. Once a social worker, school or GP makes a referral to this agency an appointment is offered to the family, and at an initial interview some form of assessment of the problem is made and a treatment plan devised. This might take the form of fortnightly centre-based sessions for the parents with the child guidance social worker; the child might be seen once or twice by the educational psychologist, who in turn would liaise with the child's school. Regular appointments at the child guidance centre might be made with the child psychiatrist or psychotherapist. Superficially this approach appears sensible and well founded. Many would agree that the family has a considerable influence on a child's behaviour and emotional state. So what is wrong with focusing on changing family relationships and thereby helping the child? There are three problems.

The first problem relates to *what* is being offered. The difficulties usually experienced by parents referred to child guidance centres revolve around problems of appropriate management of their child's unsettled or disruptive behaviour. The child guidance team might view this inappropriate behaviour simply as a symptom of faulty or inadequate communication between parents, and the treatment focus might well be centred on family 'dynamics'. Parents are often disappointed by this interpretation of the problem, and feel that discussions about family issues are irrelevant and intrusive. They frequently vote with their feet, appointments are missed and 'cases' are 'closed'.

The second problem with child guidance is *where* it is offered. Child guidance workers have traditionally valued the quiet and calm of the interview room where there are no distractions to get in the way of the 'treatment'. Parents, however, prefer home-based appointments. Those in low-paid, unskilled work experience great difficulty with making arrangements to attend interviews at child guidance centres during work hours. Again, appointments will be missed and the file closed.

Third, and perhaps most important, is the problem of context and generalisation. Even supposing appointments are kept and a good relationship established with parents and child, the problem (be it truancy, lying, stealing, running away from home) in the real world of home and school tends not to change. Typically, teachers of difficult, disruptive children who are 'under' child guidance do not report an improvement in behaviour. Shepherd *et al* (1971) established that children receiving help from a child guidance service made no more progress than those who were not. It has become apparent that the focus of child guidance treatment is too narrow.

However successful a particular form of therapy is in one setting (eg a child guidance centre), there is no guarantee that there will be a carry-over effect into another setting (eg a secondary school).

Similar problems have bedevilled the work of educational psychologists and their use of tests. The intelligence scale was originally devised in order to separate children into two groups – those who should be educated in mainstream schools and those who should not. But many psychologists became unhappy with their test-bashing image, as the extreme limitations of an instrument whose main function was to distinguish between children who should or should not be referred to special school became apparent. Ingenious attempts were made to use the test material as the basis for remedial teaching. For example, where children scored poorly on items where skills of visual matching seemed to play a part (eg making jig-saw puzzles within specified time limits) it was suggested that similar sorts of activities should be employed by the class teacher to build up this skill. These early IQ tests were not designed as remediation packages, however, and any material used in the classroom to strengthen certain skills had to be devised by the teacher or psychologist. This was inconvenient and time-consuming.

Because of this mismatch between what teachers wanted and what psychologists were providing, in the 1960s and '70s psychologists developed ability tests which were purpose-made for follow-up work in the classroom. These were based on the idea that academic skills such as reading and writing depend on the existence of a core set of sub-skills. It was proposed that if one could measure a child's abilities in these underpinning areas it should then be possible to identify deficits, present the child with suitable activities to compensate for these weaknesses, and thereby improve the child's performance in a range of related academic skills. These tests represented a valiant attempt to help children with learning difficulties rather than simply segregating them in special provision. But subsequent research has shown that this approach failed (Newcomer and Hammill, 1975). Children who are given tasks aimed at developing skills of visual sequencing, visual matching and auditory discrimination do later perform such skills better than before, but what fails to occur is any improvement in 'academic' skills. The hoped-for carry-over effect fails to materialise. The painful lesson learned has been that children get better at tasks they practise, not at those they don't.

The traditional *remedial service* for children with learning difficulties has also often failed. It has been based outside schools and has typically offered two forms of help: peripatetic, school-based teaching, usually once a week, generally outside the classroom, or withdrawal to a special class for perhaps two or three sessions each week. This arrangement has the merit that teaching is focused on important academic skills – more often than not, reading. However, success has not been demonstrated. There is no strong evidence that children who receive intermittent help from a remedial service make more progress than children who do not.

There are several possible explanations for this state of affairs. One problem has been the legacy of the sub-skills approach inherited from the 1960s and 1970s. Many of the remedial services were set up at a time when sub-skill training was in vogue. Unfortunately, curriculum development in some remedial services seems to have fossilised at that stage, or at least appears rather to lag behind many of the developments found in mainstream schools.

A further problem endemic in remedial services is the question of who is responsible for what. One inevitable consequence of dual teacher input is the fragmentation and dilution of responsibility and planning. The existence of specialist 'experts' in particular curriculum areas may undermine class teachers' confidence in their own competence, unless this liaison is approached with considerable skill and diplomacy. This often results in class teachers assuming that curriculum areas taught by the 'experts' are no longer their own responsibility. So, ironically, peripatetic support from a remedial teacher sometimes results in children actually receiving less teaching in the problem area than they did before.

The main culprit in the failure of traditional remedial services is neither the class teacher nor the remedial teacher: it is the focus of the approach – which is narrowly individual-centred. It ignores a factor whose significance over the last few years is becoming more and more apparent, namely, that intervention should be based in the natural contexts in which we expect learning to occur.

The list of approaches described so far have all been characterised by a failure to demonstrate improvements for children with special needs. To those experienced in working in support agencies, the shortcomings of child guidance, the limitations of IQ tests and the poor results of traditional remedial teaching are widely acknowledged. Professionals who recommend or support such approaches are often regarded cynically by teachers, who assume that the buck is being passed and that such suggestions are made because the professional concerned does not have the skills to intervene in any other manner.

A more recent development that has attempted to change very explicit aspects of children's behaviour, and which does not suffer from some of the ambiguities and lack of clarity that typify many earlier approaches, is *social skills training*. Social skills courses vary in their nature, but typically they are organised for adolescents experiencing difficulties in social relationships. The youngsters at which such courses are aimed might be shy and unassertive, or aggressive and overbearing in their behaviour in certain circumstances. Social skills courses are based on two assumptions: first, that many of these inappropriate mannerisms are simply learned habits; second, that these habits can be changed and new, alternative skills can be taught and learned. Social skills courses may be held in schools, or in specialist settings such as observation and assessment centres. Usually the course content is well planned. Weekly meetings are often arranged, with perhaps five to ten sessions held in total. This approach lends itself to evaluation, as its objectives are explicit, tangible and measurable. But research studies typically show that social skills training *fails* to result in the much hoped-for lasting changes. Why is this?

Furnham (1983) ends his critique of social sills training on a cautiously positive note, stressing that there is evidence that this approach can result in positive changes in social skills for limited periods. But he comments that the Achilles heel of social skills training is the issue of *generalisation* (ie the question of whether the trained skills can be used in a range of settings or are specific to one). Research has failed to show generalisation over time, over situations, over skills and from the laboratory to real world settings. The same can be said of many of the traditional approaches to special needs intervention.

A common thread is tangled through these cameos of existing practice: that of an intervention focus which is too restricted and too narrowly centred on the individual child and his or her deficits. It is a focus which fails to take proper account of the natural context in which learning occurs. All too frequently, generalisation does not occur in classrooms because plans have not been made for this to happen. Researchers and practitioners seem to have failed to recognise that classroom life is highly complex. The lesson we have learned from the past is that we ignore natural contexts in which children learn at our peril.

THE CHALLENGE OF INTEGRATION

Today such complacency is being challenged by the integration movement. It seems likely that in future increasing numbers of children with learning difficulties and other problems will be educated in mainstream schools rather than in special schools or off-site units. To a certain extent the interest in integration has been fuelled by recent special education legislation. In the past, the focus of legislation was the individual child and his or her problems. The 1944 Education Act referred to children with special needs having a 'disability of mind or body'. The terminology was medical and implied that certain children suffered from disease-like conditions that required specialised treatment. This notion was further reinforced in 1945 by the introduction of eleven categories of handicap such as 'educationally subnormal', and 'maladjusted'. For over forty years the medical model of diagnosing, labelling and treating children in segregated provision dominated thinking in special education.

It was not until the 1970s, in particular with the publication of the Warnock Committee's report in 1978, that it was formally recognised that to categorise children's difficulties under fixed headings was both artificial and unhelpful to the children, their parents and their teachers. The Warnock Committee viewed special needs as a *relative* concept, and stressed that assessment should include not only a child's problems, but also any shortcomings in the resources available to help the child. The Committee's report laid the foundation for the 1981 Education Act. One of the important general principles underpinning this legislation is the notion that an analysis of a child's difficulties must encompass the *context* in which learning takes place:

> A child's special educational needs are thus related to his abilities as well as his disabilities, *and to the nature of his interaction with his environment*.
>
> (Circular 1/83 – *our italics*)

A very important principle is that, as far as possible, children should be educated in mainstream schools. It has been argued (Bookbinder, 1983) that the provisos linked to this aim in the 1981 Act will make it very easy for education authorities to turn a blind eye to the spirit of integration embedded in the Act. These provisos lay down that integration of children with special needs should occur only where this is compatible with: the child receiving the special educational provision that s/he requires; the provision of efficient education for the children with whom s/he will be educated; and the efficient use of resources. But it seems probable that segregated special provision *will* diminish. Parent pressure groups are becoming more vocal in their demands for integration; generic teacher training is replacing specialist courses so that all teachers will be better equipped to teach children with difficulties. In London, a recent report commissioned by the Inner London Education Authority (Fish, 1985) was whole-hearted in its endorsement of an integration policy:

> All those responsible for providing services to children and young people, whether or not they have specific responsibilities for those with disabilities and significant difficulties, should accept the aim of integration for all.

Unfortunately, ready-made strategies for helping children with special needs do not exist. Although some approaches appear to result in certain improvements, many of the helping agencies which are traditionally associated with special needs children in this country do not have an impressive track record when systematically evaluated.

Until very recently teachers in mainstream schools in many parts of the country could afford to ignore the failure of these traditional methods of intervention. If problems persisted for long enough and severely enough, eventually the problem could be removed somewhere else – to a special class or school. Certainly the process of removal might take a long time and, if parents objected to segregation and special school placement, it might not happen at all. Even then, however, the very existence of the vast, complex network of special provision meant that the issue of *responsibility* for the child with special needs could be largely ignored by the mainstream teacher. Teaching and management of pupils with special needs is often viewed as coming within the province of the specialist, the 'expert': teachers in special schools, teachers in special units, educational psychologists, speech therapists, child psychiatrists. Why else are such people employed? Today, however, it is widely recognised that problems of social isolation, stigma and limited curricular opportunities often result from segregated provision.

The integration movement is gathering momentum, and with it will come the need for class teachers to assume much greater responsibility for teaching children with special needs. Until recently the teacher in the ordinary school could afford to ignore issues such as how to teach special needs children, what to teach, how to measure progress, how to record progress and how to organise learning resources and materials. These questions have been left largely to special school teachers and other specialists. Unfortunately, answers have not yet been found. Special needs has for too long been the Cinderella of education. Most teachers and advisers in mainstream education have adopted an out-of-sight, out-of-mind attitude. They have not begun to ask the questons that their colleagues in special schools have for so long been grappling with – grappling, with some notable exceptions, without success, for planning, accountability and structure have not been the hallmark of special schooling. This is not the fault of the teachers concerned but rather the result of an ideology which has isolated special education.

Integration will surely change this. Mainstream schools will be expected to take on roll increasing numbers of children who formerly would have been placed in special schools, and they will have the additional duty, imposed by the 1981 Act, of monitoring the progress of those children.

Parents will be less prepared to accept certain aspects of the special curriculum once their children are educated alongside their peers in mainstream schools. For years many parents have expressed concern about the 'soft' curriculum offered in special schools, where too often there is not enough emphasis on actively teaching useful skills. In the coming years teachers in mainstream schools will be expected to demonstrate that *all* children have access to a full curriculum. Teachers will have to plan their time with particular care so that the children with difficulties receive an appropriate curriculum, accompanied by an appropriate teaching method. The closed door of the traditional classroom will have to be opened to let in other adults: classroom assistants, support teachers, parents and visiting professionals. If this is mismanaged, the classroom will become a disorganised muddle, where the class teacher views such other adults as intruders. But, if managed well, the classroom can become a place where a rich variety of well-planned teaching strategies can be implemented so that all the children benefit, and where discovery learning can be used in parallel with a more finely focused and structured approach for those children who require such teaching.

LIMITED RESOURCES AND THE NEED FOR PLANNING

The last 20 years have been a period of growth and expansion in education. There is no doubt, however, that this cannot last. The *Zeitgeist* of the eighties is characterised in education by school amalgamations, cuts in services and general restrictions on expenditure. In *Better Schools* (HMSO, 1985) the Department of Education and Science has clearly signalled that no extra resources will be available in the foreseeable future. Local education authorities will be firmly encouraged to make the best use of what is now available, to use present resources to 'yield the best possible return'.

One of the major criticisms of the 1981 Education Act has been that its spirit of integration has not been backed by the provision of additional resources. What is becoming clear is that we will have to devise ways of 'unlocking' the teaching skills and materials which are currently to be found in special schools, in order that these can be made available to mainstream schools. In other words we will need to organise ways of getting presently available resources to children rather than children to resources.

Perhaps the limits on spending and the limits on resourcing will be a blessing in disguise. This may sound like ivory-tower talk to hard-pressed teachers faced with larger classes using books and materials which may have been provided by an active parents' association rather than by their LEA, but it does appear that one of the inherent dangers of generous resourcing is that it has made easy the buying of specialist teaching which takes place *outside* the classroom and indeed outside the mainstream school. The existence of disruptive units, remedial services, child guidance units and other services where 'treatment' or intervention occurs outside the classroom has resulted in the erosion and fragmentation of the class teacher's role. Faced with such a vast array of specialist agencies staffed by 'experts', it is hardly surprising that teachers do not feel that they are centrally responsible for teaching children with special needs. This fragmentation of the class teacher's role has frequently resulted in piecemeal and unplanned teaching strategies. All too often the primary class teacher will assume that the school's remedial teacher will teach the school's slow readers. The secondary school subject teacher will expect general learning difficulties and unsettled behaviour to be dealt with by the special needs department or head of year. Unfortunately, the very existence of a specialist service can have the effect that the children who need well-planned, consistent, regular teaching actually receive less than if that service had not been formed.

With the demise of specialist, off-site provision, and with no option of buying extra resources, the mainstream teacher will need to play a far more central role when plans are made for children who are experiencing difficulties. As support services become more school- and classroom-focused, so class teachers will increasingly take a central and active part in deciding what arrangements should be made for the children in their care. What will be critical is the use of time. In order to make the most of the time that children spend in schools teachers will have to organise their own time with great care. Decisions must be made about how much time each week should be devoted to whole-class teaching, how much to small-group teaching, and how much to individualised teaching. Such decisions must be based on the needs of the children in the class, and must reflect carefully organised curriculum planning both for groups of children and for individual children. Laissez-faire, unstructured approaches to teaching will require some revision and re-working. The 'discovery learning' method has been the hallmark of the British primary school and certainly has much to commend it, but for some children there will be occasions where significant adaptations to the method need to be made. The secondary teacher will also have to adopt a different approach, and become less subject-bound, more child-centred. Learning resources and materials will have to be carefully matched to suit different levels of ability. In order to achieve the correct balance for all children in a class or group, teachers will need to make meticulous plans for the pupils' use of valuable learning time at school.

Planned use of time will extend to others. Adults other than teachers are to be found more and more in classrooms (Wolfendale,

1984). Although Warnock's notion of a partnership between
teachers and parents is still only rarely found, nevertheless participation between the two is now much more commonplace. As we have
indicated already, it is important that parents' time in the classroom
is well spent. The notion that simply having parents present in
school somehow produces a magic called 'parental participation',
which mysteriously enters the soul of the child and miraculously
results in improved learning, is a myth that needs de-mystification.
Hewison (1982) has shown that it is possible to tease out the 'active
ingredient' of parental enthusiasm. In one project which studied the
impact of parents helping their young children to read, the
important factor isolated by the research was whether or not parents
listened to their children reading at home. Many parents are
enthusiastic, concerned and involved with their children's education. Certainly positive parental attitude to schooling will provide a
sound foundation for improving childrens' learning. But what will
count for much more – what will have a direct impact on childrens'
learning – is what parents do. The person who must plan and
organise what parents do in school and how their precious time can
be best employed is the teacher.

Perhaps an even more important aspect of time organisation
relates to the use of other professionals' time – in particular, that of
other teachers. As we move more towards the Warnock vision of
special schools becoming resource bases which offer a service to a
local network or cluster of schools, there will be more opportunities
for outreach work to take place, where support teachers work in
collaboration with their colleagues in the mainstream. This may
well involve some direct teaching, but what is more appropriate is
that this becomes an opportunity for the support teacher to advise on
suitable teaching strategies and supply the necessary resources and
materials. This advice must mesh in with a well-planned whole
curriculum. The class teacher is by far the best positioned to plan
short-term and long-term goals; by far the most appropriate person
to act as a key-worker or educational manager. This position brings
with it the responsibility of organising the ways in which the support
teacher's time is used. What is important is that the support
teacher's involvement does not result in the child with difficulties
receiving an isolated teaching slot which has been simply tagged on
to the remaining part of the curriculum. This will inevitably lead to
the same sorts of problems that have dogged traditional remedial

services – unco-ordinated teaching arrangements where no clear boundaries exist between teaching roles and where consistency is hard to achieve.

In the future, accepting that special resources will be shifted away from segregated provision and will be brought directly into mainstream schools and classrooms and given that these resources will be limited, the need for careful and effective planning by teachers will be of paramount importance.

The need for a different perspective: the ecological model

A radically different perspective is needed in special education for two main reasons: first, changes in the world outside education demand that this should be the case; and, second, the way in which we have traditionally focused upon problems and labelled them 'special' has been shown to be in itself defective. How has this state of affairs come about? The view taken here is that the area has stumbled into blind alleys and wrong turnings because of the very way we think about the problems which may arise in the classroom.

Ideas about special needs have traditionally been formulated within psychological paradigms. Although these paradigms have differed markedly in the way that they view problems and the way that they generate solutions, they have one thing in common: a focus on the singular. In other words, the method of psychology has been to isolate problems and focus on them in some detail; its methodology strips away the difficulties often found in real situations (such as classrooms) and it creates solutions (of varying efficacy) which usually share a disregard for the larger situation. Examples can be clearly seen: the edifice of special education is in itself testimony to the belief that problems could be isolated and then worked on with little consideration of the wider social, moral or ethical issues involved in such segregation.

The model of diagnostic/prescriptive teaching which became popular in the early seventies and which tried to isolate children's problems and remediate for them has been shown to be of very limited utility (Newcomer and Hammill, 1975; Johnson and Pearson, 1975); the task-analytic and consequence-management technologies which have developed out of behavioural psychology and which have dominated solutions in the late seventies and early eighties usually require a heavy input of teacher to individual child effort and often are unsuccessful for this reason. The paradigms of psychology, its traditions and its methodology have never quite meshed, either with the goals of education or with the realities of classroom life.

Frequently when teachers were promised programmes from psychologists which rested on these traditional paradigms their response would be 'That's all very well – but what do I do with the rest of the class?'. Such a response is justified. The fact that traditional psychological method does not meld with educational practice is partly due to the fact that changes in practice which are derived from such methodology are theory driven, or 'top down', the result of an effort to bend the methods of the pure to the practicalities of the applied situation.

The kind of solutions which arise out of such an approach are neatly summarised by Hargreaves (1978):

> In short there appears to be an interesting cycle of events. After the initial phase in which the original ideas and instruments are developed by psychologists there follows a phase in which over-zealous educational psychologists make somewhat premature applications of, and exaggerated claims for, these ideas and instruments and use them in ways which are not strictly warranted. Then follows a third phase in which teachers receive these ideas in a severely attenuated form, and as the ideas become diffused they also become distorted and abused. This stimulates a fourth phase in which the abuses are subjected to critical scrutiny and this in turn generates a final phase in which the original enterprise is denigrated and held to be wrong in principle.

An entirely different perspective is necessary to break away from this kind of cycle. Rather than continually generating theory-led solutions which inevitably meet with failure in the face of real-life problems, it is necessary to build up a body of knowledge and practice based in *ad hoc* solutions to practical problems.

Given discussion and communication about the ideals of education and taking into account the constraints within which those ideals have to be realised, teachers are now generating solutions which are uniquely adapted to their own situations. Such solutions are likely to be appropriately focused without ignoring important realities of the situations in which they are applied. They will take into account the specific problems of the children involved and the specific constraints of the environments in which they are developed. Some will be more successful than others; through a process of dialogue and through action research (see Nixon, 1981, see also the chapter by Trickey and Stobart in this volume, p 67) important common strands might be drawn out of situations in which people have had similar experiences. It is only through such a 'bottom up' explication of problems that we are likely to make progress. Such a bottom up methodology enables us to see from an entirely different vantage point the problems which have traditionally confronted special education.

Our understanding of the world rests, then, on a set of traditions and methodologies. The ways in which we view the world and thus the way in which we perceive problems and forge solutions are moulded by these traditions. These methodological and philosophical traditions, or paradigms, have dominated educational thought in a fashion that has not been wholly helpful. By their presence they have narrowed the way for the emergence of a body of knowledge which is linked centrally to the concerns of education; they have introduced artificial barriers between 'pure' and 'applied' concerns, and they have diminished the confidence of teachers in finding solutions to the problems which face them, which are grounded in their own experience.

One by-product of the fact that paradigms have dominated the theoretical side of education has been a fighting for ground amongst the protagonists of different ideological camps. The contention here is that such discussion is not only irrelevant to the needs of teachers but that it is also damaging for an understanding of the processes which go on in education. It is inevitable that top down or paradigm-led understandings of practical problems will conflict with one another. The view taken here is that an ecological model, in developing understanding out of practical subject matter, by its very nature avoids the pitfalls of paradigm-led understanding.

The ecological model is a synthesis of the individual-centred and the context-based understandings of situations. It takes as its starting point the fact that a child's behaviour cannot be separated from the context in which it occurs. Given such a simple starting point, it is not discordant with models which have traditionally been separated by wide differences both on methodology and content. In establishing the importance of context as a tenet, the model provides useful guidelines for traditional ways of viewing problems. Thus, behavioural psychology, for instance, is encouraged to pay greater attention to that element of the model which seeks an understanding of behaviour in *antecedents* to that behaviour rather than concentrating on its traditional preference for an understanding based in *consequences* of children's behaviour.

THE ORGANIC CLASSROOM

With the emergence of an ecological perspective it is possible to foresee the development of an entirely different set of expectations and procedures relating to the way in which classrooms and schools are organised to identify and cater for children who are experiencing difficulties. Such classrooms will be adaptive and flexible, responding to problems as they arise. They will be organic, enabling the evolution of practices and curricula which can change as conditions change.

But such a view of classrooms will have to go beyond idealistic suggestions about the desirability of child-centred education. They will have to draw upon research about classroom processes, about the dynamics of people working together and about the ways children learn. Informed by this kind of understanding teachers will be able to produce in real situations strategies and ways of operating which are uniquely adapted to their own needs.

It is through adaptations in classroom conditions that the most likely benefits for children who are experiencing difficulties will arise. It is through variations in classroom conditions and through an analysis of the way in which the classroom operates that the class teacher will come to understand how changes in the organisation of time, resources and people in the class will benefit the children. If, as has been indicated by a number of studies (eg Tizard *et al*, 1982; DeVault *et al*, 1977; Bloom, 1984), it is not so much *how* children are helped but rather *how much* they are helped which is crucial in determining children's progress, the teacher will more profitably be expending his or her energies on understanding these classroom processes than in devising specific remedial programmes for a selected set of children.

In an organic classroom the focus is distracted from the idea that problems stem from (and are encapsulated in) individual children. Rather, the focus is upon the way in which teachers are instrumental in realising the goals which they have set themselves. In formulating goals, teachers may set communication high on a list of priorities; they may feel that it is important to give large amounts of individual attention to the children; they may in different circumstances believe that it is important for a warm family atmosphere to exist in their classes. In focusing on ecological variation as a means toward achieving those goals, teachers are able to look, for instance, to the use of jigsaw groups or room-management procedures. They may, in the secondary school, look to entirely different ways of working, and be attracted by the possibilities of introducing support teaching instead of withdrawal as a move towards a whole-school approach to special needs. These possibilities are outlined later in this book.

The view of the organic classroom espoused here is one in which the classroom is unhindered by processes such as formal assessment, and unrestrained by factors such as those which may be embodied in a fixed curriculum. It is only when these obstructions to change have been removed that it will be possible to foresee the kind of real change in classrooms and in schools which give rise to the *processes* which enable children to learn.

The importance of process in the curriculum must not be overlooked in moves to the kind of change outlined. The responsibility for the shift away from process over the past ten years or so can partly be attributed to the 'back to basics' movement and Callaghan's 'Great Debate' on education. The shift away from the fixed curriculum and the fixed set of children with special problems accompanying it will be eased by a re-emphasis on the kind of process in the curriculum that Stenhouse has outlined. Such a curriculum is more informal and more flexble in the way that it allows teachers to tailor-make aims and goals for specific children or groups of children. As such, structures which identify children as having problems become redundant. The criteria for success in a more flexible curriculum will be criteria which will be placed on the curriculum itself rather than on children's success or failure at meeting objectives within a more formal curriculum. Aiming to help children co-operate, communicate, be flexible, and to work in a group, outlined earlier as important goals in a new society, will form part of a reformulated curriculum. Seen to be relevant to the society in which these children live, such a curriculum will in itself do much to reduce the casualties engendered by current educational practice.

Yet it must be clearly stated that the child-centred ideals which gave rise to much of the discontent associated with post-Plowden thinking and practice – discontent embodied in the notion of the 'continuous wet playtime' – cannot by themselves achieve the results for which we hope. Indeed, the espousal of these ideals in teachers who are unsupported by any kind of superstructure for maintaining the dynamic accompanying the ideals is likely to lead to more rather than fewer children who are ultimately assessed as having special needs. The organic classroom therefore is about a synthesis of child-centred ideals with a carefully worked out menu of analytic instruments and organisational formulae available to teachers in the classroom which will enable them to respond with sensitivity to individual problems while effectively managing the activity of the larger number of children for whom they are responsible.

References

Bloom, B. S. (1984) 'The search for methods of group instruction as effective as one to one tutoring in *Educational Leadership*, May, 4–17.

Bookbinder, G. (1983) 'A new deal or dashed hopes' in *Special Education*, 10, 1.

Clutterbuck, D. and Hill, R. (1981) *The Remaking of Work* London: Grant McIntyre.

DeVault, M. L., Harnischfeger, A. and Wiley, D. E. (1977) *Curricula, Personal Resources and Grouping Strategies* St Ann, Mo: ML-Group for Policy Studies in Education, Central Midwestern Regional Lab.

Fish, J. (1985) *Educational Opportunities for All* Report of the committee reviewing provision to meet special educational needs. London: ILEA.

Freire, P. (1972) *Pedagogy of the Oppressed* London: Sheed Ward.

Fuller, R. B. (1970) *Utopia or Oblivion* London: Allen Lane.

Furnham, A. F. (1986) *Social Behaviour in Context* Boston: Allyn and Bacon.

Galbraith, J. K. (1974) *The New Industrial State* Harmondsworth: Penguin.

Handy, C. (1984) *The Future of Work* Oxford: Blackwell.

Hargreaves, D. H. (1978) 'The proper study of educational psychology in *Association of Educational Psychologists' Journal*, 4, 9, 3–8.

Hewison, J. (1982) 'Parental involvement in the teaching of reading in *Remedial Education*, 17, 4, 156–162.

Illich, I. D. (1973) *Deschooling Society* Harmondsworth: Penguin.

Johnson, D. D. and Pearson, P. D. (1975) 'Skills management systems: a critique in *Reading Teacher*, 28, 757–765.

Macrae, N. (1984) *The 2024 Report* London: Sidgwick and Jackson

Newcomer, P. L. and Hammill, D. D. (1975) 'ITPA and academic achievement' in *Reading Teacher*, 28, 731–742

Nixon, J. (ed) (1981) *A Teacher's Guide to Action Research* London: Grant McIntyre.

Schumacher, E. F. (1973) *Small is Beautiful* London: Blond and Briggs.

Shepherd, M., Oppenheim, B. and Mitchell, S. (1971) *Childhood Behaviour and Mental Health* London: University of London Press.

Stenhouse, L. (1975) *An Introduction to Curriculum Research and Development* London: Heinemann.

Thomas, G. and Jackson, B. (1986) 'The whole-school approach to integration' in *British Journal of Special Education*, 13, 1, 27–29.

Tizard, J., Schofield, W. N. and Hewison, J. (1982) 'Collaboration between teachers and parents in assisting children's reading' in *British Journal of Educational Psychology*, 52, 1–15.

Toffler, A. (1980) *The Third Wave* London: Collins.

Toffler, A. (1985) *The Adaptive Corporation* Aldershot: Gower.

Touraine, A. (1971) *The Post-Industrial Society* New York: Random House.

Wolfendale, S. (1984) 'A framework for action: professionals and parents as partners' in E. De 'Eath and G. Pugh (eds) *Working Together: Parents and Professionals as Partners* London: National Children's Bureau.

2 The end of traditional assessment

Anthony Feiler

Since the turn of the century we have become used to the notion that
children with special educational needs should be assessed.
Although certain aspects of traditional assessment are worthwhile,
unfortunately many are not. Indeed they add very little to our
knowledge of how to help children with difficulties, and often reflect
outdated ideas which were only briefly in vogue. Traditional assessment approaches can result in a dangerously narrow focus on the
individual child and his or her problems, where scant (if any) regard
is paid to the situational factors such as curriculum content, teaching
method, etc, which may need changing. These assessment devices
have tended to describe and categorise problems and to identify
possible underlying causes, rather than generate solutions.

This chapter will trace the roots of these developments and
examine the distorting effects they have on our views about children
with special needs. It will explore some of the reasons that lead
Frank Smith (1986) to claim that tests are hazardous and should be
stamped with the warning, 'Inhaling this test could be dangerous to
the health of the child.' Some of the more positive recent trends in
practice will be outlined and suggestions made for the adoption of
certain general assessment strategies.

The problems with traditional assessment

EARLY DEVELOPMENTS

Perhaps the instrument most commonly associated with assessment
has been the intelligence test. In 1904 the Minister of Public Instruction in Paris asked Alfred Binet to construct a test that would distinguish between children who should be educated in ordinary schools
and those who should not. The scale that was first published a year

later was never conceived as an instrument to help children learn more effectively. It was simply designed to measure children's performance on a series of tests. This was then summarised and expressed as a mental age. Possibly one of the test's strengths was the comparative objectivity it lent to the difficult process of deciding which children would be denied access to schooling. But neither this test nor others like it (such as the Wechsler Intelligence Scale for Children) were originally developed in order to provide the basis for intervention. A number of misconceptions still persist about the capabilities of intelligence tests. For example, it is still widely believed that intelligence tests can do the following:

1 Measure a child's learning potential and predict future academic performance.
2 Identify important or significant learning strengths and weaknesses.
3 Provide a basis for a suitable teaching approach.

Unfortunately they do none of these. Intelligence tests are not good at predicting a pupil's future educational achievement. It is now recognised that future performance depends upon a complex interaction of both *external* factors such as teaching methods, curriculum, learning materials, etc, and *internal* factors such as motivation, current relevant skills, problem-solving, study skills and so forth.

Intelligence tests cannot pinpoint significant learning strengths or weaknesses. The profiles of abilities and deficits which result from some intelligence scales have little direct relevance for a class teacher who is planning a curriculum for a child or group of children with learning difficulties. The area sampled in intelligence tests can give only a very crude indication of verbal and non-verbal reasoning skills. These are so remote from educationally significant learning areas that their usefulness is highly questionable. Certainly they cannot provide a framework or basis for planning a suitable teaching approach.

During the 1960s the failure of intelligence tests to provide practical help for teachers resulted in a proliferation of 'diagnostic' or sub-skills tests. Acknowledging that general intelligence scales were not designed to highlight educationally significant learning strengths and weaknesses, test-constructors devised techniques for measuring certain abilities which appeared to underpin academic performance in subjects such as reading and spelling. As discussed in Chapter 1, research evidence has demonstrated that attempts to train supposed sub-skills such as visual-matching and auditory discrimination failed to help children improve their reading or spelling. The hoped-for transfer of learning did not occur. We now have to accept that there are no easy short-cuts to developing improved learning. Children get better at what they practise. A substantial number of research studies have demonstrated that the most effective way to help children learn new skills is to teach directly what we want them to learn (Becker, 1978). The most effective way to teach children to read more proficiently is to teach children to read, not to teach them to match abstract designs. Unfortunately this lesson has not yet been fully appreciated. There still remain a number of unwelcome residual effects which date from the sub-skills movement of the 1960s, and which continue to undermine the development of sound assessment strategies which will be of practical value to teachers.

The destructive legacy of the testing movement

One of the most damaging aspects of the traditional testing movement has been its restricted focus on the individual child. Typically, a child's intelligence and basic attainments were tested and the resulting formulation tended to reflect the view that once the deficits were eliminated, progress would be made. This style of assessment has its origins in medical practice. A search is made for an underlying sickness or pathology, a diagnosis is given and a pre-determined treatment is prescribed. Unfortunately, when this model is applied to education, it results in practitioners labelling children with disease-like conditions such as dyslexia, maladjustment, hyperactivity and so forth. The problem becomes 'fixed' in the child, and the resulting label can become obstructive as it focuses attention on what is wrong rather than on what strategies might be devised to overcome it. The intervention focus is far too narrow, for it fails to include an assessment of the teaching approach, the curriculum and the setting in which the child learns. The jargon used to describe children's difficulties and the test constructor's insistence on a rigorous adhesion to standardised testing procedures has served to exclude those who are in the best position to assess – namely, teachers.

Since the turn of the century the model of outside professionals assessing children in unnatural contexts away from the school setting has eroded and undermined teachers' confidence in their own assessment ability. It is only comparatively recently that professionals have been urged to share or 'give away' their skills to those who are in direct and regular contact with children (Mittler, 1981). It is hardly surprising that one of the most frequent requests made by teachers in mainstream schools, when plans are being formulated for children with special needs, is for in-service training.

An insidious effect of the traditional testing movement has been the notion that children's learning potential is fixed and invariable. This has largely arisen from some of the powers originally attributed to intelligence tests. In the past, extravagant claims were made by some psychologists. Intelligence was supposed to be inherited, uninfluenced by teaching, could be measured accurately, and was unchanging over time (Burt, 1933). It is now widely accepted that intelligence quotients do not remain constant over time and that performance on such tests is influenced by cultural and educational factors (Clarke and Clarke, 1976). Nevertheless, the notion that intelligence is pre-determined and unalterable has had a great impact on educational theory and its influence is still in evidence. For example, major decisions about which band or set might be appropriate for secondary-age pupils are still influenced by their performance on verbal or non-verbal reasoning tests.

Despite evidence to the contrary (Reynolds *et al*, 1976), there is an insidious belief that schools do not make much difference anyway, and that children's potential is an inherited, permanent entity that is impervious to teaching.

Finally, the testing movement has had a restricting influence on the curriculum for children with special needs. Many of the tests devised between the 1930s and 1960s contained items which involved visual matching skills, sequential ordering of pictures, drawing lines between parallel lines and so forth. Naturally, these were assumed to be of educational importance and many curricula in special schools still reflect these test items. Children in special schools and units can still be found working extensively at form-boards, jigsaw puzzles and sorting and matching activities. These are sometimes justified as being 'pre-reading' activities or developing 'hand–eye co-ordination' skills. As we have seen, the problem is that these activities tend not to result in the development of academic skills. If children are taught to sort and match objects, their sorting and matching skills will probably improve, but there will not necessarily be an improvement in their general ability to classify or group and compare in different situations.

Why do such inappropriate ideas infiltrate the curriculum and become established with uncritical acceptance? Part of the reason is that in the past assessment and teaching have been divorced from each other. Those involved in devising tests to measure children's functioning were not involved in teaching. It is only comparatively recently that an assessment-through-teaching model has gained credence. This will be discussed further later in the chapter.

The traditional testing movement has left a destructive legacy which we must now challenge, for it has resulted in approaches which reinforce the assumption that problems and deficits reside within children. There has been far too great an emphasis on causes and categories and not enough on solutions and strategies. The jargon and semi-scientific procedures adopted by the authors of traditional tests have undermined teachers' confidence in their own assessment skills. Far too great a chasm still exists between teaching and assessment. Teachers need to grasp the nettle of evaluation and become much more involved with the construction of assessment approaches that reflect their own schools' values, policies and objectives. This development has not been helped by an idea that has become part of the educational folk-lore in Western society, insinuating that children's intellectual potential is an unchangeable genetic inheritance and that teaching and education will not make a difference. A final problem with traditional testing procedures is that many of the out-dated ideas which they reflect have become fossilised in the special education curriculum. The shelf-life of educationally fashionable trends can be extended dramatically once they are embedded in a test, and they can prove very resistant to change.

On a more positive note, in recent years there has been a 'wind of change'. Outside professionals are beginning to come out from their medical rooms and broom-cupboards and work collaboratively with teachers (Roulstone, 1983). Assessment instruments are more directly related to relevant curricular aims (Cameron *et al*, 1986) and are more closely linked with teaching. Nevertheless, there still exists a number of unsound assessment practices, and these will be examined in greater detail in the next section.

Misuses of assessment

An assessment should aim to help a child who is experiencing difficulties in learning or adjusting. Its primary purpose should be to enable those directly involved with the child to plan suitable changes in the child's learning environment in order that progress can be made. Put another way, the single most important function of an evaluative exercise should be to make decisions about how to change the teaching approach (be it the curriculum, the learning materials used, the amount of small-group teaching arranged, etc) in order to help the child acquire new skills. Regrettably, concern for the welfare of the child does not necessarily underpin requests to outside professionals for assessments.

Often, the masked reason for a referral for assessment is the school's desire for the child to be removed – to a special school or unit. It is hoped that the assessment will confirm the school's view that the child's needs would be best met in specialist, off-site provision. Schools may be forced to approach outside professionals because frequently these workers hold the key that unlocks the door to additional resources. Outside professionals are often the gatekeepers to special provision. Nevertheless, an attractive feature (to schools) of this process is that 'experts' can be used to legitimate decisions which may be profoundly distressing to parents. What may appear to be a school's rejection of a child can be presented to parents as an earnest endeavour to secure the resources the child needs.

The legitimation of special school placement is not the only misuse of the assessment process: it may be used to assign blame to the child or family. All too often, when a traditional assessment is undertaken, and where the major emphasis is on identifying deficits and underlying causes for the problem, the burden is borne by the child or family. Conditions such as 'low IQ', 'limited concentration span', or an 'unsettled family background' are typically identified, and serve to deflect questions from curriculum, teaching approaches and general school issues. The danger of this scenario is that the assessment is used as a vehicle for fault-finding rather than as a means for devising suitable intervention strategies. Family factors do indeed play an important part in children's attitude to and motivation for schooling (Plowden Report, 1967). Nevertheless, they are often difficult to alter, and it can be tempting to devote too much time dwelling on these rather than exploring factors within school which are more amenable to change.

A major problem with traditional assessment is the manner in which it encourages single, one-off contacts between professionals and children. This has been referred to as 'hit-and-run' assessment. Many tests are designed to allow hard-pressed professionals a minimum time assessing children. Indeed, the brevity of administration is highlighted as an attractive selling feature in advertising literature. The result of such brief encounters is often a written report either recommending the placement of the child in a special school or perhaps making some rather general statements about various approaches teachers might adopt. Many of the traditional tests still widely used discourage assessing professionals from working collaboratively with teachers and parents. Instead, they tend to result in assessments carried out in the secrecy of clinics or medical rooms, isolating the child and assessor in a cocooned and unnatural setting, protected from the distractions of the real world of school and home. The resulting report which highlights the child's performance on certain tasks may well stay in the child's school file for the duration of his or her educational career. Unfortunately, the fact that a child has been assessed by a psychologist or other professional can later arouse a host of suspicions and expectations which may be unwarranted and ill-founded. Knowledge that a child was referred to a psychologist in the past is all too often quoted as proof that there must be a serious problem. This notion can be further reinforced by the style and language used in the report itself, for the strengths and weaknesses are often described as if they were permanent and impervious to change. Reports written after traditional, one-off assessments tend to have a quality of rigidity, and can lead to a static view of the child and his or her needs.

Assessment is frequently misused for a variety of reasons. It is exploited to justify recommendations for children to attend special schools or units – to provide the legitimising professional rubber stamp on unpopular or controversial decisions made by schools. It allows responsibility for action to be transformed into blame on the child or family, and it can result in the child being labelled as a problem. This is particularly likely to occur when the assessment is accompanied by a traditional report which highlights the child's deficits. These problems are endemic when assessments are carried out by outside professionals who fail to work closely with teachers. The next section will examine in more detail the role played by outside professionals, and the dangers that exist when their work is too far removed from the school and classroom settings.

The power and mystique of assessing professionals

In his article *The Professional–Lay Relationship: A Victorian Legacy* Eric Midwinter (1977) eloquently describes the chasm that exists between schools and the community, between professionals and consumers. Although we adopt modern approaches and techniques, we still adhere rigidly to an outmoded Victorian framework. Professionals continue to approach their roles with an air of dispensing 'charity'. This has the unfortunate consequence of distancing professionals from others, casting professionals in the role of the aloof expert, and preventing them from working co-operatively with their colleagues and parents in a spirit of conjoint problem-solving. It is important that professionals based outside schools work effectively and collaboratively *with* others as the role they play in the arrangements made for children with special needs is considerable.

During the last thirty or forty years there has been a substantial mushrooming of professionals who assess children with special needs (Tomlinson, 1982). It is now becoming more common for the following to be asked for advice: specialist teachers; education welfare officers; educational and clinical psychologists; speech and occupational therapists; physiotherapists; child psychiatrists; social workers; doctors; and health visitors. We invest considerable power in the hands of these assessing professionals. They have control over resources and make crucial decisions concerning which children should receive additional help and which children should be recommended for off-site placement. Why is so much power conferred on groups of professionals who spend relatively little time in schools and whose role in the main thrust of the educational system is comparatively marginal? Part of the answer lies in the mystique that surrounds the people who assess. Their status is high, and their actions made mysterious by work carried out in specialist centres, behind closed doors, protected by secretaries who stress how busy and overworked they are. A less tangible reason for teachers delegating such power to the assessing professionals is the knowledge that their observations and expertise can be used to coerce parents into accepting decisions they might otherwise reject. Suggestions for special-school placement which are couched in semi-scientific terms made by neutral professionals can be very difficult to refute. It is almost as though an unwritten contract exists between schools and the outside professionals, which dictates that their status will be maintained in exchange for collusion in the process of removing difficult or troublesome children.

Relations between schools and advisory workers are not always harmonious. There is a range of mismatches between schools' expectations and professionals' aspirations (Lovejoy, 1985). Nevertheless, on the whole there exists a reasonable working relationship, even though (or perhaps because) this partly depends on a 'you scratch my back . . .' understanding.

Turning now to inter-professional relationships, how effectively do professionals work together? Much emphasis is placed on the value of multi-disciplinary assessment. Ideally, advisory professionals should work closely with each other, each contributing insights based on their own experience and expertise in order to devise intervention strategies that are both well-informed and comprehensive. However, it is no secret that successful multi-disciplinary work is difficult to accomplish. This is openly acknowledged in DES Circular 1/83.

> Effective multi-professional work is not easy to achieve. It requires co-operation, collaboration and mutual support. Each professional adviser needs to be aware of the roles of his colleagues and should seek to reach agreement with them on their several roles and functions.

What is perhaps less well appreciated is the acrimonious rivalry that exists between different professional groups. Occasionally, openly critical accusations are made. For example, the friction between speech therapists and educational psychologists is described by Pip Wallace in her article, *Blame it on the Psychologists* (1986). More frequently the competition and rivalry between, for example, doctors and psychologists or psychologists and advisers, is camouflaged beneath a veneer of co-operation. Unfortunately, the dissension between professionals does not readily result in improved strategies being devised for children with special needs. Rather, proponents of one particular ideology or approach will defend it by attacking its critics, and the result can be sudden swings in fashion which are both confusing and unhelpful for teachers, whose work might be directly influenced by such debates.

One unfortunate consequence of allowing outside professionals so much control in the assessment of children with special needs is the influence they subsequently exert on the approaches used in special units and classes. This can result in a curriculum and teaching approach which is deficit-centred and deficit-led. The approaches adopted in many special schools and off-site classes tend to focus too narrowly on children's disabilities rather than on helping them gain access to a broad, mainstream curriculum. Too often, when children attend special provision, the approach centres on a dangerously limited area of learning such as language skills or phonics. What such children need is help to master skills and concepts which form a broad-based mainstream curriculum, rather than remedial teaching which takes place away from the ordinary school and which by its very isolation tends to be artificial and fragmented.

The argument developed so far in this chapter has been that, although the testing movement may have had its roots at the turn of the century in educationists' desire for objective and fair decision-making, the problems generated have been immense. These include the assigning of labels, which places the problem within the child rather than generating problem-solving solutions. In addition, the initiation of the assessment process is frequently a first step to removing the child from the school rather than a genuine attempt to help the child. Finally, the expansion of the testing movement has been accompanied by a substantial increase in assessing professionals whose activities have resulted in many children being placed in off-site classes where the teaching approach can be narrow, fragmented and out of date.

Assessment today

RECENT POSITIVE TRENDS

Perhaps one of the most welcome changes during the last decade has been the drift away from labelling. During the 1970s there was growing concern about the effects that categorising children with labels such as 'maladjusted', 'ESN', etc, had on children (Roe, 1978). In a penetrating study by Hargreaves and others (1975), attention was drawn to the danger of the self-fulfilling prophecy when teachers in secondary schools identify and label pupils as deviant or disruptive. The authors suggested that the behaviour rather than the pupil should be the focal point of the labelling.

The Warnock Committee (Warnock, 1978) introduced the concept of special educational need and laid the ground for the later abolition of the eleven categories of handicap (1981 Education Act). The importance of the distinction between describing a child's needs as opposed to assigning a label cannot be over-emphasised. The concept of need carries with it an implicit questioning of the adequacy of resources, and therefore leads more directly to the formulation of helping strategies.

The 1981 Education Act lays down statutory procedures for cases where formal assessment is to be carried out. This applies to a relatively small number of pupils where it is felt necessary to secure 'provision additional to, or otherwise different from, the facilities and resources generally available in ordinary schools in the area under normal arrangements' (DES Circular 1/83). The formal assessment procedure can result in additional resources being provided in mainstream schools (typically extra human resources in the form of part-time help from a classroom assistant), or possibly a recommendation for placement in a special school. Formal assessment is carried out for a small proportion of pupils (roughly 2–3%), but embedded in the Act are a number of sound principles which it is hoped will diversify to other forms of assessment. It is stated, for example, that children with special needs should be educated in ordinary schools. This is subject to three conditions: that the child receives the special educational provision which he or she requires; that there is provision of efficient education for children with whom he or she will be educated; and that the use of resources will be efficient. Although the Act does not impose a duty on LEAs to provide additional resources in mainstream schools, nevertheless, the spirit of integration has been promoted and many welcome this as a significant step forward (ACE *Special Education Handbook*, 1983).

A number of other positive features of the 1981 Education Act are worth highlighting. The involvement of the child's parents in the assessment process is viewed as essential, and it is urged that the assessment is seen as a *partnership* between professionals and parents. It is stressed that assessment should always be closely related to education and that professionals should work together with the teacher. The pivotal role of the teacher is emphasised in the assessment process – professionals are reminded that it is the *teacher* who is directly responsible for his or her pupils, and is in a key position to observe their performance in the classroom and try out different approaches to help meet the child's needs. Finally, circular 1/83 warns us that assessment is not an end in itself, 'but a means of arriving at a better understanding of a child's learning difficulties for the practical purpose of providing a guide to his education and a basis against which to monitor his progress'.

Linked to the current interest in devising *practical solutions* rather than merely identifying underlying causes, teachers, psychologists and others have begun to develop assessment and teaching materials which are specifically designed to help children with learning difficulties (Lister and Cameron, 1986). This has resulted in tests which measure particular skills, reflect a mainstream curriculum, and have direct implications for teaching. There is now a range of criterion-referenced tests which provide sequenced lists of learning targets, enabling teachers to design learning programmes for children who may require this element of structure. For examples of this sort of approach see ELSA (Early Learning Skills Analysis) (Ainscow and Tweddle, 1984); and SNAP (Special Needs Action Programme) (Muncey and Ainscow, 1983).

These materials reflect a growing awareness that children who experience learning difficulties need an instructional approach that focuses directly on teaching new skills. Fortunately, the indirect approaches of the 1960s, where children with learning difficulties were given activites aimed at developing so-called sub-skills, are now being abandoned. We are also seeing a waning of interest in norm-based tests, which aimed to compare a child's performance with that of a comparison group of peers. Educationists' concern to develop tests which provide more objective measures of children's learning skills has not been confined to the area of special needs. The authors of *Better schools* (HMSO, 1985) openly acknowledge the weakness of the traditional GCE and CSE examination systems, which give very little information about absolute levels of attainment. One of the key aspects of the General Certificate of Secondary Education will be the manner in which grades will depend on pupils' capacity to demonstrate specific levels of skill, knowledge and understanding.

A key question about any test for pupils with learning difficulties is: does it indicate clearly which significant learning skills have and have not been attained? This information is crucial if an intervention strategy is to be devised. Another welcome trend in current assessment approaches has been the recognition that it is not only the pupil that merits assessment. Certainly we need information about the pupil's strengths and weaknesses in order to plan an appropriate learning programme. But there is now a growing body of knowledge about the effects that schools – their organisation, curricula, and general ethos – have on pupils' progress. Studies which contrast and compare different secondary schools whose pupil intake is roughly comparable on various predetermined criteria demonstrate that there seem to be links between internal school factors and academic success. For example, Rutter and a team of researchers (Rutter *et al*, 1979) found that more successful secondary schools tended to praise and encourage pupils' good work; they maintained the pupils' direct involvement in lessons; pupils were given more responsibility at school; and teachers had higher expectations of academic success (Ouston, 1981).

Linked to the realisation that the legitimate target for assessment should not only be the child is an increasing interest in contextual factors. Until recently psychologists have tended to pay particular attention to the outcome of learning when working with children with special needs. For example, by making the consequences of learning more pleasurable – by systematically introducing rewards – it was hoped that children would become better motivated. Clearly, whether or not a child finds the completion of a task rewarding or not is only one of a large number of factors that may be contributing to learning difficulties. There is now much more interest in developing preventive approaches, and in assessing whether teaching methods and the curriculum may need modification in order to help children learn more effectively. This topic will be covered in greater depth in Chapter 9.

Returning to the role that parents might play in an assessment, as mentioned earlier, their involvement has now become statutory when formal assessment procedures are initiated under the 1981 Education Act. By law, parents must be asked for their views on their child's needs. In addition, reports now written for the statementing procedure are not only circulated amongst professionals but are also sent to parents. In the past we have questioned the extent to which parents can provide useful, objective information on their children's needs. However, there are now well-documented research projects where the value of parental ivolvement has been demonstrated.

This has been successfully accomplished in Portage schemes for parents of young children with special needs. Portage is an early intervention home-visiting service which advocates partnership with parents (Daly *et al*, 1985). Schemes have now been operating in the UK for over ten years, and there is considerable evidence that the parents' contribution to their child's assessment is an integral and highly valued aspect of the Portage system. The work of Elizabeth Newson (1976) has also underlined the importance of parents when young children are being assessed. She advocates that parents should be viewed as experts and that part of the professionals' task is to draw out from them valuable insights and information which can contribute so richly to our understanding of their child's needs. Although we are far from achieving true partnership with parents, professionals are now much more aware of the need to work towards this goal.

There has been a positive trend towards assessment *over time*, promoted in the Warnock report and re-iterated in Circular 1/83, where it is stressed that assessment is a continuous process. Professionals do now seem more wary of making decisions about children after limited contact. They will now try harder to liaise with teachers, involving them in assessment strategies and are appreciating that it is more profitable to assess children in natural contexts (eg classrooms and homes).

There are some grounds for cautious optimism. The assessing professionals are abandoning traditional tests in favour of developing assessment procedures which involve closer collaboration with teachers and parents, in natural contexts, and which take place over a period of time. Some of these approaches will be discussed later in this chapter, with suggestions for implementation by teachers. Before considering specific assessment strategies, however, one particularly important issue will be considered.

The need for a whole-school policy

For a variety of reasons it is often found that arrangements made in schools for children with special needs are uncertain, *ad hoc* and fragmented. This is frequently a reflection of the LEA's lack of a developed policy on special needs.

In schools where there is no clear policy, confusion reigns. Teachers need to know answers to a host of questions such as: what first steps should be taken in school for children with learning or behaviour difficulties? What resources already exist within school? Will outside professionals such as the educational psychologist, speech therapist and others be prepared to share their expertise and work with teachers and parents, adopting a collaborative, problem-solving approach? If there are no clear answers to these questions, one consequence will be that a considerable amount of teachers' time will be wasted in attempts to clarify the situation each time a child is identified as having special needs. Unless a whole-school policy exists, which states clearly the school's priorities and aims for children experiencing difficulties, attempts by individual teachers to make plans for children in their care will be frustrating and time-consuming. In a very useful book which examines assessment practices in mainstream schools (*Assessment: from principles to action*, Lloyd-Jones *et al*, 1986) the authors argue that the development of a clear assessment policy should provide coherence to the activities of different departments and individual teachers. In addition, the authors argue that unless a coherent assessment approach is adopted, it will prove very difficult to evaluate the school's curricular aims and objectives. In a survey of assessment policies and procedures in secondary schools (Clough, Davis and Sumner, 1984) it emerged that not all schools communicate policy on assessment as clearly as they think they do:

> In some schools, teachers are obviously unaware of guidelines laid down in those policies. . . Important judgments about children's progress are based on results of assessments, yet it does seem that there is often insufficient consideration of the value and purposes of these assessments.

Once a clear, coherent policy does exist, then it becomes possible for specific approaches to be explored and developed.

The next section will outline some of the assessment strategies that might be adopted by schools – some of which are now being used by outside professionals, and which, with a little adaptation, could be more widely utilised by teachers themselves.

Assessment strategies

FORMATIVE AND SUMMATIVE ASSESSMENT

One of the first questions that teachers should ask relates to the objectives of the assessment itself. Is it designed to evaluate progress made over a period of time, summarising what has been achieved? An example of this form of assessment (known as summative) is the traditional examination. Typically the information obtained is more useful to adults than the child, and may be used to make decisions about banding, access to further education, etc.

On the other hand formative assessment is continuous, and is built into the teaching process. It is designed to give immediate feedback to the teacher and pupil in order that this information can be used to motivate the learner or change the teaching approach. This type of evaluation differs markedly from the more traditional summative assessment. It is called formative as its aim is to influence, change or form what is being assessed. The role it plays is quite distinct from that of summative assessment, where the primary aim is to provide a summarising compendium that finishes or rounds off a period of teaching. If formative assessment is to be effective it needs to be frequent; its results readily understood by both teacher and pupil; it should measure directly what has been taught, and it should provide the basis for future teaching by outlining which new learning areas should be next introduced.

CRITERION-REFERENCED ASSESSMENT

Perhaps the most important information to gather before devising teaching strategies for children with learning difficulties is that which provides details about which skills have and have not been mastered. Norm-based tests which compare an individual child's performance with that of a representative sample of children of the same age will place children in rank order. However, such tests can give only a rough indication of skill level. In contrast, a criterion-referenced test is one which determines a pupil's performance by testing his or her skill against a set of tasks with pre-determined, built-in criteria for passing or failing. Although there are now increasing numbers of criterion-referenced tests available, there are

Figure 2.1 *A teaching and assessment model*
(Ainscow and Tweddle, 1979)

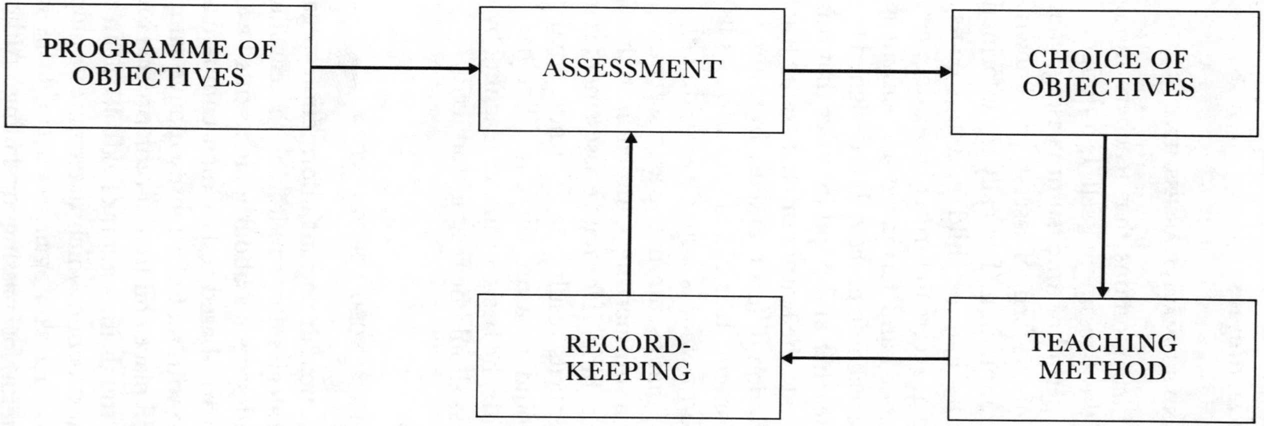

considerable advantages if teachers are able to devise their own tests which directly reflect the curriculum and teaching approach in use.

An objectives-based teaching approach can be employed. The first step is to write a series of learning steps or targets. These have three components: a description of what the pupil should do to demonstrate that learning has taken place; an indication of how well the task should be performed; and a description of relevant conditions, such as the materials to be used. Once the learning steps are sequenced in a teaching or learning order, this form of curriculum-related assessment can provide a useful tool for establishing what has been learned; for checking progress; and for planning future teaching. This approach is described in detail in *Preventing Classroom Failure: an Objectives Approach* (Ainscow and Tweddle, 1979).

TEACHING-BASED ASSESSMENT

It is useful to ensure that assessment and teaching are closely linked. If assessment is to be of practical use, it is essential that it is not an isolated activity which bears little or no relation to the curriculum or teaching approach being utilised. Ainscow and Tweddle (1979) describe a teaching model which incorporates assessment (see Figure 2.1).

Using this model, a teacher is able to use curriculum-related assessment to find out what the child can and cannot do. This information will indicate which new learning steps might be taught next. Having decided what the child should learn, an appropriate teaching method can be devised. By evaluating and recording the child's progress continuous assessment is provided which will inform decisions about which future objectives should be introduced. This model has much to commend it. For it not only establishes that assessment and teaching are inter-meshed, it also provides a basis for assessing how a pupil responds to teaching over a period of time. By doing so it allows not only the pupil to be assessed but also the curriculum and teaching method.

Nevertheless, careful thought is necessary if the problems and pitfalls of traditional test design are to be avoided. There is a danger that the assessment tail may wag the curriculum dog (Lloyd-Jones *et al*, 1986). Assessments should reflect the curriculum, not vice versa. They should, therefore, be flexible and largely based on opinions about pupils' *needs*. Decisions about which items should or should not be included in an assessment instrument should be influenced by questions such as: are the items of genuine educational significance for the pupils? Do they reflect current developments in curriculum planning? Would mastery of the skills tested help the pupil gain access to the mainstream curriculum? It is essential that the assessment does not become a compilation of items which are divorced from mainstream curricular developments, and which have been over subdivided and may result in a piecemeal approach to teaching.

PUPIL PROFILES

There is increasing interest in designing assessment procedures which provide more than a numerical measure or sketchy summary of pupils' skills and abilities. The authors of the Hargreaves report on secondary education in the ILEA (*op cit*) proposed a definition of achievement that is much broader than that assessed by examination performance alone. They distinguished four aspects of achievement. The first involves the capacity to memorise and recall knowledge or information and reproduce this in written form. This aspect of achievement is largely measured in traditional public examinations. The second aspect is concerned with the application of knowledge, and with practical problem-solving, and investigational skills. The third focuses on personal and social skills: communication and co-operation with others, self-reliance and the ability to work independently. The fourth aspect of achievement is involved with motivation, commitment and perseverence.

Clearly, it will not be easy to devise a recording system that accurately reflects the range of abilities and qualities represented in these four aspects of achievement. A development which complements these richer definitions of achievement is the pupil profile, a whole range of records and assessment devices which are applied over time and which build up a qualitative picture of pupils' strengths and weaknesses:

> A student profile is a detailed and comprehensive, but usually systematic and open, statement of the pupil's achievement – of his or her competencies and capabilities, and/or knowledge and understanding, and/or skills, learning experiences, aptitudes, personal qualities and maturity.
>
> (Lloyd-Jones *et al*, *op cit*)

A wide range of material may contribute to a pupil's profile. For example, it may include reports from class or subject teachers; comments from parents; results from tests and examinations; the views of pastoral staff; and even self-assessment materials from pupils themselves. The flexibility and comprehensiveness of this form of assessment is well suited to less able pupils. It is of particular value where the aim of assessment is to help formulate future teaching plans. It allows teachers and pupils to embark on prospective assessment, where future learning goals can be identified. This particular aspect may well be of benefit to pupils in secondary schools in their fourth and fifth years who have experienced learning failure and who are daunted by what Hargreaves (*op cit*) describes as a vague two-year educational journey towards nebulous and distant goals. He proposes that teachers should consider re-structuring secondary school courses during these years in order that half-term units can be introduced. It is suggested that a curriculum organised around shorter-term objectives appeals to *all* learners regardless of age, sex, class and ethnicity.

SELF-ASSESSMENT FOR TEACHERS

Many of the approaches and strategies described so far in this chapter have implications for teaching and curriculum change. Criterion-referenced assessment, formative assessment and pupil-profiling can all be used to assess whether teaching has been effective and whether the teaching approach should be altered. It may be appropriate for teachers to approach self-evaluation more directly. A straightforward and flexible method has been devised by the authors of *Curriculum in Action*, at the Open University, described in Hargreaves (*op cit*). The teacher answers six questions:

1 What did the pupils actually do?
2 What were they learning?
3 How worth while was it?
4 What did I do?
5 What did I learn?
6 What do I intend to do now?

This is one of many checklists written for teachers, enabling them to evaluate the effectiveness of their teaching and classroom management skills. A particularly clear and useful example is included in

John Robertson's *Effective Classroom Control* (1981). It is divided into seven sections and covers the following areas: achieving more successful teaching; sustaining pupil attention; improving the momentum and smoothness of lessons, conveying authority when giving reprimands or instructions which interrupt pupils' activities; avoiding challenges to one's authority; reducing unwanted behaviour; and using reprimands and punishments effectively.

The need for good organisation when teaching children with special educational needs cannot be over-estimated and is a theme which will be elaborated throughout this book.

Conclusions

This chapter has outlined some of the problems associated with traditional assessment and the dangers of teachers becoming over-reliant on outside 'experts'. Certain trends in assessment procedures have been highlighted as they contain elements of sound practice which can be usefully adapted and applied by teachers of children with special educational needs.

In future years, as teachers, parents and professionals work more collaboratively to help children with special needs in mainstream schools, there will be an increasing necessity to design many new different types of assessment device. These will need to be flexible, simple to administer, yield results which are readily understood by teacher, parent and pupil, *reflect* the curriculum rather than determine it, result in improvements in teaching strategies, and be readily applied in the rich variety of natural settings in which learning occurs.

Frank Smith (*op cit*) has warned us that tests can be dangerous. If we are to avoid the pitfalls of traditional assessment, we would do well to remember the wisdom of his pronouncement: 'The only fundamental justification for testing is to facilitate the child's learning.'

References

Ace Special Education Handbook (1983) London: Ace Publications.
Ainscow, M. and Tweddle, D. (1979) *Preventing classroom failure: an objectives approach* Chester: John Wiley & Sons.

Becker, W. C. (1978) 'The national evaluation of follow through' in *Education and Urban Society*, 10, 4.

Burt, C. (1921) *Mental and Scholastic Tests* London: London County Council.

Cameron, R. J., Owen, A. J. and Tee, G. (1986) 'Curriculum Management (Part 3): assessment and evaluation' in *Educational Psychology in Practice*, 2, 3, 3–9.

Clarke, A. M. and Clarke, A. D. B. (1976) *Early Experience: Myth and Evidence* New York: The Free Press.

Clough, E. E., Davis, P. and Sumner, R. (1984) *Assessing Pupils: A Study of Policy and Practice* Slough: NFER/Nelson.

Daly, B., Addington, J., Kerfoot, S. and Sigston, A. (1985) *Portage: the importance of parents* Slough: NFER/Nelson.

Department of Education and Science, Central Advisory Council for Education (England) (1967) *Children and their Primary Schools* London: HMSO (The Plowden Report).

Department of Education and Science (1978) *Special Educational Needs*: Report of the Committee of Enquiry into the Education of Handicapped Children and Young People, London: HMSO (The Warnock Report).

Department of Education and Science (1983) Circular 1/83: *Assessments and Statements of Special Educational Needs* London: HMSO.

Department of Education and Science (1985) *Better Schools* London: HMSO.

Galton, M. and Simon, B. (1980) *Progress and Performance in the Primary Classroom* London: Routledge and Kegan Paul.

Gillham, W. E. C. (1979) 'The failure of Psychometrics' in W. E. C. Gillham (ed) *Reconstructing Educational Psychology* London: Croom Helm.

Hargreaves, D. (1984) *Improving Secondary Schools: Report of the Committee on the Curriculum and Organisation of Secondary Schools* London: Inner London Education Authority.

Lister, T. A. J. and Cameron, R. J. (1986) 'Curriculum Management (Part 1): Planning curriculum objectives' in *Educational Psychology in Practice*, 2, 1, 6–14.

Lloyd-Jones, R., Bray, E., Johnson, G. and Currie, R. (1986) *Assessment: from principles to action* London: Macmillan.

Lovejoy, S. (1985) 'What do they expect? – Headteacher, teacher and social worker expectations of educational psychologists' in *Educational Psychology in Practice*, 1, 3, 108–111.

Mittler, P. (1981) Foreword in J. McBrien and T. Foxen *Training staff in behavioural methods* Manchester: Manchester University Press.

Muncey, J. and Ainscow, M. (1983) 'Launching SNAP in Coventry' in *British Journal of Special Education*, 10, 3, 8–12.

Newson, E. (1976) 'Parents as a resource in diagnosis and assessment' in

Early Management of Handicapping Disorders IRMMH Review of Research and Practice No 19. Associated Scientific Publishers.

Ouston, J. (1981) 'Differences between schools: the implications for school practice' in W. E. C. Gillham (ed) *Problem Behaviour in the Secondary School* London: Croom Helm.

Reynolds, D. *et al* (1976) 'Schools do make a difference' *New Society*, 29 July.

Robertson, J. (1981) *Effective Classroom Control* London: Hodder and Stoughton.

Roe, M. (1978) 'Medical and psychological concepts of problem behaviour' in W. E. C. Gillham (ed) *Reconstructing Educational Psychology* London: Croom Helm.

Roulston, S. (1983) 'Out of the broom cupboard' in *British Journal of Special Education*, 10, 1, 13–15.

Rutter, M., Maughan, B., Mortimore, P. and Ouston, J. (1979) *Fifteen Thousand Hours: Secondary Schools and their Effects on Children* London: Open Books.

Smith, F. (1986) 'Making the grade: the dilemma of assessment?' Paper presented at the University of Reading.

Tomlinson, S. (1982) *A Sociology of Special Education* London: Routledge and Kegan Paul.

Wallace, P. (1986) 'Blame it on the Psychologists!' in *Special Children*, 6, 10–11.

3 Effecting change in schools: working in the organisation

Jane Weightman

As teachers we are all familiar with having to think about both content and method for our pupils. Similarly, when we are planning change we need to think about what it is we want to change (content) and how to bring it about (method). This chapter is about the second strand: implementing change – not what change to implement.

Innovation

Innovation and change are not dark forces about to disturb our ordered calm. They can be interesting activities undertaken by people at work to keep their organisations lively and up-to-date by exploring possible new activities and changed methods of doing things. It is important, however, that proposals meet two criteria:

> Innovation and creativity have to do with the development, proposal and implementation of *new* and *better* solutions.
>
> (Steiner, 1965, 4)

Someone else's reluctance to support our innovations may be because the person is dull, unimaginative, obstinate and behind the times but, equally, the proposed innovation may not be very good! The main stages of innovation are: first, invention or creativity (dealt with elsewhere in this book – see, for example, Chapter 4); second, dissemination and development of the proposal, where an understanding of the school as an organisation is critical. The third stage is the consequence of the innovation in practice. Like all social action, change has some unintended consequences as well as those intended. It is important to anticipate as many of the unintended consequences as possible without quashing useful innovation. One argument for changing in small steps rather than one large step is that we have the opportunity to adjust, modify and reflect upon the consequences before taking the next step. For change to be effective other people need to be involved and this requires an understanding of our particular setting.

Power

Many teachers have an idea that the school should be collegiate: they feel any good idea will be taken up readily by their colleagues. This is not so. It seriously underestimates the variety of views present in a school. By their very nature, schools have a wide range of individuals, groups and interests. This inevitably leads to conflict. Any activity that seeks to ensure a particular outcome, where various options are possible, involves behaving politically. That is using power.

The title 'head of special needs' or 'learning support co-ordinator' does not necessarily mean the individual has sufficient influence or power to make changes. Titles, or positions of power, need the support of other sources of power, such as control of resources, to make things happen. Teachers frequently reject the idea of behaving politically as it seems insincere or devious, but those who understand and use power are more able to get things done. As Dahl says:

> The graveyards of history are strewn with the corpses of reformers who failed utterly to reform anything, of revolutionaries who failed to win power. . .of anti-revolutionaries who failed to prevent a revolution – men and women who failed not only because of the forces arrayed against them but because the pictures in their minds about power and influence were simplistic and inaccurate.
>
> (Dahl, 1970, 15)

The various sources of power are summarised in Figure 3.1.

For the special needs specialist the two most obvious sources of power are control of resources and skill. Both of these enable specialists to help other people who are uncertain or unsure what to do. For example, in one comprehensive school a modern language probationer was helped by the special needs co-ordinator providing her with tape-recorders for a lesson. In another school, a science teacher with a mixed-ability class was helped by having a special needs

Figure 3.1 *Sources of power*

1 *Resources*
Control of what others need, whether subordinates, peers or superiors
It includes the following
Materials
Information
Rewards
Finance
Time
Staff

2 *Skill*
Being an expert, having a skill others need or desire.

3 *Motivation*
Some seek power more enthusiastically than others.

4 *Debts*
Having others under obligation for past favours.

5 *Physical prowess*
Being bigger or stronger than opponent; not overtly used in organisations except as control of resources. (However, statistically leaders tend to be taller than the led.)

6 *Persuasion skills*
Bargaining and personal skills that enable one to make the most of one's other powers, such as resources.

7 *Control of agenda*
Coalition and other techniques for managing how the issues are, or are not, presented.

8 *Dependence*
Where one side depends on the other for willing co-operation the power of removal exists. Teacher action, or threatening to resign *en bloc* are two examples.

9 *Charismatic*
Very rare indeed. Much discussed in management circles as part of leadership qualities. Usually control of resources can account for claims of charismatic power, as many ex-head teachers have found.

From Torrington, Weightman and Johns, 1985, p 100

teacher in the class. In a third school, a special needs teacher helped the head of fourth year devise a reward system to complement the sanctions used by the pastoral team.

As well as understanding one's own power it is useful to consider where else in the school there is power and influence. To do this one needs to consider the school as an organisation.

Organisation culture

Each school is different from all other schools. Some are formal, precise places where people wear uniforms, address each other as Mr, Mrs, Dr, Miss, and have procedures and systems for everything. Others are informal, first names are the norm and people concentrate on the end result rather than how to get there.

Charles Handy (1986, 84–85) has developed Roger Harrison's ideas on a four-fold classification which can help to make sense of a particular school. His four cultures are club, role, task and person. *Club culture* is like a spider's web; the closer to the spider you are the more influence you have. These are very personal organisations, full of stories of past events. They are high risk and very dependent on the quality of the central character. *Role culture* is like an organisation chart with job titles, not names, in each box. These are joined together in an orderly way by regular procedures, memoranda, formal meetings and standards. The whole is organised, not led. In *task culture* a team is applied to a problem of task and can be re-grouped when the task changes. *Person culture* puts the individual before the organisation's purpose. This is mostly seen in professional practices. Handy found that primary schools were usually seen as task cultures or benevolent club cultures. Secondary schools were predominantly seen as role cultures with a club culture on top.

Understanding the nature of a particular school is essential if one is to influence it. For example, presenting a case for curriculum reform to a role culture by chatting in the staffroom might not be as effective as preparing a well-argued document, whereas the reverse might hold in a task culture. Whatever culture the school has, it is important to get others involved in the process of change.

Involving others

To work effectively in schools we need both formal and informal contacts. Depending on the organisation and the task, we may use the formal channel of a heads of departments meeting to present our new idea, or our informal contacts in the pub on Friday lunchtime. Figure 3.2 is an exercise to help you think about your network of contacts at work, both formal and informal.

Figure 3.2a   *Formal contacts*

Draw a personal organisation chart, with yourself at the centre, using □ to indicate job positions and showing the names of those currently holding those posts. The chart should include *formal* relations you have inside and outside the school. The circle represents the school and your drawing might look something like this:

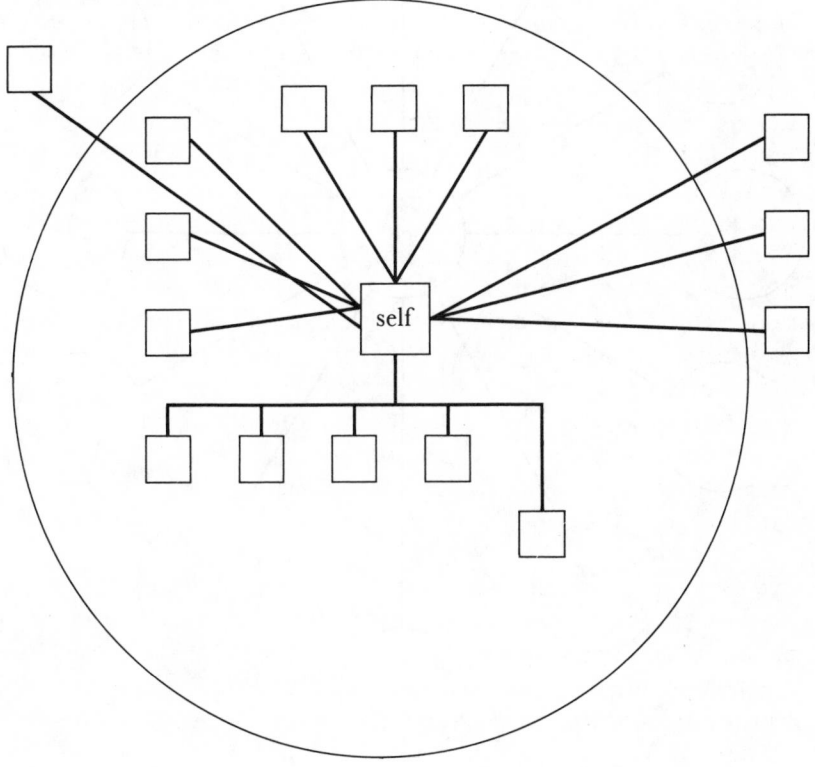

Figure 3.2b *Informal contacts*

On a second chart list all the individuals or groups who can affect your effectiveness in your job, but with whom you do not have a formal working relationship included in the first chart. Give both names and positions. The drawing, which may look something like the one below, will describe your informal network.

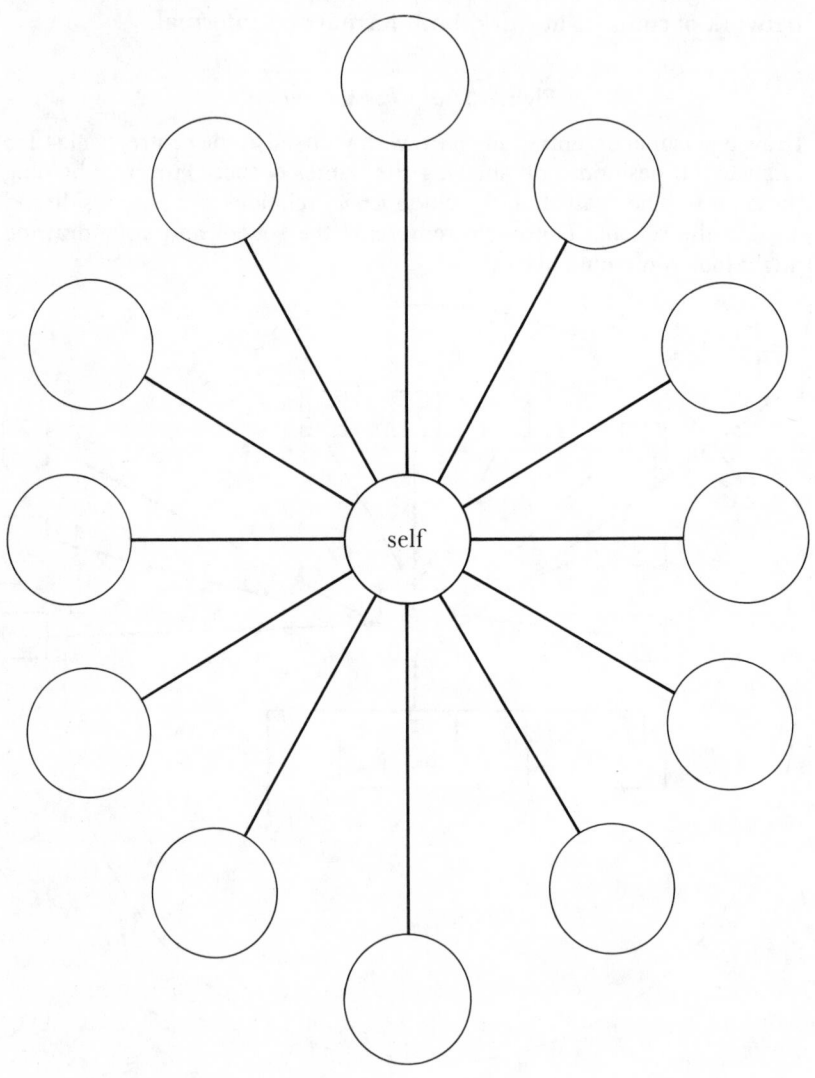

Figure 3.2c   *Evaluating the network of contacts*

1 Rank order the contacts, formal and informal, in their importance to you in getting your job done effectively.

2 Rate each contact on a scale between —3 and +3, according to how helpful the person is to you.

3 What can be done to improve communication with those you have rated between —1 and —3?

rank	contact	—3	—2	—1	0	1	2	3	Improvement by ...

4 Is there anyone who should be in your network but is not yet?

How we approach the individual to whom we are related formally or informally can, of course, also be either formal or informal. The formality of the approach will be influenced by the school's culture, our own style and the importance of the task. The important point is that people need to be involved in making the decisions about change as they are then committed to giving them a try. Decisions handed down as a *fait accompli* only challenge folk to find reasons why it should not work. Usually some sort of meeting is involved.

Meetings

We all feel ambivalent about meetings. On the one hand they take up a lot of time; on the other, there is a need to feel that we can demonstrate our democratic right to participate in decision-making. For teachers there is the additional need to come together with others and feel the security of a group after their solitary and isolated role in the classroom. Perhaps the main advantage of meetings is that, although the decisions made may have taken several people a lot of time, the decision starts life with all members committed to its success. It is important that membership of meetings is made up of those who have some contribution to make. Too many passengers can kill a meeting's sense of purpose. The contribution may be expertise, resources, political clout, personal skills, membership of another network or some other role. There is no point in having a meeting to discuss something if the decision has already been made – that only leads to frustration and distrust. Figure 3.3 gives some guidance notes on meetings.

Figure 3.3   *Meetings: some guidance notes*

The chairperson

Before the meeting

1 What is the meeting for – decision-making, team-building, briefing, generating ideas or something else?
2 Review papers for the meeting to considering timing and pacing.
3 Review meeting arrangements, eg minutes and agenda distributed.

During the meeting

4 Introduce new members.
5 Call for matters arising from minutes of last meeting (if relevant).
6 Introduce agenda items.
7 Call on members to speak, seeking a balance of views, style and authority.
8 Focus discussion on disagreements that must be resolved.
9 Periodically summarise discussion and point a new direction.
10 Ask for clarification from a member whose comments others find puzzling or unacceptable.
11 Pick a workable hypothesis from the discussion and choose the right time to put it to the meeting for acceptance.
12 Agree who is going to do what and write it down.
13 Finish on time.

After the meeting

14 Check with secretary that the notes or minutes of the meeting are drafted, agreed with you and circulated.
15 Ensure that those who have to take action know what to do, and do it.
16 Review your role as chair; what will you do differently next time?

The meeting member

Before the meeting

1 What is the meeting for?
2 What is your role – sage, brake synthesiser, diplomat, delegate, adviser, stimulus or something else?
3 Review papers for meeting and notes you plan to use.
4 Check that you have taken the action agreed for you at last meeting.

During the meeting

5 Use social skills to persuade others.
6 Be objective in seeking solutions that will be acceptable to others.
7 Avoid personal attacks on others that would isolate you from other members.
8 Support and develop contributions by others that you regard as constructive and potentially acceptable after modification.

9 Constantly monitor the mood of the meeting to judge when best to make your contributions – facts, opinions, suggestions or hypotheses.
10 Always work through the chair, recognising the authority that the group always invests in that role.

After the meeting

11 Consult with those you represent to advise them of meeting decisions and required actions.
12 Study the minutes when circulated, noting corrections needed and consider suggestions for future agenda items.
13 Take action on those items requiring your action.
14 Review your participation; what will you do differently next time?

(From Torrington, Weightman and Johns, 1985, 78)

Effecting change in practice

Having discussed the general principles of working in the organisation, how does it look in practice? The following are the four key stages in effecting change:

1 **Collecting facts about whether a change is needed** Talking to people on courses and in other schools suggests new ideas. Pressure for change also comes from the government and local education authorities. As a result of reading relevant literature, listening to others and talking to colleagues, change may begin to seem a good idea. At this stage it is important to have information about the different options by gathering written examples of syllabus, profiles, structures or whatever is to be changed. It is probably sensible to talk (where appropriate) to the headteacher, deputy for curriculum and head of department about possible change.
2 **Consultation with those affected and those interested** A common way to start is by producing a discussion document on the proposed changes and distributing this to relevant staff for comment. One head of special needs started by getting a representative from each department to come to a meeting to discuss how best to support slower children (Thomas & Jackson, 1986). From this consultation process must come a finalised document which can be presented to the staff, governors, etc. You will need to argue for, and be committed to, the plan.

3 **Implementing the plan** Communication and training are two of the things needed here; this will include a continual repetition of what will happen and how it works and a patient explanation of the details to various individuals and groups. A written document helps, but people prefer to hear things as well. Being accessible when you feel most hectic is the art of managing change successfully.

4 **Follow up** You need some system to ensure that, a far as possible, things are going to plan. One school made a member of staff in each department responsible for liaising with special needs staff. In another, the head of special needs was also head of years one and two and obtained feedback about the children that way. Some formal system is necessary as well as the informal corridor feedback to ensure that all areas are monitored.

Conclusion

Effecting change is not easy. It needs careful planning. It involves an understanding of the organisation in which we work and an understanding of our own sources of power and influence. It requires the involvement of others, because only with involvement comes commitment. The most effective people in organisations are those with a clear understanding of the way their set-up operates, a clear agenda of things they are trying to do and a network of good personal contacts who can help to achieve those things.

The aim of this chapter has been to try to help readers achieve such an understanding of their organisational context. The changes in in-service education for special needs associated with GRIST (Grant Related In-Service Training) require that in-service training will be school-focused. The expectation is that school focused in-service will actually lead to changes happening. That is a forlorn hope unless those who are in the forefront of effecting change in special needs provision in their schools understand the kinds of obstacles which are likely to obstruct them and have strategies for working with the organisation. It is hoped that the outline and exercises given here will provide some framework to that end.

References

Dahl, R. (1970) *Modern Political Analysis* New Jersey: Prentice Hall.
Handy, C. (1986) *Understanding Schools as Organisations* Harmondsworth: Penguin.
Steiner, G. (1965) *The Creative Organisation* University of Chicago Press.
Thomas, G. and Jackson, B. (1986) 'The whole school approach to integration' in *British Journal of Special Education*, 13, 1, 27–29.
Torrington, D., Weightman, J. and Johns, K. (1985) *Management Methods* London: Institute of Personnel Management.

4 Linking innovation, evaluation and classroom practice

Geoff Trickey and Gordon Stobart

The thesis

The thesis developed in this chapter is that an effective and dynamic special education system requires the closest possible relationship between research and educational practice, with the locus of innovation firmly rooted at the point of delivery – in the school and the classroom.

The effects of eighty years of educational research and evaluation are barely discernible. The relationship with clasroom practice and innovation has often been remote and at worst irrelevant. Innovation and influence has largely been seen as the prerogative of 'the establishment' – ie the government or the education authority – generally a 'top down' process that is instigated outside any systematic evaluative framework. Day-to-day classroom practice has been generally assumed to be somewhat apart from either of these more esoteric activities.

It is argued that effective change in the school or classroom requires a far greater integration between the processes of innovation, research and classroom practice, and that the means to synthesise these three elements are readily available through practitioner research. This is broadly defined as planned, monitored and evaluated innovation by those in the best position to know the practical problems and to recognise likely solutions to them.

The style and structure of special education would benefit from being practitioner-led in the search for the most effective means to achieve particular educational aspirations.

In order to consider this proposition it will be necessary to review the professional practices of teachers, administrators, and others involved in the machinery of education; to clarify the requirements for relevant and effective innovation; and to consider the role and locus of evaluation and research in education – its methodology, its limitations, and its possibilities. This analysis may cast some light on the frustrations of educational practitioners at all levels, the extraordinary impotence of mainstream educational research in this country, and the curious meanderings of educational fashion.

This is not an exhortation to unfettered individualism, since the importance of policy development and proper procedural frameworks is recognised. We do not imply that there is a need for experimentation for its own sake – that what is new must necessarily be better than what is old and familiar. It is a matter of revising professional roles and outlooks and of making rational and effective use of available expertise. Practitioner research in education requires a framework which recognises the actual state of the art, the need to proceed on the basis of evaluated outcomes, and gives appropriate status to the contribution of primary care agents – particularly the classroom practitioner.

Educational practice

If teachers were to itemise the main roles which they fulfil, one could guarantee that the list would be long and varied (pastoral adviser, curriculum planner, parent counsellor, lost property officer, arbitrator, etc) but 'researcher' may not loom large. The reason for this may be that tradition dies hard and for a long time research has been done *to* teachers *by* others.

It has frequently been asserted that the major influence determining the professional style and repertoire of teachers in the classroom is the modelling process afforded during their own classroom experiences as pupils. Trainee teachers have spent some two and a half thousand days as school pupils, directly observing the differing styles, strengths and weaknesses of numerous teachers. Given the typical length of time devoted to teaching practice during teacher training, it would be surprising if these fifteen years of accumulated exposure to the professional skills of others were not a major formative influence.

If the practice of classroom teaching has been almost an oral tradition, this may be one factor contributing to the conservatism of the teaching profession and the acceptance of a limited role in relation to the wider issues. It is not difficult to think of other factors that might contribute to a self-effacing professional style – the status of the classroom teacher in a very hierarchical academic structure; the remote relationship between teachers and their municipal employers; the limited external influence allowed in the cycle from classroom to college and back to classroom; the sheer size of the profession. All are likely to contribute in different ways to a situation where teachers generally have not seen a role much beyond the classroom or school, and have perhaps been too accepting of the implied greater wisdom of others higher in our hierarchical educational system. In other words, the existing frameworks and authority structures may effectively de-skill teachers and undermine confidence in the wider relevance of their professional contribution.

Class teachers have found themselves the focus of a torrent of advice about how they should set about their work from an ever increasing number of non-teaching staff, starting within the staffing structure of the school and extending far beyond. They have been subjected to 'expert advice' from senior colleagues, LEA advisers, educational psychologists, government inspectors, working parties, training colleges and institutes of education, government reports, and the relentless and ever-increasing flow of paper from the educational press and from the machinery of government. For every expressed view there is a contrary opinion, rarely is advice consistent across the various sources, and successive fashions countermand each other.

The important point here is that there is little expectation that the class teacher will play a significant part in determining the shape of things to come. In the main, teachers are to be in-serviced, advised, exhorted and directed. Whoever is directing operations, it is not the class teacher. If there is to be innovation, it will be someone else who takes care of it.

Where good classroom practices have been fostered and pro- moted, either by the exponents themselves or by other advocates, the indications are that they can be very influential. Certainly, innova- tion from this source can be expected to have credibility with colleagues.

Innovation

It is doubtful whether there would be much agreement about who is responsible for plotting the course of special education and for bringing about the present confused situation. Responsibilities are fragmented, being shared between central and local government, and at the local level they are frequently poorly defined and in many cases nominal. What are the respective contributions of advisers, inspectors, education officers, governors, headteachers and the rest of the teaching profession in determining special education policy?

Management influences may filter down through the system to impinge on the class teacher in a diffuse and confused way, which does more to inhibit effective action than to provide a responsive system capable of amplifying effective practices and methodology. The lack of progress with the integration of special needs children highlights the inadequacies of established mechanisms for effective institutional change. Somehow, a worth-while humanitarian aspiration with its roots in community and parental concerns, and backed by a limited but useful measure of creative good practice, has become the vehicle for disappointment, confusion and uncertainty.

At the DES level, the 1981 Education Act encourages parents to press for integrated placement for their children, but no resources have been allocated for the major restructuring of services that this implies; the resourcing formula (DES Circular 4/73), based on a system of segregated special schools, is now fourteen years old. At LEA level this places officers in an impossible situation in attempting to meet legitimate demands for flexibility (Trickey and Stobart, 1986). Rather than generating an era of exploration, development and change, the uncertainty and ambivalence of the DES and the LEAs has resulted in confusion and inertia. A recent survey by the Spastics Society, *Caught in the Act* (1986), has exposed the lack of definitive policies reflecting the 1981 Education Act, and another NAS survey, *Education in Crisis* (1986), has highlighted the lack of physical preparation for integration. The displacement activity at the local level seems to have been a preoccupation with appropriate paperwork and bureaucratic procedures for statementing.

It often appears to practitioners that authority, rather than promoting positive action, is exercised in ways that inhibit creative developments on site. Yet, when it comes to day-to-day practicalities rather than theory or general policy, the detailed understanding necessary to achieve a workable system is to be found in the work place. It is unlikely to be fully appreciated at the level from which developments are generally presumed to descend. The broad brush of policy easily obliterates the fine detail of professional practice.

This has been exactly the case with integration policy. There has been too little concern about the practicalities of implementation. While, from the human rights viewpoint, there is general agreement that, wherever possible, handicapped pupils should be educated alongside their peers, it still remains unclear how this can be achieved. Each sector of the educational community waits somewhat apprehensively for someone to arrive with the master plan. At every level, from classroom to government, everyone seems to be looking to somebody else to provide the keys to unlock the door to a new era.

These developments within special education during recent years provide a powerful illustration of the importance of aligning innovation, professional practice and research. A very positive grass roots movement has been emasculated through its elevation to policy and law long before the means of implementation had been devised. Rather than fostering and supporting early developments and the achievement of ever-improved practices and strategies capable of demonstrating the feasibility of the approach, it became transposed from a practitioner movement to a 'top-down' policy. The problem has now become: how can the authorities follow through and disseminate the fine grain of intended service delivery when the logistics and techniques required have yet to be developed?

Perhaps the Warnock Report set aspirations at an unrealistic level, given contemporary evidence of what was practically feasible. Perhaps the 1981 Education Act contributed by failing to recognise resource requirements in either material or human terms, let alone the magic ingredient required to combine these two elements into a viable system.

The total cost of professional time devoted during the past decade to this issue alone has been prodigious. We leave it to the reader to speculate about the expenditure devoted to research, conferences, standing committees, working parties, and in-service training, all occurring at central and local levels, and repeated throughout the country. So often this activity has done little more than produce descriptions of how everybody is attempting to muddle through.

Perhaps the example that should be guiding us at this stage is to be found in the development of the Portage project. In the late seventies this scheme, designed to assist parents in promoting the development of special needs children, was being operated by a handful of centres on shoe-string budgets and relying on the enthusiasm of those participating. It was far from clear at that stage whether it would survive the many hazards in its path, particularly those involved in developing a service across Health and Education Authorities. However, as results demonstrated that it was a highly effective way of meeting obvious needs, its influence has been rapidly accelerated through the use of educational support grants.

The 'top-down' approch to educational innovation is at least as likely to destroy the fine detail of effective organisation as it is to achieve benefits. The probability of achieving lasting and effective change through the promotion and refinement of on-site innovation would seem far more likely. By introducing the discipline of evaluation at the classroom and school level and supporting the systematic accumulation of practitioner research findings, much could have been done to build a body of knowledge and experience relevant to the issues of the day.

Educational research and evaluation

Evaluation in education has generally been conspicuous by its absence. Intuition, common sense, conviction, political dogma, tradition, and fashion have reigned virtually unchallenged. Where evaluation has made an appearance, it has often been so narrowly interpreted as to ensure its irrelevance.

Where research has been conceived within the confines of formal experimental design paradigms the results have been predictably uninspiring. Attempts at the controlled experiment within the educational context throw up their own particular brand of nonsense, in which 'teacher variables' become some form of contamination which interferes with the objectivity of the exercise and limits the extent to which scientific findings can be generalised. Educational research, until quite recently, seemed almost to contrive to dissociate itself from the day-to-day business of educational practice. Associated with the paraphernalia of higher education, qualifications and professional journals, it became a closed academic communication network, content to be ignored by educational managers and practitioners alike. The term 'research' acquired associations and connotations amongst the teaching profession that were the antithesis of practicality and common sense.

Teachers feel the research to be irrelevant, school administrators and board members find it to be of little value. Research fails to solve problems of classroom and society.

(Kemmiss and Grotelueschen, 1977)

More recently Carol Weiss, in a paper about participatory evaluation, has summarised decades of criticism:

... it sometimes seems that more papers have been published criticising evaluation practices and procedures than reporting results of studies conducted.

(Weiss, 1985)

In this paper she uses five broad headings to group the most frequently cited failings of educational evaluation. These respectively emphasise that it is unrealistic, narrow, irrelevant, unfair and that the findings go unused.

At the very least there has been a failure in communication. The contribution of formal educational research and evaluation has been insufficiently familiar amongst the majority of practitioners even to allow debate about its relevance. Teachers have long since given up looking in that direction for assistance in solving the problems that confront them daily in the classroom. Blackman (1972) talks of the 'acknowledged inability' of educational research 'to make any impact on the educational enterprise'.

When it comes to decision making there often seems to be little expectation that the status of ideas tossed into the debate need be above that of personal opinion. Amongst the conflicting political and philosophical perspectives and their various interests and claims on education the researcher, striving to restrain dialogue within the bounds of acceptable objectivity, is presented with formidable difficulties. Certainly, major changes in educational organisation have been launched, and successive waves of educational fashion have permeated through the system with little consideration of the desirability of systematic evaluation. These factors reflect the low value accorded to formal research and evaluation by both managers and practitioners in education.

On the other hand, practitioners have had at times a profound influence on their peers. The memorable names in the history of education and the most frequently recurring names in contemporary discussions about special educational needs are those of practitioners. Colleagues may agree or disagree with the views and approaches of such innovators but their credibility amongst colleagues is difficult to question.

We are presented with an ironic comparison between the unmanaged, unpredictable but pervasive influence of untested fashionable ideas which sweep all before them – the band-wagon effect – and the remoteness and unfruitfulness of formal educational research.

The picture has improved perceptibly due to new and more practical styles of inquiry, the early fruits of action research and some attempts to come to grips with issues of dissemination. But the structural and institutional arrangements which sustain a divide between the academic and the practitioner remain. Within this context, it is difficult to see how current styles of research could achieve the desired impact on education.

Aware of these long-standing criticisms, academic institutions have made considerable efforts to achieve a new relevance. Recent special needs research sponsored by the Department of Education and Science has made heroic efforts to focus on good practice in some local authorities, and the practicalities of classroom management of special needs. It has also taken a much more positive approch to the dissemination of findings. This is probably the best that could be achieved within the traditional institutional roles. Nevertheless, the success of this enterprise is likely to be limited by a number of questionable assumptions:

• that solutions to logistical and service delivery problems can usefully be generalised between local authorities with very different characteristics and patterns of services;
• that effective innovative planning of professional networks and inter-professional relationships can take place off site;
• that it is realistic to hope to influence the practice of significant numbers of teachers as a secondary process through in-service training;
• that the skills and attitudes of effective teachers can somehow be 'packaged' for the use of others.

Neither surveys of established practices and *post hoc* evaluation, nor narrowly framed and controlled studies hold much promise for the future. They have little potential for ensuring that professional practice and research move forward together. Current ownership of the research enterprise, its off-site origins and its inherent expertism create obstacles to the processes of professional development and institutional change that may seem to outweigh any benefits. Established research and evaluation practices confirm the teacher as object and recipient of the exercise rather than participant or initiator, and this undermining of confidence and endorsement of a restricted and passive role can only be viewed as costly. Its effect on professional practice is therefore exactly opposite to that which it sets out to achieve.

Practitioner research: a potent new partnership

Current practitioner research methodology is at a sophisticated stage of development and has been well articulated. It has its roots in the action research model of Kurt Lewin (1946), the work of Stephen Corey (eg 1953), and more recently in the thinking of John Elliott (1978). Lawrence Stenhouse (1975) used the term 'case study' to describe a second major formative strand of development concerned with the examination of problematic educational situations with a view to explaining them, but without initiating an intervention. He was a strong advocate of the teacher as researcher:

> It is not enough that teachers' work should be studied, they need to study it themselves. It will require a generation of work [and] the teacher's professional self-image and conditions of work will have to change.
>
> (Stenhouse, 1975)

An approach using action research and case study strategically in combination is described by Gordon Bell (1985). He uses the term 'action inquiry' and sees this as a potent and flexible methodology with significant learning benefits for the practitioners. In an important recent paper he considers five different models of action inquiry, giving priority to the INSET aspects of the processes involved (Bell, 1985). He has adopted Reginald Ravens's term 'action learning' to refer to the professional development inherent in the use of these techniques. He contrasts this approach with professional development using the more familiar didactic and authoritarian methods:

> This trend in thinking that there surely is someone somewhere who knows what is best and can decide for one is a form of

self-domination that is profoundly ironic. As a preferred mode of INSET, it is a procedure destined to promote the infantilisation of teachers rather than secure their growth.

(Gordon Bell, 1985)

Education will always be confronted with change and new challenges as society crosses new frontiers at an accelerating rate. Education must find ways of keeping abreast of, and adapting to, economic and technological development with its implication for patterns of employment and leisure, and all the complexity of social change that inevitably follow.

Any static view of an educational system is now untenable. Education must reflect society *today*, if method and content are to remain relevant and if it is really going to contribute to the process. Since change has become a feature of all our lives, the systems for institutional change within education need to be incorporated as an essential part of the whole rather than as an optional extra, an inessential luxury to be considered only when we can afford it.

Practitioner research offers a great deal in relation to these ends. What is required is a supportive framework within the LEA that encourages and resources the systematic evaluation of the initiatives of its own professional staff. There have been several developments along these lines.

Frameworks for innovation

During the summer of 1984 the London Borough of Barking and Dagenham established a Projects Advisory Committee with the primary function of providing advice and support to LEA practitioners wishing to develop a project relating to their special needs work. They also served to reassure the officers of the LEA that proposals were responsible in their aims and methods. Committee members with a variety of backgrounds were invited from inside and outside the borough to serve for a period of one year. In particular, four areas of specific expertise were sought: project design experience, experience of special/mainstream collaboration, awareness of recent innovation, and the parental viewpoint. Their brief was to help to tighten up project design, to ensure that project aspirations were realistic, relevant and responsible. It was hoped that the field experience of committee members would assist with the anticipation of practical difficulties. The variety of backgrounds and experience available was expected to ensure that project participants would have access to information about other relevant work.

All local teachers were encouraged by various means to consider establishing projects relating to the particular difficulties that they confronted in the course of their work. The role of the committee was to be collaborative and to be involved at an early stage; to be constructive and supportive rather than judgmental. During the following year a diverse series of local projects was successfully launched in this way. The skills of the committee in assisting project teams improved over that period and the process became increasingly efficient. The project programme achieved tangible results and the scheme provides one useful example of a framework designed to facilitate practitioner research.

Since 1983 Leicestershire have employed ten curriculum support teachers with the brief to develop a range of action research projects. The aim has been to develop a wider range of options for children with special educational needs. Successful projects may then receive Authority sponsorship on a wide scale.

Each year all mainstream and special schools are invited to submit bids for funding from a pool, which in turn is allocated from a total £450,000 set aside since 1983 for Priority Area INSET. The bids are channelled through nine Area Special Needs Co-ordinators to a Special Needs In-Service Steering Group, which includes representatives of all those involved in special education in-service provision and the administration.

A second school-focused system drawing from the same funds allows schools to submit bids for additional supply time to support school initiatives. Schools may acquire from two to forty days' additional teaching time through this scheme.

There is provision in this Leicestershire programme for particularly successful schemes to be extended or adopted on a permanent basis. Project teams are invited to submit interim and final reports on their activities and some may develop to become INSET priorities in their own right, being included in subsequent annual bids to the Education Committee. Where projects demonstrate an ability to meet a particular need effectively they may be taken into the main special education budget as an established part of local authority provision.

Both the Barking and Leicestershire schemes support the innovative talents of practitioners and provide the means through which they can play a part in determining the future pattern of provision. The importance of operational frameworks of this kind is that they positively encourage innovative exploration of alternative working arrangements and broaden local debate about responsibilities, problems and possibilities. They also recognise the unique nature of local circumstances and arrangements as the necessary starting point for local developments as well as for the appraisal of developments in other authorities.

In managing such arrangements, the LEA has to keep in mind the ultimate long-term goal: the achievement of a coherent pattern of local special needs provision. To this end it is vital to encourage a level of evaluation adequate to allow projects to inform discussions and future policy decisions.

Practitioner research as in-service training

A significant difficulty arises with the physical and psychological remoteness of traditional educational research from the practice of teaching. Even supposing that the other difficulties of methodology and relevance were to be overcome, the additional problems of dissemination would remain. The lack of influence of research on education has sometimes been considered to be due to difficulties in communicating findings to practitioners. We have already suggested that there may be other important reasons for this, but whether or not dissemination is the root cause of what Henry Chandler called 'the fractured interface' (Chandler, 1981), it is clear that the dislocation of research and practice does create a need for communication that is very different from that required in the case of practitioner research. When the problem researched is derived from the difficulties arising on site, and the practitioner confronted with the difficulty participates directly in the analysis of the problem and the evaluation of possible solutions to it, dissemination of findings has very different functions. After all, the practitioners are the first to know the results, not the last, and will not need to be convinced that the findings are relevant to their situations.

The difficulties of achieving change through in-service training are certainly apparent to advisory services and to others with a professional development role within the LEAs. Quite apart from issues about the efficiency of the exercise there are the problems of access and attendance. Typically, the same enthusiastic minority attends the majority of courses, and these teachers are unlikely to be those most in need of inspiration and motivation. The limitations of INSET as a vehicle for institutional change have been emphasised in *The Myth of the Hero Innovator* (Georgiades and Philimore, 1975).

Over recent years new and exciting alternatives to the didactic model have been developed. The cascade model in particular has been prominent in special needs awareness training, and workshops are generally considered more effective than lectures. The major common component in these approaches has been that of active participation. Direct involvement of some kind is recognised to be far more likely to achieve changes in professional practice than passive exposure to information. Practitioner research represents one extreme of a continuum in this respect. Involvement in the processes of problem clarification, project planning and evaluation could hardly be more direct.

Practitioner research in education is concerned with teacher participation in the process of developing a body of practical professional knowledge. This is a somewhat novel exercise.

> Perhaps it is timely to recall that hitherto teachers have been largely excluded from developing knowledge of their own practice except under the control of academics, outsiders, or professional researchers.
>
> (Bell, 1985)

This is a process in which the professional development of the participants is an intrinsic part rather than a secondary consideration. The emphasis is on personal professional responsibility rather than on dependence on outside authority. Generalised across the profession, this approach can only enhance the self-esteem of teachers. Practitioner research, therefore, has the potential to promote development of the profession as well as individual professional growth.

Under previous INSET funding arrangements the traditional role of the academic institutions was endorsed and there was little incentive to develop closer working links with the LEAs. In spite of this, some attempts have been made to achieve greater collaboration, through DES regional courses, for example. It has not been an easy matter, however, to change the traditional working relationship between the academic network and practising teachers within the LEAs. The results of a recent survey conducted by the authors indicated that teachers interested in this approach still find little support and need great determination and persistence as they pursue their interests in relative isolation. The recently revised INSET funding arrangements provide a new flexibility and give the LEAs far more opportunity to shape their own arrangements. Some have already seen the value of devoting INSET funds to practitioner research and it is to be hoped that this possibility will become more widely recognised.

Conclusion

It has been our intention to reappraise the relationship between research, innovation, and professional classroom practice. We have argued that much of what is wrong in special education has arisen from a lack of synchronisation in the traditional relationship between the aims and methods of education, the impetus and demands for change, and the processes of evaluation. In our view, far greater coincidence is required between these three areas and we have argued that innovative classroom enterprise within special education should be recognised as capable of an important role in providing practicable solutions to educational problems.

The fostering of such 'bottom-up' policy development, based on teacher-led innovation, would require the development of support-ive and facilitative frameworks at the LEA level, and encouragement and recognition at a national level – perhaps through Grant Related In-Service Training or Educational Support Grant.

The main impediment to progress would appear to be that teachers have been conditioned to view their professional role in rather restrictive ways. This perception is confirmed by the established educational structures which characterise research as an advanced academic activity and place school teachers at a lowly point on the academic scale. We are convinced that Lawrence Stenhouse is correct in the view that the self-image of teachers and their conditions of work will have to change in order for practitioner research approaches to be maximised. He estimated that it would take a generation of work to achieve this. We hope that this time scale is pessimistic.

There have already been developments in advanced training where the value of practitioner research as a training process has been exploited. Similar developments are to be encouraged as being of considerable potential, benefiting both the professional skills of participants and the course of development of educational practice. The same emphasis also needs to be incorporated into initial teacher training.

We now have a sound methodology, well-defined working practices, and a rapidly growing body of practitioner research experience on which to build. All that is needed is the courage on the part of the teaching profession to accept the professional challenge and responsibilities of participation, and the maturity on the part of the training establishments to accept a different but more relevant role. Given these two elements, we could achieve a truly dynamic and responsive education system, in which practitioners build from their own unique, front-line perspective to enable education to meet the continuing challenge of change.

References

Bell, G. (1985) 'INSET: Five types of collaboration and consultancy' in *School Organisation*, 5, 3, 247–256.
Blackman, L. (1972) 'Research in the classroom: Mahomet and the mountain revisited' in *Exceptional Children*, 39, 181–191.
Chandler, H. N. (1981) 'Research and teachers: The interface remains fractured' in *Journal of Learning Disabilities*, 14, 10, 604–606.
Corey, S. (1953) *Action Research to Improve School Practices* University of Columbia: Teachers College.
Elliott, J. (1978) 'What is action research in schools?' in *Journal of Curriculum Studies*, 10, 4, 355–357.
Georgiades, N. J. and Phillimore, L. (1975) 'The myth of the hero innovator and alternative strategies for change' in C. C. Kiernan and F. P. Woodford (eds) *Behaviour Modification with the Severely Retarded* Associated Scientific Publishers.
Kemmiss, S. and Grotelueschen, A. (1977) 'What is "educational" about educational research?' in *Journal of Educational Research*, 71, 1, 48–52.
Lewin, K. (1946) 'Action research and minority problems' in *Journal of Social Issues*, 2, 34–36.
NAS/UWT *Education in Crisis* London: NAS/UWT.

Rodgers, R. (1986) *Caught in the Act* The Spastics Society, CSIE London.
Stenhouse, L. (1975) *An Introduction to Curriculum Research and Development* London: Heinemann.
Trickey, G. E. F. and Stobart, G. (1985) 'Special needs administration takes shape' in *Education* 167, 16, 362–363.
Weiss, C. H. (1985) 'Towards the future of stakeholder approaches to evaluation' in E. R. House (ed) *New Directions in Educational Evaluation* Lewes: The Falmer Press.

PART II
The whole school

Introduction

In this section our contributors examine reform of the curriculum as a whole-school issue and they look at some of the ways in which the school as a whole can respond to a changing concept of special needs.

Will Swann, in Chapter 5, contends that our understanding of the difficulties children experience is often simplistic. It is rooted in the notion that the curriculum is a body of knowledge to be imparted. But some children will have difficulties for evermore if the curriculum is seen in this way. He argues that the only kind of curriculum in which a portion of children will not always be experiencing problems is one which is less didactic and more pupil-centred – one which is embedded in the context of pupils' experience.

Ingrid Lunt, focusing on the primary school, argues (Chapter 6) that substantial changes are required to avoid the problems associated with traditional withdrawal for remedial work, for this model isolates children from the contexts in which they are experiencing difficulty, separating them from their peers and from the mainstream curriculum. A more context-based focus is required. Several approaches are described, which involve moving additional help to children – rather than children to the additional help.

Geof Sewell (Chapter 7) reminds us of the backdrop of unemployment against which we attempt to improve the achievements of secondary pupils. He argues that the alienation brought on by the bleak outlook of these young people is often aggravated by the stigma engendered by the remedial systems of some secondary schools. He outlines a 'free flow' model, in which boundaries between the conventional special needs department and the rest of the school are substantially diminished. Low-achieving pupils *can* do well, and they need to be seen doing well. Teachers in secondary schools are urged to form like-minded small groups and to reach out forcefully and imaginatively to raise both expectations and achievements.

5 Learning difficulties and curriculum reform: integration or differentiation?

Will Swann

Introduction

My aim in this chapter is to consider some aspects of the kind of curriculum which will make it easier for pupils with special needs to participate in ordinary schools. I include in this remit those who are excluded from ordinary schools and are educated in special schools and those who experience difficulties in learning in ordinary schools and whose involvement in the life of their school is, for this reason, tenuous.

+ I shall split the former group into two sub-categories: those who have sensory or physical disabilities and those who do not. Children who are segregated into special schools by reason of their ability and behaviour form a much larger group than those who are segregated because of disability. Among pupils with disabilities are a great many who have learning difficulties as well. Tony Dessent (1983) remarked that most educational psychologists have encountered the relative ease with which ordinary schools will accommodate pupils with disabilities, by comparison with the problems they face integrating pupils with learning difficulties. His comment is well supported by national trends in special-school placement. From 1978 to 1983, there were significant falls in the numbers of pupils with sensory disabilities in special schools, after taking into account the general fall in school rolls. Numbers in schools for pupils with physical disabilities were static, but there is plenty of evidence that many spent much of their time in ordinary schools while still on a special-school roll. But, at the same time, numbers in special schools for pupils with learning difficulties and behaviour problems were growing (Swann, 1985). We also know that where schemes to integrate children with physical disabilities have got under way, it is those without marked learning difficulties who have been most readily integrated (Swann, 1987). The slogan for the early 1980s, then, was integration by disability but segregation by ability. What has happened nationally since then is anybody's guess in the absence of usable statistics.

One reason for this situation lies with the relative demands made on ordinary schools, their staff and their curricula by pupils with disabilities and those with marked learning difficulties. No one should underestimate the expertise needed to support children with disabilities in ordinary schools. But, generally speaking, the changes needed are *additions* to the curriculum provided for all pupils. These may involve support staff, micro-technology, adapted materials, inservice training, changes to accommodation, and systems to monitor and co-ordinate individuals' progress. Rarely do pupils' disabilities present a challenge to the curriculum itself in the way that learning difficulties do. By challenge I refer to the inappropriate nature of many curricula, to the overt opposition to schooling expressed by many older pupils and to the sense of frustration and failure many teachers encounter in trying to provide appropriate work for some pupils. Any significant reduction in the number of pupils with learning difficulties in special schools is going to depend on the ability and willingness of ordinary schools to change their curricula so that they can encompass a wider range of ability than hitherto. I shall not say anything here about strategies for including pupils with physical or sensory disabilities. There is an extensive literature now available on this topic (see, for example, Booth and Swann, 1987; Hegarty and Pocklington, 1981; Jamieson, Parlett and Pocklington, 1977; Lynas, 1986).

Although many teachers around the country have found imaginative ways to increase the participation of pupils with learning difficulties in ordinary schools, there are still very few published accounts of the everyday classroom experience of pupils with learning difficulties which would provide a sound basis for widespread development. One of the side-effects of the domination of special education by educational psychology is that books and journals fill up with studies of how pupils respond to experimental learning programmes, while the stock of observations from ordinary classrooms, which would tell us about how ordinary teachers cope with learning difficulties from day to day, is all but non-existent. In this respect, 'ecological' thinking has yet to make an impact. But knowledge in education is no guarantee of consensus. An important feature of our current situation is that there are deep disagreements about desirable styles of teaching and learning and the organisation of schools and curricula. Even supposing we knew in detail what we wanted to do to the curriculum, 'we' might not have the power to do so. The education system in this country is prey to the competing forces of many interest groups. An awareness of the constraints on ordinary schools, trying to improve the lot of pupils with learning difficulties, is a great asset in making reasonable plans for change, and a vital part of the 'ecosystem' of schools. Later in this chapter I shall consider some of these constraints.

Conceptions of learning

Many responses to learning difficulties in the past have been based on the idea that they can be treated as if they were disabilities. Children who have failed to learn have been treated as if they had a mental disability. Curriculum development in special education has been dominated by these 'deficit theories' of learning difficulties, which hold that such difficulties arise because some children lack certain skills and abilities which are necessary preconditions for learning in school. Learning difficulties have been ascribed to deficits in language, attention, perception, memory, and capacity for incidental learning, in addition to all-pervasive accounts of general intellectual deficiency. Deficit theories have also flourished in the rapidly expanding study of and provision for children described as dyslexic, where learning difficulties have been attributed to factors such as incomplete cerebral dominance and defective eye-movements. Despite extensive criticism, deficit theories remain an important part of the educational scene. For Gulliford (1985), the central deficit of pupils with learning difficulties lies in their 'difficulty in learning the basic skills of reading, writing or mathematics . . . If not remedied, the *disability* becomes an increasing handicap as the child gets older and as schoolwork depends more on reading and writing' (Gulliford, 1985, 2, my italics). The solution to learning difficulties, therefore, lies in putting back into children the missing skills which will enable them to join the mainstream curriculum again. I want to argue that this view is seriously mistaken for two reasons. First, it treats children's skills and behaviour as if their expression is independent of the learning environment. It assumes that if a child can't do something in one setting, then s/he can't do it at all. Correspondingly, if you teach skills in one setting, children are free to use them in another. Second, practices based on deficit theories are unrealistic about the demands that the mainstream curriculum imposes on children. In exploring these two issues, I shall not just be trying to show what is wrong with deficit theories but also arguing for two features of an alternative, curriculum-centred approach.

Deficit theory has always been a popular explanation for educational failure. In the 1960s it gained political prominence in the American 'war against poverty' and in British attempts to overcome the educational failure of poor, working-class children. Interest centred on the apparent linguistic problems of such children. Some of the strongest claims were advanced by the Americans Bereiter and Englemann, who argued that many children came to school without any useful language. They claimed dramatically that 'many disadvantaged children of pre-school age come very close to the total lack of ability to use language as a device for acquiring and processing information (Bereiter and Englemann, 1966, 39). The solution they proposed was to inculcate in these children the basic linguistic resources that they need in order to profit from schooling. Although this theory has long since been debunked in the mainstream literature (Edwards, 1979; Stubbs, 1976), it continues to exercise influence in special educational circles. Bereiter and Englemann's programme was the forerunner to the approach known as Direct Instruction, the most well-known example of which is the DISTAR programme (Carnine, 1977). This has been widely advocated by some educational psychologists (Branwhite, 1983; Gregory, 1983).

The failure of the early linguistic deficit theories lay in their pessimistic assumptions about what children could do. The linguist William Labov (1970) showed how dramatically the communicative performance of children could be reduced by the situation in which they were expected to perform. Judgments about children's competence were frequently made on the basis of their ability to respond in individual tests. Labov argued that such tests were unfamiliar and highly threatening to many children. The result was that they adopted a defensive, minimal response strategy. In less threatening situations, where child and adult had more equal status in the conversation, children revealed themselves as much more competent communicators. To use their behaviour in a test as a reliable guide to their communicative competence was clearly mistaken.

Since Labov's pioneering work, there have been many studies of the relationships between children's linguistic performance and their communicative environment, particularly in classrooms. Many classroom studies have been notable more for revealing the ways in which opportunities for pupils to use their linguistic resources are limited, than for how they are enhanced (Edwards, 1980; Willes, 1983). Tizard and Hughes (1983) and Wells (1985) have both shown how the style of interaction adopted by teachers in pre-school and primary classrooms affects pupils' linguistic performance. Children who appear fluent and convey complex ideas with complex language in one conversation can appear to have linguistic and conceptual difficulties in another. Take, for example, a four-year-old, working-class girl, June, whom Tizard and Hughes observed talking to her nursery teacher at school and to her mother at home. An extract from a conversation at school reveals an apparently rather limited child. Here, the teacher has just cut a piece of paper in half for June.

Teacher	How many [pieces of paper] have you got now?
Child	[No Reply.]
Teacher	How many have you got?
Child	[No reply.]
Teacher	How many pieces of paper have you got?
Child	Two.
Teacher	Two. What have I done if I've cut it down the middle?
Child	Two pieces.
Teacher	I've cut it in . . .? [Wants the child to say 'half'.]
Child	[No reply.]
Teacher	What have I done?
Child	[No reply.]
Teacher	Do you know? [Child shakes head.]
Child	Two.
Teacher	Yes, I've cut it in two. But . . . I wonder, can you think?
Child	In the middle.
Teacher	I've cut it in the middle. I've cut it in *half*? There you are, now you've got two.

(Tizard and Hughes, 1983, 194–5)

This conversation is all the more remarkable since June began it by asking her teacher, 'Can you cut that in half?' Compare this with June's performance during a game of knock-out whist with her mother.

Mother	[Deals out six cards each.] You have to call. [Child won the previous round, so she decides trumps this time.]
Child	Oooh, I got a good hand here again, but I can help it. [Arranges the cards in her hand] I got two aces here.
Mother	You shouldn't tell me what you got. Go on, call trumps.
Child	I call heart, I not putting a heart down.
Mother	Hearts. [Mother wins the first trick.] That's mine. [Child wins the second trick.] That's yours. [Child wins another trick.]
Child	No, diamonds.
Mother	Oh, you've changed your mind. That's mine. [Child wins the last trick: she has won four tricks to her mother's two.]
Mother	So how many you got?
Child	Three.
Mother	You haven't. Count. And I've got . . .?
Child	Two. An' how many did I have?
Mother	Four [Child says something unclear. Mother deals five cards for the next round.] Five.
Child	Oh, I got a good hand here as well again . . . Ace of spades.
Mother	What you gonna call?
Child	Diamonds.

(Tizard and Hughes, 1983, 52–53)

The explanation for the difference in June's performance will lie partly in the history of her relationships with her mother and teacher and partly in the specific features of these conversations. One difference between these two settings lies in the extent to which adult and child are collaborating towards achieving shared goals. Wells, Tizard and Hughes argue that children are able to be more competent communicators when adult and child share a common purpose and interest in communicating and when young children can contribute in ways meaningful to them.

Just as context influences children's linguistic performance, it also has a powerful impact on other aspects of learning. Let me take mathematics as an example. Easen (1987) provides an excellent illustration of the way in which the format of a task can make a difference to a child's apparent ability. Charlie, a thirteen-year-old who was receiving remedial support in his comprehensive school, was asked to subtract 70 from 109 using the standard notation and a standard vertical layout. His answer was 100. His techer then asked him, 'If you had £109 and you spent £70, how much would you have left?' Almost immediately, Charlie replied, '£39'. He explained how he worked it out. 'It's £70 . . . 70, 80, 90, 100 that leaves £30 and there's 9, so £39'. The second formulation of the problem gave Charlie the scope to deploy his existing strategies, which were denied him in the written form. A wider demonstration of similar processes has been provided by Carraher *et al* (1985). They investigated the arithmetic skills of nine- to fifteen-year-old children who worked as street vendors in a town in northern Brazil. First, they bought goods from the children in the streets. This involved the children in solving problems involving the four basic rules of arithmetic. They had to calculate the price of a number of items from a unit price, work out the change due, and so on. These problems were all recorded and later presented to the same children in their homes in two other forms: as word problems involving imaginary people and transactions, and as problems in the standard arithmetic notation. The children solved 98 per cent of the real commercial transactions, 74 per cent of the word problems and 37 per cent of the problems in arithmetic notation. Why? One difference between these settings that may be important is the relative ease with which they permit children to deploy their existing knowledge and well practised strategies. Another is that the children's mental activity in the street is sustained by a real purpose and a context which is personally meaningful. Arithmetic in the street made sense to these children in a way in which school arithmetic did not. So, children may well be more competent than they are given credit for, possessing what Hull (1985) describes as 'unconscripted knowledge', that is, knowledge relevant to the tasks they face in school, which is excluded by the way they are taught.

What I have said so far leads to the conclusion that at least some learning difficulties are *created* in interactions between children, teachers and curricula, rather than *discovered* in children. I do not mean by this that learning difficulties are the result of any intent by teachers to persuade children that they are incompetent. Classroom interactions are the end result of a complex interweaving of factors which constrain what teachers and children can do. None the less, understanding how learning difficulties arise in interactions is the first stage in overcoming them.

How do pupils' existing understandings go unacknowledged? Let me suggest part of the answer to this question by considering a brief exchange I had with a girl in a reception class recently. This was five-year-old Tanya's first week in school. She was tracing round some flat plastic shapes. We talked about what the shapes were called. Most of the time Tanya looked puzzled. I asked her how many sides the square had. In response she took three other squares from the box and laid them out in a line, the sides touching each other. I put them back again and asked Tanya to show me a side of the square. She pointed to the centre of the top surface of one square. My initial reaction was to suppose that Tanya did not understand the word 'side', but this conclusion is unsatisfactory. Although her reponses appear to be random guesses, they may not have been.

Tanya will have met the word 'side' many times outside school, in expressions such as 'put it to one side', 'which side are you on?', 'side by side' and 'the side of the cupboard'. In the exchange I have just recounted, 'side' takes on another, less familiar meaning. Tanya's responses make sense if we treat her as an active interpreter of my questions. Her first response was to put some squares *side by side*; her second response was consistent with interpreting a side as a plane surface of an object, as in 'the side of the cupboard'. Tanya will have had some knowledge about sides and she seems to have made sense of my question in terms of her existing knowledge. I suspect her 'difficulty' was largely illusory, and is more accurately described as a communication failure, but on whose part? There are important similarities and differences between my role and Tanya's role in this exchange. We were both actively engaged in making sense of each other, and we were both doing so through our existing understandings. But the relationship is highly asymmetric. I had the power to define and control the purpose and content of the exchange; Tanya did not. I had the power and resources to test her understanding but she had no power to challenge mine. It seems to me that it was the overwhelming control over the exchange that I exerted that guaranteed Tanya's understanding would be obscured. The encounter provided me with material to reflect on and to learn from; it is unlikely to have provided Tanya with anything positive and may well have left her with a sense that she had failed to perform appropriately for a powerful adult.

There is an obvious danger in over-extending the notion of unconscripted knowledge. Taken to extremes it might seem that all teachers have to do is devise contexts in which children can reveal their hidden genius. This is not a defensible position. The first implication of my argument so far is that teaching and learning should start from the child's existing understanding. This is far from a new conclusion. There has been a growing interest in many branches of the mainstream curriculum literature in the ways pupils bring their everyday understanding to bear on the curriculum. This has been particularly marked in science education, where there is now a sizeable literature on the 'alternative frameworks' pupils use to understand concepts such as force, power and energy (Driver, 1983; Osborne and Freyberg, 1985). But in the field of learning difficulties the exhortation to take account of pupils' current understanding has generally been interpreted in a much more limited fashion, as locating pupils on a predetermined, ranked checklist of skills. The checklist published with the SNAP materials is characteristic (Ainscow and Muncey, 1983). This approach is as likely to obscure as to reveal a child's knowledge. The infinite variations of pupils' understandings in such methods are reduced to a limited number of can do/can't do categories, which do nothing to recognise the context-dependent nature of children's performances.

The second implication of my argument concerns the conditions under which pupils' understanding and competence is likely to be revealed. There are two aspects to this. First, children are more likely to express their competence in contexts that are personally meaningful to them. This requires on the part of teachers a degree of sensitivity which is made more difficult by the imposition of curricula whose content and structure is defined in isolation from and prior to contact with specific pupils. This sensitivity must entail treating judgments about children's competence as provisional, and as always related to a context. In this sense, the trouble with many behaviourist-inspired teaching programmes is that they are *insufficiently behavioural*. Whilst recognising the 'problem of generalisation', they assume too readily that the behaviour a child displays in one setting tells us what we can expect in others. Second, it seems more likely that children's competences (and limitations) will be most effectively revealed where they have some personal commitment to and control over their activity. Children are more likely to be able to use what they already know, to relate it to new knowledge, and to transform their existing understanding when they can exert a measure of control over the way they learn. And teachers are more likely to be able to exploit pupils' own resources for learning. As Steven Rowland puts it: 'the challenge with which children who experience learning difficulties present us is to listen more carefully, and take bolder steps towards understanding their world as reflected in the choices they make and the interpretations they form of their environment.' (Rowland, 1987, 58.)

Curriculum demands and curriculum support

To be effective as a basis for remediation a deficit theory would have to identify precisely the 'skill gap' between the curriculum and the child, and fill it. The traditional approach to remedial education has assumed that the gap could be filled by the development of basic literacy and numeracy, but rarely has there been any more specific description of the skills required. Difficulty in reading, writing and calculating do form major barriers to pupils' participation in the mainstream curriculum, but none of these is a unitary process. The *particular* skills with which children are equipped in segregated remedial teaching may not be sufficient, or in some cases necessary, to cope with the mainstream curriculum. When we examine the range of skills and abilities demanded of children, it becomes clear that the notion of withdrawing children and reintegrating them later is theoretically weak and practically unrealistic. There are three arguments against deficit theory here. First of all, the skills demanded of pupils in the mainstream are extensive, complex and content-specific. It is quite possible to teach children reading, spelling and handwriting skills in separate remedial lessons, but none of these will overcome the more fundamental *conceptual* difficulties that children encounter. Hull (1985) describes some of the problems that 14 and 15 year-old pupils to whom he taught 'supplementary English' encountered:

Some of the questions they asked me seemed quite rudiment-
ary: 'Which way is clockwise?' 'Is descending going up?' 'Is
glucose a plant?' At the same time they made seemingly bizarre
errors in comprehension. 'Animals harbour insects' meant
they ate them. 'The lowest bridge town' was a slum on a
bridge. 'Flushing (22,000)' meant they caught 22,000 fish there.
Expressions such as 'molten iron', 'physical feature', 'factor',
'western leader' were often insuperable obstacles to comprehension.

(Hull, 1985, x–xi)

Second, while some pupils are withdrawn for remediation, the
rest of the world moves on. Even if withdrawal teaching could
prepare pupils with the necessary pre-conditions for learning in the
mainstream, by the time they return their peers have progressed to
new work, presenting new difficulties. Third, and most important,
the difficulties in the mainstream curriculum that give rise to the
need to withdraw or exclude some children affect many more than
can possibly be accommodated in special provision. The most valuable analyses of learning difficulties so far have come not from the
field of special education, but from mainstream educators concerned to improve the curriculum for all children in ordinary
schools. For example, studies by Davies and Greene (1984); Lunzer
and Gardner (1979) and Perera (1984), all firmly rooted in the mainstream, have greatly enhanced our understanding of the difficulties
presented by written material, and of ways of overcoming them.
Children labelled as having learning difficulties benefit from
strategies aimed at difficulties that all pupils encounter. Davies and
Greene (1982), for example, describe the use of 'directed activities
related to text' (DARTS) which involve the use of small-group
discussion of extracts from textbooks. These aim to encourage pupils
to explore and extract the meaning of the text in an active manner
using a framework provided by the teacher. Amidst the overall
success of the strategy, Davies and Greene found that teachers were
surprised by the high level of performance of children labelled as
'remedial'.

Teachers responsible for pupils with special needs might look
askance at the idea that the best chance for preventing learning difficulties lies with their mainstream colleagues. Whatever ideas
permeate the educational literature, practice in schools is often quite

different. Subject departments in secondary schools, in particular, rarely place pupils with learning difficulties high in their priorities. So, as criticisms of the traditional model have gained ground, special needs teachers have begun to see themselves as change agents working in the mainstream in the interests of pupils with learning difficulties. Other chapters in this book make it clear that there has been a major shift over the past few years from the delivery of remedial education by withdrawing pupils or segregating them in remedial streams towards providing children with learning difficulties with support in mainstream lessons across the curriculum. The key words in the new approach are *support* and *access*. Staff responsible for pupils with learning difficulties are often now referred to as 'support teachers'. Their job is to give pupils 'access to the curriculum'.

Support teachers have penetrated the curriculum to varying degrees. In some cases they have found themselves acting mainly as teaching aides, with no control or influence over lesson content and methods, and able to do little more than supervise and interpret for some pupils. Many have questioned the value of this use of their time and expertise. As one remarked to me: 'I told him, I didn't have any role in that situation. I was just going to be standing there'. Other support teachers have found that mainstream teachers have welcomed their services as revisers and adapters of curriculum materials. Worksheets have been noticeably improved in many schools, with clearer text and layout, better illustrations, more explicit instructions, and imaginative supplementary exercises. In some cases this strategy has gone beyond these surface features, and has involved a more thorough analysis of the conceptual difficulties presented by learning materials. Williamson and Williamson (1986) have provided an excellent example in their work on some recipe cards. Their analysis goes well beyond the limited use of readability tests. In fact, this material had low readability scores, the result of an elliptical, terse style that actually made them very difficult to follow. The cards contained many words and expressions that pupils had not encountered before (eg *rubbing-in method*), and other words used in a specialised and unfamiliar sense (eg *grease*, *risen*); they failed to specify some parts of the task, like turning the oven on and off, and the order of instructions did not correspond to the order in which operations had to be performed. The revised cards were longer, more explicit and consequently easier to follow.

Revising materials is a role that special needs departments can undertake with relative ease. It helps mainstream teachers, and poses little threat to their status and autonomy. Decisions over content and method remain largely in the hands of the subject- or class-teacher. Yet is it far from clear that it is always a profitable strategy. Learning difficulties may be generated by more fundamental problems in learning methods that cannot be overcome by changes in the language and structure of materials. Robert Hull (1985) has recently written a penetrating critique of the secondary curriculum. One of his targets is the *unreal* nature of many tasks that pupils face. Children have to deal with material which describes and analyses the world about them, yet Hull argues that these tasks often fail to connect with concrete reality. Children have to learn at second-hand. The result is that concepts which from the teacher's perspective deal with reality have to be learnt by pupils in a purely abstract manner, because there is no way for them to give the task any empirical grounding. In analyses of several lessons Hull shows that a number of pupils appeared to have understood the lesson, from their written responses, but deeper enquiries revealed that what they understood by the words they wrote did not correspond to their teacher's understanding or to reality. Without any way of giving the words of the teacher or the worksheet a concrete meaning, the only meaning available to these pupils is in terms of other words. They must learn a set of logical relationships between words and sentences. If they are able to do this, they progress, but the value of what they have learnt is in question. If they cannot manipulate the language of the task in this purely formal way, their difficulties will quickly become evident. The solution to such problems does not lie in improving the language of materials, but in bringing that language into closer contact wih the real world, by giving pupils chances to learn from first-hand experience, and to develop their own language to account for the experience. This conclusion calls for a larger practical component across the curriculum: an insertion of reality into classrooms and an insertion of pupils' learning into the world outside the school.

These problems have not been lost on many support teachers who have had to face the dilemma of supporting a curriculum that they feel is fundamentally inappropriate and in need of a more radical overhaul than they have either power or resources to conduct. As Susan Hart (1987) points out, a support teacher may enable children to copy notes down from the board more effectively, but to what end? Should pupils be engaged in such a task in the first place? In such circumstances, the support teacher's role might be better described as an additional classroom control device than as a support for pupils' learning. Controlling difficult pupils was always one of the functions of the traditional model, yet there was at least the possibility (not always translated into reality) that pupils would receive an appropriate curriculum during the time they were segregated. If support teaching brings no fundamental challenge to the curriculum that gave rise to demands for withdrawal, it may be *less* valuable than its antecedents – a device to sweep an unresolved problem under the desk. For this reason, the notion of 'access to the curriculum' is a singularly unhelpful metaphor. It conjures up images of support teachers prising open the doors of a department store for the benefit of the masses. 'The curriculum' is there for the taking, if the key can be found. This view of learning difficulties is not far removed from the deficit theory it purports to replace. It may be more useful to think of the curriculum, not as knowledge to be conveyed, but as a set of *teaching and learning relationships* by which that knowledge is conveyed. And it may be more useful to think of the job of support teaching as improving the quality of those relationships.

Reforming the curriculum

Pressure for fundamental curriculum reform aimed at improving the lot of pupils with learning difficulties has built up during the 1980s from many directions. Here I shall concentrate on initiatives from central government and one local initiative that has had a national spin-off – the ILEA's review of its secondary school provision in the Hargreaves Report (ILEA, 1984). These developments have concentrated predominantly or exclusively on the final two years of compulsory schooling, which will be my concern in this part of this chapter. The two themes for curriculum reform I have identified so far – pupil control and practical reality – are to be found here as well.

In 1982, Sir Keith Joseph announced the Lower Attaining Pupils Project, since then better known as LAPP. It began in 1983 with projects in thirteen LEAs, part funded with some £2 million of urban aid money, part funded from LEAs' own resources and EEC funds. By 1986 it had expanded to cover seventeen LEAs. Its target population was the 'bottom 40 per cent' of pupils aged 14 to 16, for whom the public exam system was not designed. The original guide-lines for the programme were not highly detailed. Sir Keith Joseph's speech announcing the programme set out 'areas for development' with a strong flavour of vocationalism and the basics. They included work experience; the development of inter-personal, literacy, numeracy and communication skills; practical learning methods and the appreciation of industry and commerce. The projects that have been funded over LAPP are very diverse in content, methods and organisation. In 1986, HMI reported on the first two years of full-scale operation (DES, 1986). The programme is also the subject of extensive local and national evaluation, although substantial reports have yet to appear (Weston, 1986). As HMI portray LAPP, it contains some of the seeds of a curriculum that might respond to the need for greater pupil control over and participation in their own learning, and for a more practical, empirical approach to learning.

Manchester's Alternative Curriculum Strategies (ACS) project is one of the larger LAPP projects. Pupils' freedom to define their own programmes is an important element of this project. In one school, for example, this has allowed one pupil to devote one day a week to studies of Rastafarian culture (*The Times Educational Supplement*, 27 Jan, 1984, 9). However, this principle has been taken up in vary-ing degrees by the schools involved. Hustler and Ashman (1985), who are involved in the local evaluation of the project, are enthusi-astic about the extent of pupil involvement: 'experiential learning is the *sine qua non*, and pupils are involved again and again in making choices, in negotiating with staff and each other, in making decisions and taking responsibility for these decisions . . . for the initial target group of pupils something different does seem to have been created'. One way to lessen teacher domination of learning, and to increase participation by pupils, is to make more use of discussion and collaborative learning methods (Barnes and Todd, 1977). More oral work has been a feature of most projects, particularly Wiltshire's Oracy Project, designed to increase the use of collaborative discus-sion as a learning method. HMI were generally optimistic about the early results of this aspect of LAPP projects.

Practical reality in LAPP projects has a number of interpretations.

In one version it means an increase in time spent on technical, vocational and practical *subjects*, often in colleges of further education linked to schools. In one project in Lincolnshire, for example, pupils spend up to three days a week at a local college, doing courses in engineering, construction, catering and commerce (*The Times Educational Supplement*, 27 Jan, 1984, 8). In another version, practical reality involves responses to the criticisms I considered earlier of the second-hand curriculum, divorced from reality. Several schools have made extensive use of the local environment of the school as a resource for project work. Pupils taking part in the Lincolnshire project embarked on the study of the life, industry and inhabitants of a local village in addition to their vocational work. Many courses have used residential field trips to give pupils first-hand learning experiences. Reid and Hodson (1987) describe how one Manchester school used residential weekends to involve pupils in active learning about topics as diverse as the influence of people on their environment, astronomy, and canoe-building. However, more information is needed to judge how far these resources outside the school have been successfully exploited: Hull notes how the teachers he observed used the outside world as a more attractive backdrop for the same unreal tasks.

These features of some LAPP projects have been reflected in the Hargreaves Report (ILEA, 1984), which has since received attention all over the country. The report claimed that the key to combating under-achievement lay not in the content of the curriculum, but in finding methods of teaching that could actively engage pupils in learning. It argued for an alternative strategy to traditional didactic exposition, excessive reliance on worksheets and teacher-dominated lessons. Practical and oral work were important elements in this strategy. There was to be a much greater use of the resources of the local community and local industry to provide real learning opportunities beyond the school, unfettered by the constraints of subject boundaries and the timetable. This would allow for genuine investigation, in which pupils could control the direction of their work. Oral work was to be used for several purposes: to diversify styles of presentation in lessons, to enable pupils to learn through sustained dialogue, and as part of the process of writing.

A curriculum for all?

At this point readers may begin to wonder why I have chosen to mention these initiatives, since there is very little in them that is new, as HMI pointed out in their survey of LAPP projects. Many schools which do not form part of any co-ordinated national or local initiative have been using such methods for years, although they are in the minority. A recent book produced at the Open University (Booth, Potts and Swann, 1987) is full of accounts by teachers of pupil-centred methods involving collaborative oral work, the use of first-hand experience, and practical learning approaches. It is the *context* of the initiatives I have described rather than the curricula themselves that I want to emphasise.

LAPP is a programme targeted at a group defined by their exclusion or partial exclusion from the examination system, promoted by a government committed to increasing differentiation in schools. Sir Keith Joseph remarked in a TV broadcast in 1984: 'If it be so, as it is, that selection between schools is largely out, then I emphasise that there must be differentiation within schools' (quoted in *Forum*, Spring 1987). Although LAPP may have the seeds of a more real and responsive curriculum in it, it also contains the seeds of a separate curriculum for non-examination pupils. Some LEAs, conscious of this danger, have made their projects available to all pupils, not just those not taking any public exams. Others, like Manchester, aim to use their LAPP project as an educational Trojan horse – the first stage of a much wider reform of the fourth and fifth year curriculum for all pupils. How realistic this aim is will depend on whether the curriculum developed in the more imaginative LAPP projects can be grafted on to the requirements of new GCSE exam syllabuses and timetables. There are grounds for pessimism here. GCSE has been said to encourage more active learning strategies, although others have doubted the extent to which it will change practice (Scarth, 1987). However, through the establishment of national criteria it reduces opportunities for teachers to define their own syllabuses and methods. Teachers' discretion will be further limited by the introduction of grade criteria. These are currently under development. Work is in progress to split subjects into domains with sets of specific attainments in each domain (Murphy, 1986). This more detailed specification of curriculum content may increase the pressure on teachers to control the pace of work according to the need to cover the syllabus rather than in response to the needs of pupils, and it may make pupil-centred methods harder to establish. Moreover, grade criteria may lead to differentiation of syllabuses within the exam system, making the prospects for mixed-ability work across the whole ability range remote.

The shades of two alternative scenarios can be detected within LAPP, if it remains a differentiated programme for 'non-examination pupils'. In the first version, pupils negotiate their own broad-based curriculum and engage in active learning based on relevant first-hand experience. The other scenario is less encouraging. The programme as a whole has already been the subject of criticism by HMI for reproducing many of the well-worn features of provision for less able pupils in times past and present: too much emphasis on basic skills, lack of breadth and balance, low expectations of pupils, pupils not sufficiently involved (DES, 1986). When the programme was first announced, *The Times Educational Supplement* berated its 'paltry funding' and maintained that it 'only makes sense if this is to be seen as the beginning of a much more radical attempt to initiate curriculum differentiation around the age of 13 or 14, leading to courses for the bottom 40 per cent' (*The Times Educational Supplement*, 16 July, 1982). Should such a programme be introduced on a mass scale, there is no guarantee that even the 'paltry' resources available for the pilot schemes could be reproduced everywhere. Resource-based learning, field trips and practical work are expensive. With limited resources, lacking the commitment of pioneers and the support of local and national evaluators, what would be the prospects of a broad, active and challenging curriculum?

The Hargreaves Report's attitude to curriculum differentiation is more ambivalent than the views that underlay LAPP. This can be seen in two features of the report: its views on mixed-ability teaching, and the status of the 'aspects of achievement' which are at the heart of the report's recommendations. One of the strengths of the report is the great care with which it weighs arguments and counter-arguments before adopting its own position. Yet its willingness to take a stance varies. The arguments for and against a core curriculum are systematically rehearsed, but in the end the report comes down firmly in favour of a substantial compulsory core. This is not because the counter-arguments have all been refuted. There is a measure of moral commitment to a core curriculum which causes the authors to give greater weight to some arguments than to others. This is perfectly proper, for the decision has a necesary value base. However, commitment is less evident when the report comes to consider mixed-ability teaching. Here again arguments are presented to which people with different values might reasonably attach differing weight. But the report eschews any definite posture. Although the committee 'inclines to favour mixed-ability grouping, especially but not exclusively in the first three years of secondary schooling', they are cautious because they are unable to link any particular form of grouping to higher achievement. Hargreaves himself, in the book that is the intellectual forbear of the report, argued that, although most of the core curriculum could be taught in mixed-ability groups, for academic option work pupils would need to be 'streamed or setted if the most able pupils are to be stretched' (Hargreaves, 1982, 173).

Herein lies a crucial ambiguity in the thinking behind the report. Its recommendations were based on a theory of achievement designed to supplant standard uni-dimensional notions of ability. It distinguished four 'aspects of achievement'. One was the achievement tested by public exams – the capacity to express ideas in written form, to recall, select and manipulate propositional knowledge. The other three aspects were practical skills, social skills and personal skills including self-motivation and responsibility. This theory allowed the committee to redefine the problem of underachievement. No longer was this limited to underachievement in the conventional academic sense. Pupils could underachieve on any or all of the four aspects. The exam system was attacked for guaranteeing underachievement by excluding social and personal skills. But the question arises, are these four aspects of achievement equally important for all pupils, or should some pupils concentrate on some at the cost of others? Here the report is inconclusive. Whilst it inveighs against the polarisation of academic and practical skills at one point, at others it uses the terms 'able' and 'academic' interchangeably. Less able pupils are equated with less academic pupils. This equation suggests that new non-academic aspects of achievement have not been introduced in order to revalue practical, social and personal skills for all pupils. Rather they form an alternative theory on which to base an alternative curriculum for less academic *and therefore* less able pupils.

Conclusion

I have argued in this chapter for two directions in which the curriculum might be reformed in the interests of pupils with learning difficulties. I have also argued that, however desirable it might be to move in these directions for all pupils and thus to enable pupils of very diverse abilities to learn together, there are sizeable ideological and practical barriers in the way of reaching this goal.

Ironically, we may find that other pressures, notably parents, will persuade ordinary schools to include some children who are dramatically less able than most, whilst at the same time they continue to force many children to the margins or consign them to special schools and units bearing the label 'moderate learning difficulties'. Recently, I was involved in writing about the school experience of a profoundly and multiply handicapped girl, Samantha Hulley, who had begun her school career in the special care unit of a special school for children with severe learning difficulties. She then moved to an ordinary junior school and is now at a comprehensive school (Hulley *et al*, 1987). How is it possible for a girl with very limited linguistic and cognitive skills to share in mixed-ability groups, when so many children whose distance from the intellectual norm is tiny by comparison remain in special schools, units and groups? Beyond the particular features of her programme, its organisation and resources lies, I believe, a more fundamental answer. It is that Samantha has been *exempted* from the normal system of expectations, standards and role requirements. Her inability to perform like most other pupils at her junior school was acknowledged and accepted, and on that basis she was able to learn at her own pace as she and her teachers exploited the learning opportunities afforded by a vibrant junior classroom. But the exemption of one pupil is no signal that the system of expectations as a whole has been relaxed.

References

Ainscow, M. and Muncey, J. (1983) 'Learning difficulties in the primary school: an in-service initiative' in *Remedial Education*, 18, 3, 116–124.

Barnes, D. and Todd, F. (1977) *Communication and Learning in Small Groups* London: Routledge and Kegan Paul.

Bereiter, C. and Englemann, S. (1966) *Teaching Disadvantaged Children in the Preschool* Englewood Cliffs, NJ: Prentice Hall.

Booth, T. and Swann, W. (eds) (1987) *Including Pupils with Disabilities* Milton Keynes: Open University Press.

Booth, T., Potts, P. and Swann, W. (eds) (1987) *Preventing Difficulties in Learning* Oxford: Basil Blackwell.

Branwhite, A. B. (1983) 'Boosting reading skills by direct instruction' in *British Journal of Educational Psychology*, 53, 291–298.

Carnine, D. (1977) 'Direct Instruction – DISTAR' in H. G. Haring and B. Bateman (eds) *Teaching the Learning Disabled Child* Englewood Cliffs, NJ: Prentice Hall.

Carraher, T. N., Carraher, D. W. and Schliemann, A. D. (1985) 'Mathematics in the streets and in schools' in *British Journal of Developmental Psychology*, 3, 1, 21–30.

Davies, F. and Greene, T. (1982) 'Effective reading: using pupil resources for comprehension and learning' in *Remedial Education*, 17, 4, 163–173.

Davies, F. and Greene, T. (1984) *Reading for Learning in Science* Edinburgh: Oliver and Boyd.

Department of Education and Science (1986) *A Survey of the Lower Attaining Pupils Programme: the First Two Years* London: DES.

Dessent, T. (1983) 'Who is responsible for children with special needs?' in T. Booth and P. Potts (eds) *Integrating Special Education* Oxford: Basil Blackwell.

Driver, R. (1983) *The Pupil as Scientist?* Milton Keynes: Open University Press.

Easen, P. (1987) 'All at sixes and sevens: the difficulties of learning mathematics' in T. Booth, P. Potts and W. Swann (eds) *Preventing Difficulties in Learning* Oxford: Basil Blackwell.

Edwards, A. D. (1980) 'Perspectives on classroom language' in *Educational Analysis*, 2, 2, 31–46.

Edwards, J. (1979) *Language and Disadvantage* London: Edward Arnold.

Gregory, P. (1983) 'Direct Instruction, disadvantaged and handicapped children: a review of the literature and some practical implications' in *Remedial Education*, 18, 3, 108–114 and 131–136.

Gulliford, R. (1985) *Teaching Children with Learning Difficulties* Windsor: NFER/Nelson.

Hargreaves, D. H. (1982) *The Challenge for the Comprehensive School: culture, curriculum and community* London: Routledge and Kegan Paul.

Hart, S. (1987) 'A lesson from humanities' in T. Booth, P. Potts and W. Swann (eds) *Preventing Difficulties in Learning* Oxford: Basil Blackwell.

Hegarty, S. and Pocklington, K. (1981) *Educating Pupils with Special Needs in the Ordinary School* Windsor: NFER/Nelson.

Hull, R. (1985) *The Language Gap* London: Methuen.

Hulley, B., Hulley, T., Madden, S., Parsons, G. and Swann, W. (1987) 'Samantha' in T. Booth and W. Swann (eds) *Including Pupils with Disabilities* Milton Keynes: Open University Press.

Hustler, D. and Ashman, D. (1985) 'Personal and social education for all: apart or together?' in E. C. Cuff and G. C. F. Payne (eds) *Crisis in the Curriculum* London: Croom Helm.

Inner London Education Authority (1984) *Improving Secondary Schools* (the Hargreaves Report) London: ILEA.

Jamieson, M., Parlett, M. and Pocklington, K. (1977) *Towards Integration: a study of blind and partially sighted children in ordinary schools* Windsor: NFER.

Labov, W. (1970) 'The logic of non-standard English' in F. Williams (ed) *Language and Poverty* Chicago: Markham Press.

Lunzer, E. and Gardner, K. (eds) (1979) *The Effective Use of Reading* London: Heinemann Educational.

Lynas, W. (1986) *Integrating the Handicapped into Ordinary Schools: a study of hearing impaired children* London: Croom Helm.

Murphy, R. (1986) 'The emperor has no clothes: grade criteria and the GCSE' in C. Gipps *et al* (eds) *GCSE: an uncommon examination* Bedford Way Paper, No 29. London: University of London Institute of Education.

Osborne, R. and Freyberg, P. (1985) *Learning in Science: the implications of children's science* London: Heinemann Educational.

Perera, K. (1984) *Children's Writing and Reading: analysing classroom language* Oxford: Basil Blackwell.

Reid, D. J. and Hodson, D. (1987) *Science for All* London: Cassell.

Rowland, S. (1987) 'Ian and the shoe factory' in T. Booth, P. Potts and W. Swann (eds) *Preventing Difficulties in Learning* Oxford: Basil Blackwell.

Scarth, J. (1987) 'Teaching to the exam? The case of The Schools Council History Project' in T. Horton (ed) *GCSE: examining the new system* London: Harper and Row.

Stubbs, M. (1976) *Language, Schools and Classrooms* London: Methuen.

Swann, W. (1987) ' "Firm links should be established . . .": a case study of conflict and policy-making for integration' in T. Booth and W. Swann (eds) *Including Pupils with Disabilities* Milton Keynes: Open University Press.

Swann, W. (1985) 'Is the integration of children with special needs happening?: an analysis of recent statistics of pupils in special schools' in *Oxford Review of Education*, 11, 1, 3–18.

Tizard, B. and Hughes, M. (1984) *Young Children Learning* London: Fontana.

Wells, G. (1985) *Language, Learning and Education* Windsor: NFER/ Nelson.

Weston, P. (1986) 'If success had many faces' in *Forum*, 28, 3, 79–81.
Willes, M. (1983) *Children into Pupils* London: Routledge and Kegan Paul.
Williamson, C. and Williamson, J. (1986) 'A recipe for success' in *Support for Learning*, 1, 3, 13–18.

6 Special needs in the primary school

Ingrid Lunt

Classrooms have been characterised by their multi-dimensionality, their simultaneity, their unpredictability (Doyle, 1977). Nowhere is this more so than in the busy primary classroom where the teacher has to cope with a large number of very different demands and abilities, any number of potential interruptions and distractions and, increasingly, various forms of special educational need.

> Teachers in almost all primary schools have to teach a broad curriculum to a very wide spread of ability. They need to ensure that the pace of learning is as suited to the brighter children as it is to the average or the less able. The importance of differentiation will become increasingly apparent as pupils get older. Teaching the broad curriculum ... places formidable demands on the class teacher which increase with the age of the pupils.
>
> (HMSO, 1985)

> What has emerged in general terms is an increased understanding of the formidable problems teachers face as they strive to implement the laudable philosophy of individualising instruction, and the equally formidable array of skills that are required to carry this out effectively.
>
> (Bennett *et al*, 1984)

There is no doubt that teaching in the primary classroom requires a feat of organisation and management of all kinds of dimensions: the physical setting, the social groupings, the psychological environment ... quite apart from the management of curriculum and teaching activities and materials. 'The classroom environment is such a potent determinant of student outcomes that it should not be ignored.' (Fraser, 1986) Yet, until recently, these crucial aspects of the classroom environment have rarely been analysed in ecological terms as demands which may either inhibit or enhance successful learning and teaching. Further, 'few assays appear to have been made, particularly in this country, into systematically changing the ecology of the classroom as a possible means of helping children who have special needs.' (Thomas, 1986)

This chapter will consider the place of children with special needs in the primary classroom and ways in which the classroom environment may be managed to meet their needs more effectively and sensitively. In particular, the role of other adults in the classroom will be considered, taking the assumption that children of a very wide range of need and ability have a right to be, and will increasingly be, educated in the ordinary primary classroom. The question to be asked is: How can the teacher organise and mobilise available resources creatively in order to provide the flexible and dynamic classroom environment envisaged in the Warnock report (1978) and echoed by the Fish Committee?

> Provision to meet special educational needs should now be seen as a flexible service responsive to individually assessed needs. Its main function should be to provide additional or different arrangements for individuals in the most appropriate place in the closest possible association with educational arrangements for all children and young people.
>
> (ILEA, 1985)

Meeting the needs of special children

Although, increasingly, teachers are being told 'Every teacher is a teacher of special educational needs', there is nevertheless the logistic problem posed by the familiar question: 'She needs so much time and help, what do I do with the other twenty-nine?' Add the further four or five children in an average classroom (Warnock's '20%') who at some time in their school career will experience difficulty in benefiting from or fully utilising the educational opportunities provided and the 'feat of organisation' is formidable indeed. Until recently the needs of children who were falling behind with their work or unable to concentrate or to benefit from the opportunities for learning provided by primary classrooms may have been met by withdrawing these few children in a small group to another room or sometimes even another building or school to receive extra or specialist help, either as individuals or more often as a small group. The emphasis was on individual help, freedom from distraction, often with specialist expertise, and certainly away from the context of the classroom. Some of the problems of the individualistic approach have been discussed elsewhere. More recently, there have been increasing moves to provide for children with special needs in the ordinary classroom and to move the additional help to the children rather than the children to the additional help. In a period of limited resources the task has been one of using presently available resources (peripatetic teachers, support teachers, parents) in as positive, creative and mutually supportive a way as possible. Before considering these possibilities, it may be useful to look at some of the problems in meeting children's special needs by withdrawing the children.

The problems of withdrawal for 'extra help'

Primary schools have been aware for some time of the importance of early identification and many have devised screening and monitoring procedures (school- or LEA-based) to ensure that children receive help and attention sooner rather than later. As mentioned earlier, until relatively recently such help has been in the form of withdrawal, perhaps two to four times a week for, say, half an hour at a time, after which the children resume 'normal' classroom activities. Apart from the fact that there is very little evidence to suggest that children thus withdrawn show greater progress than children remaining in class, there are problems in withdrawing children for 'extra help' for all parties: the child, the class teacher, the peripatetic/support teacher and the school.

The *child*, probably already behind, loses precious time in class and misses out on learning experiences and opportunities for social interaction. On return from the 'extra help' session he or she is expected to make sense and progress and pick up the threads in the very busy classroom. Further, the child with difficulties in learning may be particularly in need of continuity and consistency in teaching approach and curriculum organisation and content. Such a child may be confused by the different teaching styles and expectations, pace of learning and classroom environment, and it is questionable whether skills mastered or understanding gained in the small-group setting with its different rules, roles, expectations and relationships will necessarily generalise to the larger classroom setting. All this may serve to contribute only to further confusion for a child already experiencing difficulties with the demands and expectations placed upon him/her in the classroom. However 'attractive' the setting of withdrawal for 'extra help' (and withdrawal groups are frequently characterised by their pleasant physical surroundings, warm atmosphere and unthreatening learning situation), the child is labelled as different by him/herself, peers, teacher and parents. The dangers of labelling children as 'remedial' or having 'special educational needs' are well known, with their concomitant effects on the child's self-esteem and peer relations.

Labelling individual children and withdrawing them firmly locates the problem within the child and isolates the problem from the context; put another way, it separates the 'problem' child from the 'problem-causing' environment. More recent conceptualisations of special educational need have emphasised its essentially interactive nature and the importance of context. Both the Warnock Report and the 1981 Education Act have pointed to the necessity of taking into account the context in which the child learns. This is particularly the case with children who at one time in their school career are experiencing difficulties in learning which reflect at some level a mismatch between the child's attainments and progress and the expectations of the teacher and the learning environment. It is this mismatch which needs to be the focus of any form of intervention and this may most effectively be considered within the ordinary classroom. 'The ecological perspective, developed in psychology and applied more recently in special education, views disturbance as a "failure-to-match" in the interaction between the child and the system that surrounds him or her.' (Apter, 1982) Apart from these difficulties, the child withdrawn for 'extra help' is somehow seen and treated as 'different' and the positive intentions of *extra* help may result in quite unintentional negative effects.

For the *class teacher*, a major problem of withdrawal groups is in the professional de-skilling or lack of expertise implied by the referral out. It is as though the teacher might say, 'I was trained to teach normal children. This one has special educational needs, is maladjusted, has a specific learning difficulty, etc, and I do not have the expertise necessary to teach him'. This expression ignores the relative nature of special educational needs and furthermore categorises the child outside the classroom. Restricting the 'range' of children's abilities or needs with which the ordinary class teacher feels able to cope introduces the dangers of streaming and banding and negates the philosophy of mixed-ability teaching. The child with learning difficulties becomes somehow 'different', outside the range of the class teacher's expertise, and needs therefore to be handed over to the expert. Some of the problems of this approach have been identified elsewhere (see Chapter 1) and the failure of 'specialist' educational programmes outside the classroom has been noted. Of equal relevance is the teacher's perception of the situation and evaluation of his/her competence to cope, together with the vital importance of that intimate knowledge of and relationship with *all* pupils usually evidenced by the primary school teacher. Related too, is the problem of perceiving 'specialist' teaching as somehow different from 'ordinary' teaching, with certain pupils requiring (or benefiting from) a different form of educational régime which is somehow not available in the ordinary classroom. Handing over a child to an outside 'expert' or 'specialist' may be a simple short-term solution (to the problem of how to cope in class) for a few hours a week but does very little to enhance either the child's or teacher's competence or confidence. It has the added danger of marginalising and mystifying the process of meeting children's educational needs. The ultimate responsibility for organising all the children's learning lies with the class teacher and not usually with outside agencies.

The *peripatetic/support teacher*, too, is placed in an unenviable position by a withdrawal policy; s/he may be expected to work miracles (in isolation); s/he may be blamed for the child's problems and expected to 'cure' the child's learning difficulties – all this in isolation from the context in which the learning difficulties occur. A child does not have learning difficulties in the way he or she has blue eyes, for instance, but only in relation to the learning situation.

The ways in which primary . . . schools meet a wide range of individual needs, set objectives and place teaching programmes for all pupils, including those with difficulties and disabilities, may determine the extent of many special educational needs. These needs, and the provision made for them, can no longer be considered in isolation.

(ILEA, 1985)

In some sense, however hard the peripatetic teacher may work in a withdrawal situation, s/he is concentrating time and effort at the wrong target: the individual child rather than the mismatch between child and learning context. The problems of matching teaching style, pace, context to pupils' needs and abilities, particularly pupils above and below the 'average', has been well illustrated in a study by Bennett *et al* (1984), who found that

> high attainers were underestimated on over 40% of tasks assigned to them, a pattern similar to that reported by HMI (1978). But an equally clear pattern of overestimation was found for low attainers. Of their assigned tasks 44% were overestimated in both language and number work . . . Teachers were adept at recognising a task that was proving too difficult but were totally blind to tasks whose demands were too easy. The reasons for this are twofold. Firstly, the teachers' typical management style required them to be seated at the front of the class, and as a result supervision was limited to quick observational sweeps of the classroom. The usual image was of a class working cheerfully and industriously. This, indeed, is the second reason for a teacher's lack of recognition of too-easy tasks.

The importance of match or 'goodness of fit' between pupils' abilities and interests and teacher style and expectations is important for all pupils, and vital for pupils who are experiencing difficulties. The peripatetic teacher operating a withdrawal group is in no position to detect the mismatch, far less to reduce it, and therefore only increases the discrepancy between learner and learning environment.

Finally, and of considerable importance, withdrawal groups cause problems for the *whole school*. They cause problems of fragmented curriculum and fragmented social groupings, problems of segregation and labelling of children with special needs, and, last but not least, the practical problems of organisation, coordination and timetabling and the inhibiting effects on a whole-school policy for special needs. Further, withdrawal groups prevent the possibility of flexible provision and take little account of the essentially dynamic nature of the primary classroom and of the teaching and learning process. Teaching and learning must be seen as dynamic and social processes which take place in the context of the whole school and which are affected by that context. Hidden, or not so hidden, messages about separation or segregation do little to enhance that learning context for all pupils and do much to reduce the confidence of pupils, parents and teachers.

Bringing 'extra help' to the classroom

Fortunately, there has been an increasing trend to involve peri-patetic/support teachers in the classroom, working alongside class teachers. This trend has in some areas and schools extended to involving parents in the classroom (Jackson and Hannon, 1981). The welcome presence of several adults (support teachers, in some cases other professionals, parents) raises considerable questions as to effective use of time, personnel management, different roles and perceptions of roles and overall organisation and management. How does the already busy and complex primary classroom adapt to the presence of another adult or adults? How does the teacher ensure that individual children benefit from the extra help while remaining fully integrated and not segregated or labelled by the presence of the extra adult? How is 'extra help' absorbed by and integrated into the ordinary classroom? How is it possible to structure the dynamic and flexible arrangement of the classroom to maximise the positive and minimise the negative aspects for all children? What effect does this have on the whole school? Some answers will be sought under the following headings:

1   classroom organisation and grouping
2   management and organisation of personnel
3   the advisory role of peripatetic teachers
4   monitoring progress and record-keeping

I CLASSROOM ORGANISATION AND GROUPING

Despite encouragement by the Plowden Report (1967), the ORACLE study (Galton *et al*, 1980) revealed far less group work in primary schools than was supposed. Although seated in groups, children were usually working as individuals. The possibilities of shared and co-operative learning amongst groups of children and active engagement in a shared task have until recently been neglected, in particular when thinking of children with special needs. Although structuring the shared learning task or activity initially requires considerable time in planning and organisation, the benefits in terms of overall constructive classroom functioning are numerous (see also Chapter 9). For the child with special educational needs, meaningful involvement in a group learning task enhances confidence and self-esteem and consequently ability to learn and make progress. The scope and flexibility for creative classroom grouping may immediately be enhanced by the presence of additional adults in the classroom (peripatetic/support teachers and/or parents), though organisation is a very important factor. In one area a group of pupils originally referred to the schools' psychological service with 'specific learning difficulties' and subsequently placed in a small group for 'extra help' were returned to their classes following a reorganisation of the service. The peripatetic teacher who had previously offered a highly structured and in many ways effective withdrawal programme had become impressed by the overwhelming problems caused for the children by their attendance outside school for 'extra help'. She therefore implemented a 'support within class' programme specifically aimed to structure small-group learning activities so as to include the pupils previously withdrawn for 'extra help'. These small-group activities included peer tutoring, collaboration on specific tasks and structuring a particular project to include different roles and tasks for the different members of the group. The teacher found that the pupils previously withdrawn showed noticeable increase in self-esteem and self-confidence along with increased attainments in basic skills. The organisation of the peer learning group provides considerable opportunity for enhancing the participation and development of pupils experiencing learning difficulties.

2 MANAGEMENT AND ORGANISATION OF PERSONNEL

In a period of limited resources (particularly in terms of personnel) innovations in primary schools generally depend on a more efficient use of presently available personnel, 'maximising the potential of current staffing and resources'. (Thomas, 1986) This means that, within a whole-school policy and a whole-class practice of meeting children's needs, there needs to be considerable flexibility and yet structure in the use of additional adults in the classroom. Objections to the presence of other adults in the classroom have been that they threaten the autonomy or authority of the class teacher, undermine his/her teaching 'expertise', duplicate or overlap roles and thus confuse pupils. It is, therefore, important that the class teacher takes full responsibility for overall planning of the curriculum and the teaching arrangements and that s/he remains in charge over-all. The other adults should have specific and particular roles assigned to them, which complement each other and are clear to the pupils. Particular approaches to structuring adult involvement in classrooms, eg room management, will be discussed later (see Chapter 8).

The advantages of children with special needs receiving extra help in the classroom will be evident from the earlier discussion of the problems with withdrawal. If they are not removed from class such children are less likely to be labelled and therefore stig-matised; the work which they do is linked to and arises from work which they are expected to do in their classroom; the extra help or effort is more easily targeted where it will have maximum effect, ie at the interface between the child's learning ability and the learn-ing situation; the extra help arises from and is linked to a flexibility and dynamic within the classroom which enables an organic and flexible response to children's needs, increasing, decreasing or removing help and support as necessary; the extra help is more easily integrated with the main structure and framework of the curriculum in the classroom. In much the same way as a well-functioning whole is more than the sum of its parts (Hoffman, 1981), a well-defined, well-differentiated team of adults, each with different roles and functions but working together in a classroom, may result in considerably enhanced learning and performance by the children. This has been shown in a study adapting techniques of room management to a primary classroom (Thomas, 1985). Although less work has been done to involve parents with specific tasks in the classroom, long overdue moves towards partnership with parents and the well-known and well-documented benefits of involving parents in their children's education make this a logical extension of work already going on in classrooms with peripatetic teachers. Issues such as status, authority, professionalism and equal partnership raised by involving parents in classrooms have implications for the ethos and ecology of the whole school and will be further discussed in Chapter 12.

3 THE ADVISORY ROLE OF PERIPATETIC TEACHERS

The shift away from withdrawal groups and from the individualistic notion of special educational needs to a more relativistic and context-based focus has meant a dramatic change in the role and skills demanded of the peripatetic teacher. Not only is s/he required now to work as a member of a team alongside other adults in the classroom but there has also been a shift towards an advisory function for support services. This has been developing in parallel with a shift in other professional support services (eg educational psychology services) away from direct work with individual children to more indirect work *via* the significant adults who work directly with the children. This is partly due to a recognition that those adults in most frequent or daily contact with children, ie parents and class teachers, usually provide the most appropriate and (if adequately supported) effective help for the child, and partly due to an attempt to consolidate, rather than fragment, efforts to help an individual child. A whole-school policy for special educational needs may be more effective where the main agents are the class teachers, who retain full responsibility for all the children in the class, and where the outside services are co-ordinated in a manner to support rather than fragment efforts directed towards individual children.

This shift has implications for the training and support of peripatetic services. Peripatetic support teachers are now developing skills related to curriculum and classroom organisation and to understanding the processes of learning and teaching; the focus may no longer be the individual child so much as the learning context and how this effects (individual) children with special educational needs. While the class teacher takes a central role and responsibility for *all* children in his/her class, s/he is supported by a team of personnel; some will remain outside the classroom, others will work alongside the teacher in the classroom, and all will have an advisory function at some time. The shift is rightly away from locating problems within individual children towards identifying problems in the mismatch between learner and learning situation.

4 MONITORING PROGRESS AND RECORD-KEEPING

The Warnock Report (1978) and the 1981 Education Act emphasised the importance of assessment procedures for children with special educational needs. Increased pressures for accountability and parental participation have meant a re-examination of all forms of record-keeping. Many schools are now developing forms of pupil profiles in order to monitor children's progress in all areas of development (see also *Improving Secondary Schools*, Hargreaves Report, ILEA, 1984). Methods of assessing and monitoring children's progress have shifted dramatically from a narrow within-child, normative approach to a more within-curriculum criterion-based approach, which emphasises measurement of progress within the classroom. A mismatch in teachers' expectations and therefore in provision both for the more able and the less able pupils has been shown to occur with alarming frequency (Bennett *et al*, 1984). There is an overriding need in primary schools for the teacher to carefully match materials, tasks and classroom resources to the different levels of ability of the pupils and to make 'meticulous plans for the pupils' use of valuable learning time at school' (Chapter 1).

This task requires the class teacher to develop a system of organising the curriculum and devising forms of monitoring which relate closely and specifically to the stages of progression of each learner in the class. This curriculum framework and system of recording progress needs to be open and available so that other adults working within the classroom (peripatetic teachers, ancillary helpers, parents) are able to encourage and record progress within particular areas of the learning environment.

The shift from withdrawing children for extra help in a small group to structuring the classroom in a way which provides a flexible and dynamic learning environment for *all* children increases the necessity for curriculum-related forms of evaluating and recording progress and for a whole-school framework of record-keeping so that all relevant teaching personnel may use it to ensure continuity and consistency of provision. Under a 'withdrawal regime' it might be quite possible for the two teachers working with a child to be operating two quite different forms of curricula and teaching method, with two quite different forms of monitoring progress. Teaching and recording progress need to occur within the child's ordinary classroom (ie the natural context) and to be related to the tasks and curriculum in which the child is progressing. Opening the closed door of the traditional classroom and breaking down the isolating barriers of the static classroom will involve making the curriculum and records accessible to a much wider range of adults and this task requires a high degree of management and organisation. This includes specifying educational aims, goals and objectives for the whole class and for each child and making sure that these are carefully matched both with the individual and with the learning context. Special needs often arise from the mismatch between learner and task or from deficiencies in the learning situation. A system of relating the curriculum to the method of assessment and recording is essential in order to ensure that every child is provided with the most positive and helpful learning environment.

The whole primary school

The primary school provides the ideal setting for breaking down the barriers mentioned in Chapter 1. Opportunities to bring other adults into the classroom (and also to bring children out of the classroom) and to organise the individuals in classrooms into smaller groupings in which children with special needs work alongside other children and another adult, will ensure continuity and consistency of learning together with the provision of individual help where needed. A well-managed, integrated curriculum and integrated day which include clearly-stated aims, goals and objectives for each child, together with available adults to implement this, could provide one answer to the question: 'What do I do with the other 30?'. Breaking down barriers between teachers, ancillary helpers and parents and working towards partnership in the classroom throws open the door to many possibilities for creative thinking, learning and teaching. Involving children and other adults in assessment and record-keeping within a curriculum-related framework may break down the barriers imposed by traditional models of assessment and create a flexible and dynamic framework in which children may progress.

This chapter has looked at some aspects of primary classrooms and schools; in particular how they affect children with special educational needs, and might be structured to help these children. This perspective takes for granted the integration of the vast majority of children with many different forms of difficulty and need into the local primary school and the ordinary classroom. The implications of this assumption demand a radical restructuring of the way in which both human and material resources are used. Resources need to be brought to children within ordinary classrooms. This means the presence of several adults with differing skills, backgrounds and professional expertise within the classroom, and the effective organisation of their contribution. It means the availability of a very wide range and variety of curriculum materials, programmes and resources and an accompanying system of monitoring and recording progress, to be available within the classroom and accessible to the various adults working there. The whole school requires a policy and framework which offers support and personal and professional resourcing to the adults working with individuals and groups, but in particular to those working with children who have special educational needs. This requires an organisational and management structure at the level of the classroom (class teacher as educational manager) and of the school (deputy or headteacher as manager of whole-school policy). Only within this framework will primary schools avoid the dangers of labelling and segregation for pupils, or of unco-ordinated and unsupported services of peripatetic teachers and helpers which the 'static' classroom implies. By considering the context in which children are learning and the ecology of classroom and school, primary schools may develop a flexible and dynamic learning environment which promotes the development of *all* children.

References

Apter, S. J. (1982) *Troubled Children, Troubled Systems* New York: Pergamon.

Bennett, N., Desforges, C., Cockburn, A. and Wilkinson, B. (1984) *The quality of pupil learning experiences* London: Lawrence Erlbaum Associates Ltd.

DES: Central Advisory Council for Education (England) (1967) *Children and their Primary Schools* London: HMSO (The Plowden Report).

DES (1978) *Special Educational Needs* Report of the Committee of Enquiry into the Education of Handicapped Children and Young People. London: HMSO (The Warnock Report).

Doyle, W. (1977) 'Learning the classroom environment: an ecological analysis' in *Journal of Teacher Education*, 28, 6, 51–55.

Fraser, B. J. (1986) *Classroom Environment* London: Croom Helm.

Galton, M. J., Simon, B. and Croll, P. (1980) *Inside the Primary Classroom* London: Routledge and Kegan Paul.

HMI (1978) *Primary Education in England: A Survey by H M Inspectors of Schools* London: HMSO.

Hoffman, L. (1981) *Foundations of Family Therapy: a conceptual framework for systems change* New York: Basic Books.

ILEA: (1985) *Educational Opportunities for All* London: ILEA (The Fish Report).

Jackson, A. and Hannon, P. W. (1981) *The Belfield Reading Project, Rochdale, Lancashire* Belfield Community Council.

Thomas, G. (1985) 'Room management in mainstream education' in *Educational Research*, 27, 3, 186–192.

Thomas, G. (1986) 'Integrating personnel in order to integrate children' in *Support for Learning*, 1, 1, 19–26.

7 Free flow and the secondary school

Geof Sewell

The origins of the present concern to re-analyse remedial education in terms of its school context can probably be traced to the meeting of a small group of sociologists, educational psychologists, remedial teachers and special school staff at Birmingham University in April 1980. The meeting reflected a degree of unease amongst practitioners, parents and academics at the slow pace of desegregation and at the 'obfuscations' of the Warnock Committee (Barton and Tomlinson, 1981). What concerned us particularly was the neglect of sociological issues by the Committee (Lewis and Vulliamy, 1980) at the expense of psychologistic models of 'need' and the resolution of competing interests among the 'gatekeepers'. Despite the near universal chorus of approval which greeted the report's publication (Cooke, 1979), it had shown remarkably little interest in mainstream organisation and curriculum. Its use of the 'cascade' model had side-stepped the problems raised by efficacy research on special schools, special classes in ordinary schools and withdrawal groups. And for those of us who worked in secondary school, it appeared to have little appreciation of the day to day realities of classroom life.

What interested all of us at that meeting was the possibility that most of what Warnock called 'special educational needs' might be socially and institutionally determined, rather than inherent to the child. According to an interactionist model, 'learning difficulties' could be relocated in teaching and learning processes, wider organisational and curricular structures and ultimately in the relationship between education and the reproduction of social class. Among the questions which a decade of debates about integration and labelling theory had raised but which we felt Warnock had evaded were: if the skills and expectations of mainstream teachers were heightened through better in-service education, classroom support and resources, would the pupils traditionally associated with remedial departments and ESN (M) schools continue to have the same kinds of difficulties described by Warnock? If such difficulties are 'socially constructed', what role do special needs assessment and provision serve? And at the back of our minds was the question: how would worsening recession, restraints on educational spending and increasing youth unemployment affect the proportion of pupils in special schools and the problems of learning difficulties in the mainstream?

At that meeting, Sally Tomlinson wondered whether the expansion of special educational provision from the 2% in special schools to the Warnock 20% constituted an educational response to significant economic changes. Following three decades of rising expectations, increasing social mobility and high unemployment, pupils with the lowest attainments and fewest job prospects could well become the focus of social tensions. One of the functions of this newly enlarged special education could easily become that of signalling, through assessment, organisational and curricular procedures, that pupils were unlikely to find work because of their own innate learning difficulties. More recently (Cohen, 1986), a DES official seems to have drawn very similar conclusions:

> We are beginning to create aspirations which society cannot match. When young people can't find work which meets their abilities and expectations then we are only creating frustrations with disturbing social consequences. We have to ration ... educational opportunities so that society can cope with the output of education. People must be educated once more to know their place.

Since the Birmingham meeting things have worsened considerably. Integration does not appear to have increased: recent figures show the proportion of pupils in segregated special schools actually grew in the six years since Warnock was published (Swann, 1985). Low attainers in mainstream schools have also been progressively disadvantaged. Courtenay (1986) suggests that of the 14% of pupils who left school with no exam qualifications in 1984, 40% were unemployed a year later. This figure can be compared with unemployment rates amongst the 23% who left with more than four CSEs: in this group 16% were unemployed.

In such a climate it is not difficult for practitioners and academics to feel that anything positive they might try to do merely props up an increasingly iniquitous system. Secondary teachers most concerned with low attainers feel caught between demoralised staffrooms and despairing pupils. Two weeks after I took up my present teaching post, one of the children in my third-year remedial class asked, 'Why should we work? We're too thick to get exams and too thick to get a job. What's the point in getting *us* to work?' In very many secondary schools, this sense of futility and boredom intensifies in the last two years. Educational attainments barely rise and in some cases may even regress. Absence increases, formal work is characterised by banal, repetitive exercises and practical work is all too undemanding. If one asks 'non-exam' classes to consider staying on at school or college, the response is often derisory. Courtenay's analysis (1986, *ibid*) suggests that of the 14% who left without exams only 2% stayed on for more than another year. It is scarcely surprising that intensifying recession has made an increasing number of secondary teachers feel that educational reforms for the less able need to be accompanied by wide-ranging social changes.

However much one understands the feelings which generate such critiques, it has to be argued that some of these analyses are both simplistic and parochial. Anthropological studies like Edgerton's (1967) have shown how complex the relationship between economic structures and the social construction of learning difficulties can be. More recent comparative studies would suggest that it is not only in more egalitarian societies that pupils with learning difficulties attain higher standards. In West Germany, all pupils are expected to pass exams in their own language, Maths, Science and the Humanities. Their programmes of pre-vocational training and work experience run alongside demanding academic courses. In Japan there are mixed-ability classes until 15+ and 94% of pupils stay on until 18. Drew (1986) suggests that most pupils follow a Maths programme 'very similar to a fairly traditional O-level course'. A long-standing UNESCO survey of special education in the Soviet Union (Segal, 1966) points out that Russian schools do well enough without remedial departments or special classes. Pupils are taught in mixed-ability groups until 16+. Devereux (1966) noted that, if children found difficulty in a certain subject, they would go to the teacher concerned for help. Parents would be contacted and extra lessons arranged for small groups after school, for which subject teachers are paid overtime. The parents themselves are drawn into the process. There is additional evidence from Grant (1979) that pupils with learning difficulties attain much more than their British equivalents.

Neither in Japan nor the USSR are there formal exams at the end of compulsory schooling: teachers still attain high standards without the 'bait' of academic qualifications.

Every teacher a teacher of special needs?

At present, it is often assumed that the way out of the morass for English schools would be for government, LEAs or particular schools to formulate appropriate policies for special needs:

> We embrace the slogan 'every teacher a teacher of special needs' and turn it into an objective of in-service training ... We adopt a whole-school approach to learning difficulties, echoing the Bullock Report's view of language teaching across the curriculum.
>
> (Booth, 1985)

Yet the effects of a whole-school language approach, such as the Schools' Council DARTS project, on the attainments of poor readers have been extremely discouraging. Results suggest that pupils do not make even the rapid short-term progress they would have done with the traditional remedial approach. Meetings to write special needs policy documents often seem to be 'scudding over the clouds' (Ashcroft, 1986). Too many working parties fail to confront essential problems of teacher skill and attitude and the context of failure that informs them.

In Britain, the attitudes and skills of many secondary-school subject specialists are themselves part of the problem. Pupils with learning difficulties often experience their teachers as petty-minded snobs:

Paul   This school is a load of rubbish because the teachers think they are a class above the rest. Some of them are all right but some of them make you sick.

Sue   The teachers here really get on my nerves. They are always picking on you.

Even those teachers who do identify with low attainers do not always speak the same language as their pupils:

Sarah   I like History and I like the teacher. I get on really well with him and I did last year. But I just can't understand the words he uses. It's just too hard.

It often appears that only a minority of staff in the 'academic' subjects establish positive working relationships and help pupils with low expectations achieve high standards:

> **Jane** I didn't choose RE (in the options). But now I am having to do it, it is getting more and more interesting. At the moment we are doing a topic on Death . . . Mrs Brown is good for a laugh . . . The teacher was very good to us.

Interactionists like Brophy and Good (1974) would argue that whilst a minority of teachers treat low attainers 'in grossly inappropriate ways' and most others merely 'reinforce low expectations', there are also a few who 'reach out forcefully and successfully to involve' these pupils. Sometimes these teachers are traditional remedial teachers, but they are also to be found scattered across the subject departments. To make a start in bringing our pupils up to the levels of their Japanese or Russian counterparts, it is probably easiest to co-ordinate the efforts of this significant minority of subject staff.

Free flow

Harnessing the enthusiasm of what often turn out to be the most competent subject staff is something that comes through action rather than working parties. One needs a way of providing a shared and valued experience. Most teachers still see problems with reading as the most important source of learning difficulties (Croll and Moses, 1985). Many secondary schools still withdraw pupils for reading tuition in the first two years. One way of initiating change is for this significant minority of subject staff to undergo a short period of school-based training in reading tuition and then to take part in this traditional remedial activity. Previous research indicates (Sewell, 1982) that the children do not lose out from having non-specialists. Improvements in reading ages can be broadly similar to those achieved with fully-trained peripatetic staff (Cashdan, Pumfrey and Lunzer, 1971). Training can be carried out by the special needs co-ordinator, members of the advisory service or educational psychologists. Even with the constraints of the new contracts, it can be fitted into Year 5 and Year 7 teaching slots during the public exam season. One starts by asking a small team of staff to help out for one year, then the following year another team is involved.

Gradually one may introduce up to one third of the staff to the scheme (see DES, 1978). With many of the subject staff involved, the experience of working closely with a small group of low attainers on the basic skills can become a spur to rethinking their own part of the curriculum and its delivery. In one extreme case the head of a history department destroyed all her worksheets a few weeks after starting with her backward readers. Many others begin supplementing existing resources and talking with other staff about new approaches, different ways of structuring courses and pacing lessons. The classic problem with withdrawal work, a problem which Warnock did not address, is that after a short period of rapid gains, pupils return to their mainstream classes and progress ceases. As long ago as 1948, Collins (1961) noted that in the long term all the initial advantages are cancelled out. In Collins's (1972) words, 'remedial education is a hoax'. My research indicates, however, that if they find amongst their subject teachers a significant few who identify with them, talk to them in words they understand and know *how* to help them organise their work, low-attaining pupils continue to progress (Sewell, 1982).

It is often argued that remedial departments 'de-skill' subject teachers. For many staff, however, it is not as if they had much skill to start with. Initial training for subject specialists is still largely inadequate (Clunies Ross and Wimhurst, 1983; Sewell, 1986) and in-service education is mainly directed at existing remedial and special education specialists. For many teachers and schools a rolling programme of involvement with small groups of pupils on basic skills can be the starting point for wider change. The teachers' first lesson is that:

> There is no mystique about remedial education, nor are its methods intrinsically different from those employed by successful teachers everywhere.
>
> (Bullock Report, 1975)

Other features that can be built into the programme are collaborative teaching with remedial specialists or with probationary staff who work in the same curriculum area. Gradually one builds up a group of like-minded colleagues, who talk the same language and who feel happy to 'flow' between class teaching, small-group withdrawal in the basic skills and collaborative teaching in their own subject. After that training year, the teacher may well persuade his or her own department to let him/her work in their lessons, offering advice on curriculum delivery, preparing extra resources and supporting colleagues through collaborative teaching.

The system could well ossify, turning a growing number of staff into 'thickie teachers', if the training programme did not ensure a regular turnover. The support that collaborative teaching offers subject staff is not, in my view, the key to the programme's success. The most significant aspect of 'free flow' is that the mix of approaches – withdrawal work, consultancy and collaborative teaching – together provide these small teams of staff with an opportunity to rethink learning difficulties and teaching difficulties in terms of their own subjects. Action leads to redefinition, not vice versa, and this is vital in secondary schools, where subject boundaries still represent real problems for curriculum development. Any teacher who has taught poor readers and helped screen whole populations knows about discrepancies between test scores, and knows how much of a discrepancy there can be between a test score and how a child functions in a given context. Successful experience with a reading group helps one realise that the term 'special needs' has already become yet another means of categorising children. As the head of one science department who had recently become a free flow teacher remarked:

> Some of the kids on our special needs list can read all right in our lessons and it must be because they like science. Some of those who are not on the list get in a right muddle. And some of our A-level kids, who never got picked up because their reading was just a little bit too good, are having tremendous problems coping in the lower sixth. Yet my science teachers come to me and say, 'I haven't got time to get through all my experiments with the special needs kids in my class. Get them out, would you?' I tell tell them it's not as simple as that but they don't see it.

It is widely assumed at the moment that if only the traditional remedial teacher were to move out of his special classroom and work collaboratively across the curriculum, this would increase expectations among teachers and pupils by itself:

The aim of the whole-school approach is to move the expertise of the special class teacher into the classroom and out of the isolation of the remedial class or special 'unit'. The role of the special needs teacher thus becomes advisory or pervasive, not simply restricted to a very small number of children but influencing curriculum planning and resources throughout the school.

(Simmons, 1986)

Despite such large claims, collaborative teaching by staff from the remedial class or special unit has been largely unevaluated (Sayer, 1984). Secondary teachers are unused to having a second adult in the classroom (Clunies Ross, 1984) and it would appear highly unlikely that having been seen to fail in their more familiar approach, special needs staff will achieve much in subject areas where they have little or no expertise. As one colleague said:

This isn't what I came into remedial education for. And what's the Geography teacher going to say when I offer to help? I don't even have Geography O-level.

Children with learning difficulties are often embarrassed at the special help they get in open class from someone whom all their peers know is the 'thickie' teacher. As another teacher said:

The arguments (for support in class) are that he won't get singled out as a remedial child . . . but the three I go into, they feel embarrassed the moment I walk through the door. And they look at each other and they know they need my help and they hate it.

(Bines, 1986)

As Cockcroft (1982) pointed out in relation to Maths, children with the greatest difficulties benefit from collaborative work with the most skilled subject specialists. Free flow ensures that teachers who are not often seen as specially reserved for slow learners team teach for short periods in their own subject areas.

When in the late 70s an HMI inspected remedial provision in my previous school, he found it hard to accept that there was no clearly defined remedial department. No teacher worked full time with low attainers, those who did were only involved for a year at a time; yet the standards of the pupils did not suffer from this lack of continuity. In just a few other schools there is now no special needs department. The role of special needs co-ordinator might be devolved to a deputy head or senior teacher, but the withdrawal and collaborative teaching will be carried out by an ever-changing group of subject specialists. Some of these co-ordinators try to involve the whole staff: those with poor discipline, the rigidly authoritarian, those who cannot talk to children and the insensitive – on the grounds that it gives them all an opportunity to learn new skills. If one is serious about generating higher standards, it is probably more effective to start with the significant minority, teachers like those whom the LAPP evaluators (DES, 1986) characterised as:

> the very best practitioners (who combined) subject specialist expertise with a high level of teaching skill and capacity for relating easily and productively to pupils with a wide range of needs.

Examinations

In the early stages of free flow it is essential to keep reminding oneself of the importance of failure in secondary schools. The context of failure has functions far beyond the school gate. Low expectations are extremely obdurate; they serve

> to familiarise pupils with the logic of inequality that pervades society at large: to reduce potential opposition to such inequality; and to make many children breathe a sigh of relief when they are released from school into subordinate positions in adult life after long experience of educational failure.
>
> (Westergaard and Resler, 1975)

To withstand such pressures, one must establish vividly and publicly how high the attainments of pupils with a history of learning difficulties can be. Unfortunately, this almost certainly means coming to terms with public exams. As Clunies Ross and Wimhurst (1983) found in their survey of secondary schools:

> In school E pupils were given the opportunity to participate in exams . . . They were expected to achieve academic success and

were observed to respond well to the challenge. Alternative non-exam courses, however well constructed, do not provide the same kind of tangible goal.

Having raised the attainments and expectations of our younger pupils, our school established that no child should be excluded from an exam group on the basis of ability. In 1987, the average number of CSE passes for the 16% of our intake group originally picked out as having learning difficulties was 4.9. These passes were not predominantly in the practical subjects. Every pupil who had entered school with reading difficulties passed English, many with chronic problems in Maths passed that, and most a Humanities and a Science subject. High standards in the liberal curriculum did not interfere with their pre-vocational or work experience programme.

This group has not been penalised by unemployment nearly as savagely as those in Courtenay's MSC study (1986, *ibid*). And all this development took place against a background of worsening youth unemployment, intermittent teaching strikes and no general staff meetings.

Until our special needs department had spearheaded this raising of expectations, a small group of our pupils left school every year barely literate or numerate. The best written work that they could manage was a page of well spelt, simply written narrative. This is an extract from a story which one of the higher attainers in our 'non-exam' class wrote a month before he had left school:

> I was walking from school when a Big Black car Drove up to me. And the back door of the car open and a Big Man got out. And he had a big hat and a black suit and shoes. He got me and push me into a car.

The mother of one of the boys in that particular non-exam class came into school to see what she could do to help her younger son, then in the second year, with his reading. She commented that the younger boy was already doing better written work than that of her older son, despite the fact that his initial difficulties had been much greater. The kidnap story can be compared with two extracts from essays on 'Law and Order' by two of the 1987 fifth years with a history of learning difficulties:

> I think the main problem with the English Judicial System is that it's too soft. At York Crown Court we saw two men who

were suspect altogether of 21 criminal offences, such as theft, damage to a stolen vehicle which cost a staggering £4745 and £900 damage.

This pupil has minor problems with apostrophes, he mis-spells 'suspected' and repeats the word 'damage' but the breadth of his vocabulary, the complexity of his sentence-making and the sophistication of his approach are beyond comparison with those displayed in the earlier extract. The second extract is from a child who only reached a reading age of 9.5 in the second year:

I think the strengths of courts is that they try anything else before sending you down. Like at the Magistrate's Court this young lad burgled this man's house taking 27 pound coins . . . In the end he got put in a Community Centre for so many hours a day for six months. He could of got sent to prison for this offence but the courts was very fair to him.

The writer of this second extract confuses 'of' and 'have' and makes too much use of 'this', but once again one is struck by the ability to construct an argument and to select illustrations to back it up. The pupils came from the same group and they learned it was possible to hold strong conflicting views of the same events, something which former O-level pupils struggling to master masses of factual material often failed to do. The key to this more sophisticated use of writing was the developing of speech. As can be seen in an earlier publication (Sewell, 1986), the talk of our 'less able' pupils became strikingly more assured and reflective.

The raising of expectations in Maths forced us to address a number of cognitive and organisational problems. We realised that pupils with a poor grasp of concrete operations and number bonds were able to carry out supposedly more complex mathematical procedures. One of the reasons for the 'excessive' narrowness (Cockcroft, 1982) of Maths syllabuses for low attainers is the Piagetian assumption that arithmetic and basic practical work must precede more abstract concepts. Far from needing more Maths games and further exercises in basic arithmetic before they could move on, we found that lessons in statistics, geometry and algebra reinforced number skills. Provided the teacher scoured the textbooks for difficult prose readings, sudden leaps in the complexity of the exercises given and concepts that were poorly explained, we could use a post-Cockcroft course like IMS (*Integrated Maths Scheme*, Kaner, 1983) with the whole ability range. The sense that low attainers did not need to be excluded from work that the rest were doing itself raised attainments and we reached standards we had not originally dreamed of.

Maths departments often have very rigid ideas about the spread of ability, and generating organisational change can be very difficult. Our supposedly low attainers were doing better than some children in higher sets and when we entered our pupils for exams this indirectly raised standards for pupils in higher sets. It also made the department ready to reconsider mixed ability in the lower school.

The foundations of our work with 14 to 16 year-olds had to be laid through raising attainments and expectations in the lower school. Our significant minority of free flow staff had first to prove that fast progress could be made in the basic skills. Next we had to come to terms with what pupils were capable of from fourteen to sixteen. But this in turn made us rethink our expectations with younger pupils. Even with a strong theoretical belief that low attainment was the fruit of poor pupil self-concept and low teacher expectation, it was difficult for the teachers who spearheaded such changes to say they knew what our pupils were really capable of. Reality and the aims and objectives that buttress it seemed ours to define. We felt at times as if telling the pupils they could get good grades at CSE was a confidence trick: at other times we felt as if the under-achievement of so many 'special needs pupils' was a confidence trick. And we tried to discuss this with our children. At the last evaluation meeting we held with our first English exam pupils, in 1984, the colleague with whom I had been teaching said:

> When we took you lot on at the start of the fourth year, you were the first groups we had ever taken through to a CSE exam. Now, if you had been in the school a year earlier, you would have been 'non-exam' English. This would probably have meant we would not have put so much pressure on you, you wouldn't have had to do all the essays and reading and we wouldn't have had to get on at you as we have done. But at the end of the third year, Mr Sewell and I thought that maybe six or seven or eight (out of forty) would achieve CSE grades. We would split you up then and the rest of you would go into a special class and do drama and watch videos and go on visits

and the rest of it. But what we realised after about the summer term of the fourth year was that you were *all* really good. And that you were going to achieve something remarkable. And the feeling that Mr Sewell and I had was that we were really very proud of you. There are sets higher up who haven't achieved what you have done.

There is no doubt that exams provide 'bait' but they also make the successes of these groups appear more objective. Perhaps as we develop Mode III GCSEs in line with profiles, graded assessments and concepts like education for capability, we shall also feel that we are examining a more appropriate range of qualities in our pupils. We have to accept that, as it stands, GCSE has a lot of problems for pupils with a history of learning difficulties. When the exam was first discussed among HMI, none of those concerned with special education was involved. The differentiated questions in many exams mean that pupils would have to read through a lot of the paper before they came to the odd ones they could answer. The very grading system could lead some employers to think that F is for Failure and G is for Good. All in all, however, GCSE does present free flow teachers with an opportunity to rethink many of their own skills, attitudes and assumptions.

Changing the ecology

The possibility that one might reshape comprehensive education from the bottom up with free flow and new 14 to 16 courses could in turn just begin to affect the micro-climate of individual schools. Schools with free flow teams, which reject categorisations like GCSE and LAPP courses, may also be a little more suitable for pupils from special schools. Many LEAs are presently taking under-used teachers off the rolls of primary and special schools, giving them a period of college-based retraining and then asking them to 'support' statemented pupils in secondary schools. Primary schools are used to this form of servicing. Communication may be easier because of their size and rather more homogeneous attitudes to handicap (Sewell, 1980). Secondary schools are more heterogeneous, however. Each subject department has its own ideology of acceptable learning and behaviour. There is often a range of staffrooms. And teachers find it difficult enough to tolerate members of their own schools in their classes, let alone an outsider. Though it makes line management and administration more difficult, it might be more suitable for the statemented child if free flow teachers were given extra training and then offered support to their own schools and departments, part-time.

Traditionally, pupils with behavioural problems have been seen as the responsibility of remedial staff, whatever their abilities. A great deal of expertise has grown up, which, with the closing of special classes, could be fed back into the system. In my own department at present all the previous remedial class teachers now serve as year heads, building bridges between the pastoral and the academic, helping liaise with primary schools and parents and developing study skills programmes for all the pupils.

Raising the attainments of British pupils to the levels of other more technologically advanced or more egalitarian states, with prospects of worsening unemployment and further government restraints on educational spending provides a 'challenge . . . which should not be underestimated' (DES, 1986). Free flow and the introduction of new exams provide the individual comprehensive school with an opportunity to change its ecology, to provide alternatives to the context of failure. At our Birmingham meeting Andrew Sutton coined the phrase 'the ideology of benevolent humanitarianism' to suggest how difficult it would be to convince the special educational establishment and our practising colleagues that focusing on pupils' 'needs' could inadvertently extend the social construction of disability. Just occasionally one glimpses the alternative: how small groups of like-minded teachers can reach out 'forcefully and successfully' to raise educational standards and change attitudes, even when society as a whole is growing steadily more divided.

References

Ashcroft, P. (1986) Personal communication.
Barton, L. and Tomlinson, S. (1981) *Special Education: Policy, Practices and Social Issues* London: Harper and Row.
Bines, H. (1986) *Redefining Remedial Education* London: Croom Helm.
Booth, T. (1985) 'Training and progress in special education' in J. Sayer and N. Jones (eds) *Teacher Training and Special Education Needs* London: Croom Helm.
Brophy, J. E. and Good, T. L. (1974) *Teacher Student Relationships: Causes and Consequences* New York: Holt.

Cashdan, A., Pumfrey, P. D. and Lunzer, E. A. (1971) 'Children receiving remedial treatment in reading' in *Educational Research*, 13, 2, 98–103.

Clunies Ross, L. and Wimhurst, S. (1983) *The Right Balance* Slough: NFER.

Cohen, G. A. (1986) 'No Habitat for a Schmoo' in *The Listener*, 116, 2976, 6, 4 September.

Collins, J. E. (1961) 'The effects of remedial education' in *Birmingham University Institute of Education: Education Monographs, No 4* Edinburgh: Oliver and Boyd.

Collins, J. E. (1972) 'The remedial reading hoax' in *Remedial Education*, 7, 3, 9–10.

Cooke, G. V. (1979) *The Times Educational Supplement*, 29th December.

Courtenay, G. (1986) *England and Wales Youth Cohort Study: First Summary Report* Sheffield: SCPR.

Croll, P. and Moses, D. (1985) *One in Five: The Assessment and Incidence of Special Educational Needs* London: Routledge and Kegan Paul.

DES (1975) *A Language for Life* London: HMSO. (The Bullock Report.)

DES (1978) *Mixed Ability Work in Comprehensive Schools* London: HMSO.

DES (1982) *Mathematics Counts* London: HMSO. (The Cockcroft Report.)

DES (1986) *Lower Attaining Pupils' Programme: The First Two Years* London: HMSO.

Devereux, K. F. (1966) 'The education of children in ordinary schools' in S. S. Segal (ed) *Backward Children in the USSR* London: Arnold.

Drew, M. (1986) 'Ahead of the rest' in *The Times Educational Supplement*, 10 October.

Edgerton, R. B. (1967) *The Cloak of Competence* Berkeley: University of California Press.

Grant, N. (1979) *Soviet Education* Harmondsworth: Penguin.

Kaner, P. (1983) *Integrated Mathematics Scheme* London: Bell & Hyman.

Lewis, I. and Vulliamy, G. (1980) 'Warnock or Warlock? The sorcery of definitions' in *Educational Review* 32, 1, 3–10.

Sayer, J. (1984) 'Training for diversity' in *The Times Educational Supplement*, 14 September.

Segal, S. S. (1966) *Backward Children in the USSR* London: Arnold.

Sewell, G. (1980) 'Transfer to special schools' Unpublished MEd dissertation, Birmingham University.

Sewell, G. (1982) *Reshaping Remedial Education* London: Croom Helm.

Sewell, G. (1986) *Coping with Special Needs: a Guide for New Teachers* London: Croom Helm.

Simmons, K. (1986) 'Painful extractions' in *The Times Educational Supplement*, 17 October.

Swann, W. (1985) 'Is the integration of children with special needs happening?' in *Oxford Review of Education*, 11, 1, 3–18.

Westergaard, J. and Resler, H. (1975) *Class in a Capitalist Society* Harmondsworth: Penguin.

PART III
The classroom

Introduction

Special education is not notorious for its success in looking at the workings of ordinary classrooms. Why should it be? It has been set in a cul-de-sac where practitioners have been free to examine individual learning problems rather than learning environments. The orientation of special education has been towards efficiently identifying those children who are failing, segregating them from their peers and then providing resources to help them in a different setting. Given such an orientation the ordinary classroom environment has been almost an irrelevance. Worse, the orientation has enabled mainstream classroom practices to evolve as though a proportion of children did not exist.

Recent moves away from such thinking and towards an integrationist stance have not been matched by any serious or sustained examination of the implications.

So the third part of this book concentrates on ways of understanding and changing the classroom in order that special needs might more easily be met. A number of themes are discussed. We begin by examining some of the most pressing organisational concerns in meeting special needs in the mainstream: how to 'integrate' the resources and personal skills that have traditionally been separated from the mainstream. This is central to successful integration yet scant attention has been paid to it. From different perspectives Sarah Tann and Kevin Wheldall go on to review means by which grouping can be used to help prevent problems arising and to help children to mix and communicate. Some of the means by which newer ways of helping children with learning difficulties may actually be implemented in the classroom are discussed in Jonathan Solity's chapter. Sheila Wolfendale continues by making a detailed examination of some of the innovative ways in which parents are being involved in their children's education. This is an important area: many parent involvement projects rest on the assumption that for many children 'special needs' will simply cease to exist if there is closer communication between home and school. Andrew Pollard closes this section for us by revealing – and challenging – some of the ways in which we shape our ideas on special needs in the classroom; he suggests that no real changes can take place without changes in attitude.

8 Planning for support in the mainstream

Gary Thomas

Over the last few years a quiet revolution has been taking place in our schools. It has gone unnoticed because there has been no fanfare, no top-down initiative sparking it off. The opening of classroom doors to parents, specialist teachers, welfare assistants, support services and all kinds of volunteers from the community has truly been a revolution. It is a revolution in ideas about community participation in education. It is a revolution in thinking about teachers' autonomy within the classroom. And it is a revolution in terms of the possible advantages for children.

A number of trends have brought about this revolution. There is the general and widespread demand from the community at large for more openness in the institutions which serve it. But more specifically there are two trends which have played a major part in bringing extra people into the classroom. First, there is the trend towards increased participation of parents in their children's education. This has been translated into practice, in some cases, in parental involvement in the classroom. Equally important has been the trend to integrate into ordinary schools children who would formerly have been sent to special schools. This latter trend has resulted in provision being made by many LEAs for special children in ordinary schools: resources and personnel have been provided to help meet those children's special needs within the mainstream class. This change constitutes the single most important means by which integration is being effected.

In practice it has meant that welfare assistants have sometimes been appointed to meet special needs; sometimes specialist teachers, for instance, teachers of the hearing impaired, will be working alongside the classteacher. Sometimes teachers from 'outreach' schemes in special schools will be working with the teacher in the mainstream, perhaps providing advice or resources for special needs or perhaps working with individuals or groups of children. Peripatetic remedial teachers, instead of withdrawing children from the class-room for help, are now providing support within the classroom. Remedial departments in secondary schools are changing the way they work, so that their staffs provide help within the mainstream of the curriculum instead of withdrawing children as they used to.

A survey completed recently (Thomas, 1987) indicates that the trend has gone much further than many might have imagined. In some areas it is the exception to find primary teachers who always work on their own; instead, parents work in nine out of ten class-rooms, and a great variety of other people, from school governors to speech therapists to young people on YTS schemes, are involved in classrooms.

These developments are necessary and welcome but they are accompanied by problems. They represent a very new departure in the working practices of most teachers and they confront us with unfamiliar challenges. Prior to these developments the class teacher's territory was very much her own. Similarly, the remedial teacher had a well-defined job, taking small groups of children out of the classroom, in turn, to her own territory. Now all this has changed.

Many problems may arise when people share a task but the effects are multiplied when the practice of working individually is well-established. An analogy may be drawn between current teaming arrangements and team teaching. Team teaching, pioneered with such high hopes in the early seventies, has since declined substan-tially (see Geen, 1985) because no-one really considered the organ-isational problems in making it work. In theory it seemed like a good idea, but in practice it raised more problems than it solved.

But the current teaming arrangements are arising for very differ-ent reasons from those which gave rise to team teaching. Team teaching was an ideal in itself. Today's teaming has arisen out of reasons other than the feeling that teaming is in itself valuable. None the less, the practical problems which beset team teaching will certainly recur with current teaming arrangements.

It is essential then that we look at the possible problems which may arise when people share a task and it is essential that we look at the changed parameters of classroom organisation when other adults move into space which has traditionally been the domain of one adult.

Since our concern is for special needs in education (and since many of these extra people are in mainstream classes now to help meet special needs) we also need to look at how these changed parameters may affect the way we meet special needs. Only then will we be able to go on to suggest the best possible ways for these adults to work next to one another.

So I shall first try to make clear my understanding of the term 'special needs'. Unless a revised understanding of what 'special needs' means in a post-Warnock era is made manifestly clear there is the danger that in the move of these extra people into mainstream classes, the same practices will be going on – but simply in a different place. No meaningful shift toward integration will have occurred.

Special needs and extra people

I sometimes feel that human beings have a natural tendency to label, to want to pigeon-hole, to categorise. The manifestation of this trait is nowhere more clearly seen than in the changing of the term ESN to SEN in recent years. Despite the best intentions of Warnock, despite the 1981 Act, the term 'SEN' has become an adjective – another label. We need to remind ourselves what special needs are when considering the work of additional people in the classroom.

This is particularly relevant when thinking about additional people in the classroom because the success of integration pivots around this issue. Integration is not so much about moving the special children – that is relatively easy. The much more difficult task is to integrate and effectively use in mainstream education the resources and the personnel traditionally associated with special provision. If we are going to meet special needs in the mainstream, it is necessary to remind ourselves what special needs actually *are* in order that the best efforts of these personnel are not wasted. It would be all too easy to move from segregation in special schools or remedial rooms or medical rooms, only to see segregation actually occurring in the mainstream classroom with a special person – perhaps an ancillary helper, perhaps a support teacher – identifying 'SEN children' in that setting and proceeding from there as though nothing else had really changed.

Clearly, this would be a defeat for the aims and ideals of integration. Behind integration is the wider ideal of a comprehensive, mixed-ability curriculum for all – an ideal of schools where children are not stigmatised by being withdrawn from the class. Most teachers would now go along with the aims and ideals of integration and I do not propose to rehearse the arguments for or against here. I take it as a starting point that integration is occurring and I seek ways of making that ideal work without regressing to a kind of disguised segregation: segregation within the classroom. So, if the ways people work in the mainstream classroom alongside the class-teacher are so important for effectively meeting special needs, it is important to define what these special needs might be and how they might be met by those who are coming into classrooms.

Cerebral palsy is not a need. Downs syndrome is not a need. Brain damage is not a need. Learning difficulties are not a need. A need can only be defined in terms of an outcome. We can only say that children need a particular kind of teaching if we have a particular kind of outcome in mind. If we say that it is important to learn number bonds to ten we may then proceed to define the best way of helping children to learn that information. From there, we could go on to say that children need a particular kind of teaching in order to learn number bonds. A special need then becomes something over and above what is normally needed.

Not all goals in education are as easy to define. The goals of today's teacher will be more to do with communication, coopera-tion, sharing, developing children's language and imagination. But even here it is salutary to stop for a moment and consider the *needs* children have, with these goals in mind. Clearly, in the case of cooperation and communication it would be fruitless to have children sitting on their own in rows – they would *need* to be in groups. But one of the most interesting findings of recent research (see Tann, Chapter 9) is that even when teachers had wanted children to be doing *individual tasks* they kept children in groups. For individual tasks they would have been better working on their own; in other words, they *need* a different kind of classroom set-up, because in groups children are more easily distracted. Children who are experiencing difficulties are often particularly easily distracted, losing concentration very quickly. In thinking about their *special* needs, grouping and other classroom arrangements have to be considered very carefully in order that distraction is reduced. So, special classroom geography might constitute the special need for many children.

I introduced the point about need because it is essential for any understanding of how classroom organisation can be changed. A child's needs for doing a particular task or to become an active participant in groupwork or to master some particularly difficult concept can be defined only in terms of the teacher's goals and in terms of the particular characteristics of the classroom and school situation. Special needs then become merely extensions of the kinds of needs that all children have in mainstream classrooms.

I cannot proceed to an analysis of the ways in which additional adults may work effectively to meet special needs without carrying this exploration a little further. I shall do this by splitting these needs into *individual learning needs* and *organisational needs*.

Individual learning needs

Of all the constellation of factors which seem to affect children's ability to learn, individualised teaching seems to be one of the most important (eg Stallings, 1976). Efforts of educators and psychologists in recent years have been towards refining methods of teaching individual children. Yet evidence seems to show that it is not so much the methods themselves that are important. Rather, it is the *amount* of individual teaching we provide which is crucial in determining children's learning (Bloom, 1984). In other words, if we can be successful in providing this individual teaching within broadly defined ground rules we can be fairly sure of success in our teaching. So what are these 'broadly defined ground rules'? They might be summarised thus:

1 Regular individual help. It is a commonplace that sometimes children seem almost immediately to forget what they have learned. So they need regular help.
2 Distributed practice. Children appear to learn better from frequent, short doses of teaching than one long session. In other words, six five-minute sessions would in general be better than one thirty-minute session.
3 Keeping things in sequence. Many children can pick up ideas when they are presented in a fairly loose, unstructured way. They learn new ideas through exploration, communication and inference. But some children may be unsuccessful unless we think

more precisely about the sequence of ideas in the task we are presenting to them. Although doubt has been cast on the value of, or need for, a formal or rigid sequence in presenting material (see Bennett, 1978; Horne, 1984; Stallings *et al*, 1986), it nevertheless seems clear that some children will benefit from more careful thought being given to the building of idea upon idea.

4 Making sure the learning situation is rewarding. The situation may be inherently rewarding – for instance in an interesting task. But all the attention given to making the subject matter interesting will have been to no avail if the ambience in which learning is expected to take place is unrewarding – if we are impatient or pressurising, or if we comment negatively on those areas over which a child may be experiencing difficulty.

Accepting that we keep our help broadly within these guidelines, what are the implications for classroom practice? The most immediate and pressing concern is the fact that it will be very difficult to provide this kind of individualised teaching. Teachers may justifiably ask what they are supposed to do with the rest of the class if they are to be doing more of this kind of work with children who have special needs. The involvement of the 'integrated' personnel provides at least one possible key to this dilemma and I shall attempt to put forward a solution after having tackled some other important features of classroom organisation for special needs.

Organisational needs

I have already mentioned grouping and the need for consideration of the aims of grouping. If we are expecting children to co-operate and communicate, there is certainly a justification for grouping them. However, if children are mainly doing work individually there are probably classroom arrangements which are going to be more effective for this purpose. Moreover, some children are highly distractable and lose concentration very easily. So it may be worthwhile to think of classroom arrangements which minimise distraction and help children concentrate.

The way in which the teacher moves around the class is also relevant here. Classroom management research has shown (eg Anderson, 1980; Brophy, 1979) that effective teachers manage to circulate and provide feedback frequently. But often the arrangement of the children in the class is such that circulation cannot happen very easily. There is clearly a possibility here for thinking about classroom arrangements which will facilitate such kinds of operation. Particularly relevant as far as teaming is concerned is the finding of Cohen *et al* (1979); they discovered in the classrooms they studied that the layout of the class was the most important factor in determining whether teaming worked well in the classroom.

I do not propose to attempt an in-depth analysis of classroom management research or research on instructional efficacy here. Rather, with special needs in mind, my intention has been to pick out a few key findings in these areas which might serve as a basis from which to proceed in suggesting how additional people might work alongside the classteacher. They might be summarised thus:

- *Individual teaching* eg regular practice; distributed practice; sequence; a rewarding learning situation
- *Factors in classroom organisation* eg grouping; placement of resources
- *Factors in classroom management* eg circulating; providing feedback; providing cues to the children

Effectively using support to meet organisational and individual needs

The analysis I have just made provides some clues for thinking about the work of the extra people in classrooms. Many, as I have noted, are there in order to meet special needs, yet very little thought has been given to the way in which opportunities are created for meeting special needs in this fundamentally changed environment.

Clearly, great opportunities in terms of improving classroom organisation and the ways in which we meet individual needs are created when these extra people are present. How might we proceed to suggest a pattern for their work? One way might be to look at the difficulties which class teachers customarily experience, given the problems in both managing the body of the class and at the same time providing individual attention to children. As I have noted, individual attention appears to be all-important for children who are experiencing difficulty. The ORACLE research confirmed (Galton *et al*, 1980) what most experienced teachers know: it is difficult to manage the main body of the class if you are devoting your attention primarily to individual children. Here is the central dilemma of integration: how do you manage and teach the larger body of children while at the same time providing the 'special' children with the kind of help they need? There is no formula which will enable one person to mix the different ingredients of classroom life into a solution which is perfect for meeting the needs of all children.

Though no formula exists, guidelines might be sought in the analysis made above. The conspicuously difficult task is in *simultaneously* providing the individual help of the kind the children with whom we are concerned so often need (ie regular help in frequent short doses), and constructively managing the rest of the class. Clear opportunities exist in differentiating the teacher's task so that each participant takes on a particular role in the new shared classroom.

Such a suggestion, if it is taken up, marks a new departure for today's classrooms. Implicit in the suggestion is the notion of an entirely new kind of classroom – one where there is shared decision-making and shared responsibility for children; where a discrete group of 'special needs children' does not exist and where children's special needs are met through a variety of pedagogic or organisational devices. Such assumptions demand that those who will now be working together to provide support for special needs in the mainstream will be working collaboratively with classteachers. Although planning for the curriculum will remain the class teacher's role, s/he will increasingly be planning for the curriculum and organising the classroom in collaboration with others. Only when this happens will special needs truly have been met appropriately. Until it happens and for as long as 'special personnel' continue to work only with a small group of previously identified 'special children' we shall be perpetuating the existence of segregation: segregation in the classroom.

How might the differentiation work? As I made clear above, no prescription can be given. Each classroom is unique, with a unique collection of children, facilities, organisational problems, and other circumstances. Above all, each teacher is unique and each set of adults who may be working alongside is unique. Each supporting adult is very different: a highly skilled support tecaher may be working alongside an enthusiastic yet naïve parent. But it is too easy to type-cast. Many parents are sensitive and skilled; indeed, it is often the case that they are in the classroom *because* they have special skills to offer. Many of the welfare assistants now being appointed to help meet special needs are extremely competent individuals who could, had their circumstances or inclinations been different, have made excellent teachers. Most significantly, though, each brings a particular and a rich experience to the classroom. Each biography offers something different to the children and it is important that the most is made of these contributions. It is important that we do not become deluded by the stereotypes which have for so long constrained the ways in which we think about the contributions of additional people and about special needs.

My point is that far more imaginative ways may be sought of deploying the extra help that is now in classrooms for special needs. Welfare assistants can do more than work with one individual exclusively for, say, half a day a week. Parents can do more than help with the traditional parent activities like cookery and needlework (see Cyster *et al* 1979). And there is surely a far larger role for the support teacher than merely visiting a class once a week and working with a group of children; she must now – and often does – work collaboratively with the classteacher to help organise the response they are making for the children who are experiencing difficulty.

With the new openness now coming into our classrooms and with our changed concept of special needs we can think far more fluidly about the ways in which these extra people work. Indeed, modern work on management (see, for instance, Hackman and Oldham, 1980) indicates that if people are to work effectively and with commitment it is essential that we move outside the constraints which have hitherto bounded our thinking about their contributions. People have to be involved in the task (in this case, teaching) and not feel that they are merely 'skivvying'; they have to have variety in their work – and not always be allocated the same child or given the same work to do; they have to have some autonomy; and they have to have feedback on the way they are working.

What does this imply? First and foremost it implies that planning for special needs has to be a joint exercise involving all the adult classroom participants. It implies that people's strengths and weaknesses are identified at this planning stage. It implies that a fairly clear definition of classroom tasks and activities be made in order that roles can be devolved and exchanged. It implies that each person's contribution is valued. Last, it implies that the group (which may be only two people) meets regularly to discuss and evaluate the way that they have been working.

I should like to suggest a model which incorporates these features and which incorporates the possibility of differentiating the teacher's role in order that special needs might be met according to the crude taxonomy outlined above.

A model

To recapitulate, children's special needs may be met in a variety of ways; some of these are outlined above. When adults (from whatever background) are working together in the new shared classrooms they, too, have needs if they are to work effectively; some of these also have been identified. A model for the various different participants in the classroom to follow might now be proposed.

The model should be based on knowledge about the ways children learn and about effective methods of classroom organisation and management. It should, in very general terms, have something to say about what the teacher has to do in order to meet special needs. From these specific descriptions it should be possible to delineate the kinds of activities which need to be undertaken by the class teacher. Packages of activities – activities which hang together and are united by a theme – might be bundled together as appropriately undertaken by particular individuals. With the focus on the discrete activity it should be possible to foresee negotiations among participants on the ways in which activities are undertaken.

The following 'room management' (adapted from M. Thomas, 1985) provides one such model. It starts by specifying a number of job descriptions for the various participants.

Individual helper The individual helper concentrates on working with an individual on a teaching activity for 5–15 minutes. So, in an hour it should be possible to arrange between four and twelve individual teaching sessions.

Activity manager The activity manager concentrates on the rest of the class, who will normally be arranged in groups of between four and eight. S/he will quickly circulate, keeping them busy and providing feedback.

Mover The mover deals with all interruptions to routine, eg visitors, spillages, etc in order to keep the activity manager and individual helper free from distraction.

The model goes on to specify a number of basic tasks which have to be completed by each of the participants undertaking these roles:

1 What an *individual helper* does:
Before the session:
a has available a list or rota of children for individual help and the activities and materials required for each;
b helps the activity manager to organise the classroom for the session;
c assembles materials needed for each child's work in the area to be used for individual work. For example, if it is to be a one-hour session with fifteen minutes for each child, four children will be seen in the hour and four sets of activities should have been prepared ready for each child to start straight away when s/he is called.
During the session:
a asks the first child on the list to come and work. Fifteen minutes should be the maximum for an intensive individual activity. In order to minimise the possibility of the session becoming frustrating and failure-laden it should be stressed to the individual helper that the emphasis should be on praise and gentle encouragement;
b asks subsequent children on the list to come and work.

2 What an *activity manager* does:
Before the session:
a organises a variety of tasks/activities for each group;
b informs the individual helper when s/he is ready to begin.
During the session:
a ensures that each group member has appropriate materials/books/equipment;
b quickly prompts children to start working if necessary;
c supervises use of shared materials;
d moves around the group to praise children who are busy, and to give feedback on work.
Thus, the activity manager moves from one busy group member to the next, commenting on her/his activities, giving help and praising those who are busy. S/he also very briefly prompts group members who are not busy.

3 What the *mover* does:

Before the session:

a helps the activity manager to prepare materials for the session;

b checks there are adequate supplies of pencils, paper and other relevant materials.

During the session:

a deals with interruptions, such as visitors;

b deals with crises such as spilt water;

c monitors smooth housekeeping, for instance in the use of shared facilities;

d becomes another activity manager if everything is flowing smoothly.

Although a study (G. Thomas, 1985) has shown that such a system can work well in the primary classroom (and reports indicate that it is also working in secondary settings) it cannot be stressed strongly enough that this model cannot be proffered as a prescription. All classrooms will have their own needs and such a model, as outlined here, will only go some way to meeting them. Ultimately, teams will have to formulate their own models uniquely suited to their own sets of circumstances. It may not be appropriate, for instance, to think of including a mover; indeed, such a function would only be appropriate for a class of younger children.

However, such a model does provide at least a draft on which teachers may base teamwork for special needs in their classes. It takes account of the learning needs of the children and of the complex and difficult problems found in classrooms. It allows for people changing and negotiating their roles and working practices. It provides a framework upon which teams can build their own arrangements.

This discussion – about negotiation – leads to a second but no less important feature of successful teamwork: the processes of planning, monitoring and evaluation. The lessons learned from teamwork in other classroom settings (see, for example, Cohen, 1976) are that these processes are essential for successful teamwork. Moreover, without the participation of all team members – not just the professionals – there is unlikely to be meaningful involvement. In practice it will be difficult for teachers to find time for planning and evaluation with others. But the warnings are clear: if time is not found, this kind of complex collaborative exercise is likely to end in failure. It may well be that support teachers in particular (who will find it most difficult to find time for this kind of exercise) will have to earmark time for planning and monitoring in the re-scheduling of their work.

Such rescheduling is essential, given the innovatory nature of the changes that are taking place in classrooms. The organisational implications of changing from solitary working to teamwork have been grossly underestimated. An ill-conceived or poorly evaluated innovation may not simply disintegrate; its debris may act as a barrier to further development, or to innovation in other areas, long after the event.

What then are the ingredients for successful planning, monitoring and evaluation? Because these developments are so new in education there are few examples from which to draw in seeking advice. Spreading the net wider, though, there is advice to be gleaned from the ways in which groups work in other settings (eg Hackman and Oldham, 1980; Robson, 1982; Herkimer, 1984). Key elements appear to be communication among participants; acceptance of the ideas of others; and willingness to make changes. These may seem so obvious as elements of successful teamwork that it is hardly worth mentioning them. But it is all too clear that unless they are explicitly spelt out they are often ignored: the obvious eludes us and common sense often flies out of the window when we work under the weight of the organisational culture. These 'obvious' elements might be incorporated into the new teamworking arrangements thus:

1 The team (comprising perhaps a classteacher, a support teacher and a parent) meet to discuss the way they are going to work. Others, such as an ancillary helper, the headteacher or the educational psychologist, might also be involved. Some kind of structure is essential for this meeting if it is not to become a mini case conference postulating quasi-diagnostic explanations for individual children's problems. The focus is most usefully organisational with the draft of a system such as 'room management' used as the basis for the discussion. People need to discuss the roles they are to be fulfilling and whether, for instance, they would feel comfortable undertaking a particular set of tasks. Role swapping can also be discussed here. Depending on the composition of the group, curricular issues might be discussed – for instance, how the

support teacher is going to make adaptations to the mainstream curriculum for children with reading difficulties.

2 The planned scheme is put into operation. Participants are encouraged to look for problems and ways of improving the system. People should be encouraged to remember that the system is not sacrosanct; it has merely been devised as a way of effectively meeting special needs. As such it has to be adapted as problems are seen to arise.

3 The team meets again to discuss the running of the system. The openness of a 'quality circle' should be the hallmark of such a meeting; in other words, the atmosphere should be informal, with people being encouraged to come up with ideas. Such a meeting ought to take place regularly – at first, perhaps once a week.

Conclusions

Few attempts have been made to analyse the problems and opportunities in the organisational accompaniments to integration. The influx of extra people into classrooms is the most important of these accompaniments; it is now happening on an unprecedented scale. A host of questions has arisen about the working of the new arrangements but this is no reason to abandon them. If we wish to realise the ideal of integration we have to look for guidance to fields unfamiliar to those of us who have worked in the special sector. Though the ground will be unfamiliar in this new diversion, the road is by no means uncharted. If we follow it, the destination promises to be one where there is less segregation, more openness and a nearing of the ideal of a comprehensive education for all children.

References

Anderson, L. M., Evertson, C. M. and Emmer, E. T. (1980) 'Dimensions in classroom management derived from recent research' in *Journal of Curriculum Studies*, 12, 4, 343–356.
Bennett, S. N. (1978) 'Recent research on teaching: a dream, a belief, a model' in *British Journal of Educational Psychology*, 48, 127–147.
Bloom, B. S. (1984) 'The search for methods of group instruction as effective as one to one tutoring' in *Educational Leadership*, May, 4–17.

Brophy, J. (1979) 'Advances in teacher research' in *Journal of Classroom Interaction*, 15, 1, 1–7.

Cohen, E. G. (1976) 'Problems and prospects of teaming' in *Educational Research Quarterly*, 1, 2, 49–63.

Cohen, E. G., Meyer, J. W., Scott, W. R. and Deal, T. R. (1979) 'Technology and teaming in the elementary school' in *Sociology of Education*, 52, January, 20–23.

Cyster, R., Clift, P., and Battle, S. (1979) *Parental Involvement in Primary Schools* Windsor: NFER.

Galton, M. J., Simon, B. and Croll, P. (1980) *Inside the Primary Classroom* London: Routledge and Kegan Paul.

Geen, A. G. (1985) 'Team teaching in the secondary schools of England and Wales' in *Educational Review*, 37, 1, 29–38.

Hackman, J. R. and Oldham, G. R. (1980) *Work Redesign* Reading, Ma: Addison-Wesley.

Herkimer, A. G. (1984) 'Quality circles in healthcare provision' in *Healthcare Financial Management*, 38, 7, 34–39.

Horne, S. E. (1983) 'Learning hierarchies: a critique' in *Educational Psychology*, 3, 1, 63–77.

Robson, M. (1982) *Quality Circles: A Practical Guide* Aldershot: Gower.

Stallings, J. A. (1976) 'How instructional processes relate to child outcomes in a national study of follow-through' in *Journal of Teacher Education*, 27, 1, 43–47.

Stallings, J., Robbins, P., Presbrey, L. and Scott, J. (1986) 'Effects of instruction based on the Madeline Hunter model on students' achievement: findings from a follow-through project' in *The Elementary School Journal*, 86, 5, 571–587.

Thomas, G. (1985) 'Room management in mainstream education' in *Educational Research*, 27, 3, 186–194.

Thomas, G. (1987) 'Extra people in the primary classroom' in *Educational Research*, 29, 3 (in press).

Thomas, M. (1985) 'Introduction to classroom management' in P. T. Farrell (ed) *Proceedings of the 1983 EDY Users Conference* Manchester: MUP.

9 Grouping and the integrated classroom

Sarah Tann

Introduction

There are slender grounds for believing that integration will be successfully achieved just by moving children and resources from the special sector to the mainstream. Indeed, there is sound evidence from the USA – where the commitment to meeting special needs in ordinary schools pre-dates our own by several years – that attempts at desegregation may actually do more harm than good. Ways have to be found of adapting the methods of good mainstream practice in such a way that those children from special settings together with those who are experiencing difficulty (Warnock's 20%) can fully participate in classroom activity.

Grouping practices lie at the heart of this classroom activity in primary schools. In many secondary schools, grouping is also increasing in importance. This is especially so in the first years, where mixed-ability organisation is becoming more common, particularly in subject areas which are no longer based on traditional academic departments, such as integrated studies. The group is the main setting in which children mix, talk to one another and cooperate. It is the setting in which integration will succeed or fail. There is a real danger that integration will exist in name only – that segregation will continue within the ordinary classroom – unless we examine the practices we adopt in grouping children.

For many years teachers have been encouraged to let children learn by talking together in small groups. Plowden described the motivation and stimulation that can be derived from the 'cut and thrust' of discussion (p 757), as well as the managerial convenience of the time saved by teaching a particular point in groups (p 755). Bullock went still further in underlining the importance of using language both as an instrument of learning and thinking and in its role in social and emotional development. In fact the Report declared that 'a priority objective . . . is the serious study of the role of oral language in learning'.

However, before beginning to explore the potential of groups, it is important to distinguish between 'grouping' and 'groupwork'. 'Grouping' is a system of arranging children into smaller than class-size units, which is commonly found in primary classrooms. This usually takes the form of four to eight children seated round a table, with each child working individually. Such groups are often based on friendship/compatibility, though sometimes according to ability. This can be termed group-seating.

Where this seating arrangement is also used as a target of teaching – more commonly where the seating is by ability – the arrangement can be termed group-teaching. Alternatively, a teacher may use grouping as a means of planning which children should do a particular task. Such a group need not sit together or even be taught together, but may be thought, by the teacher, to need to work on a particular task. Such a form of grouping can be termed group-planning.

An alternative practice is to provide opportunities for children to work together, in a collaborative fashion, on a shared task. Such groupwork may initially be teacher-led, or include teacher intervention, but with the intention of encouraging the group to become peer-led and learn to work independently of the teacher. It is this form of groupwork – or group learning – which will be the focus of this chapter.

The chapter is divided into four sections. The first section examines some of the aims and claims made for the particular context of groupwork, concerning the potential for language and social development for children across the whole range of learning needs. The second section briefly reviews the evidence which indicates the extent of the current use of such groupwork in mainstream British primary classrooms. The third section focuses on the types of tasks and the range of strategies which may facilitate the development of the aims of group work, with particular reference to integrated groups. The fourth section explores some of the implications for teachers and children of using this form of learning–teaching context in terms of modelling, motivating, managing and monitoring the processes and outcomes of group-work practices.

1 Aims and claims

Researchers have identified a number of particular advantages believed to be associated with groupwork. These include the possibility that groupwork can provide an important context where children are put in charge of their own learning and can take responsibility both for handling the task and for handling the group. Such a situation requires language skills, social skills and problem-solving skills. It allows the children to define the task in their own terms and to 'talk their way in' with the greater likelihood, therefore, of being able to come to grips with the issues. The group context provides an alternative to the whole-class and individual learning situations and therefore allows children to try out different roles in relation to their own learning and to each other (see Barnes, 1969, 1976; Barnes and Todd, 1977).

A number of more specific points have also been identified. For example, Swing and Peterson (1982) confirmed findings that showed that both high-ability participants and low-ability participants enhanced their learning in mixed-ability groups. It was suggested that this was because the high-ability members often had to explain, give reasons and justify their contributions, which helped to clarify their own understandings. The low-ability members were often the target of such explanations and, thus, being actively engaged in the discussions, they also benefited. Medium-ability members, however, failed to enhance their learning. Further, low-ability children benefited more from group work than from whole-class situations (Peterson, Janicki and Swing, 1981). A cautionary note, however, was sounded by Johnson *et al* (1983), who suggested that groupwork in integrated contexts could, in fact, increase rejection of 'special' children and reinforce negative stereotypes. It would seem that particular attention needs to be paid to developing a supportive climate and to structuring the task, so that the activity involves co-operation – and not competition, either within the group or between groups.

Another interesting finding was from work done in the context of mixed-age groups. Low-ability children who were set the task of tutoring younger children improved in terms of self-esteem, clarified their own understanding and were more motivated in their own learning challenges (Feldman, Devin-Sheela and Allen, 1976). Benefits were thus both cognitive and social.

2 Evidence of groupwork practices

The dominant message from research findings relating to group-work practices during the last decade has been that very little collaborative 'groupwork' is undertaken in English primary class-rooms (DES, 1978; Galton, Simon and Croll, 1980). However, the same results from both of these researches – HMI survey and ORACLE – found that the practice of 'grouping' was highly prevalent. Group-seating, on the basis of similar ability, was common practice in mathematics and this was sometimes accom-panied by group-teaching. Conversely, collaborative groupwork was sometimes found in art/craft and topic work. Data collected during ORACLE classroom observations revealed that 90% of teachers never used groupwork although, in interview, half the teachers claimed to do so. This discrepancy may well indicate the confusion betwen the terms 'grouping', where children may be doing similar work, and 'groupwork', where work was shared. Interestingly, an analysis of the nature of teacher intervention in group situations showed that teachers spent more time giving routine instructions to groups, than to individuals or the whole class, and they spent less time on task content when talking with groups than when talking to individuals or the whole class. Thus, teachers appeared to be using groups for management purposes rather than motivation or learning development purposes.

A recent survey of 66 Aberdeen teachers has revealed some data of a very similar nature to further ORACLE results derived from 58 teachers, in terms of the distribution of teaching styles. Hence, 'class enquirers' comprised 15.2% of the Aberdeen sample (ORACLE 15.5%), 'individual monitors' comprised 12.1% (ORACLE 22.4%), 'group instructors' 19.7% (ORACLE 2.1%) and 'changers' amounted to 53% in Aberdeen and 50% in the ORACLE sample (Roberts, 1984; Galton, Simon and Croll, 1980). The higher propor-tion of group instructors in the Aberdeen sample is probably because the research related only to the teaching of mathematics, where grouping was likely to be more frequently used.

A number of reasons for these practices were offered. Class enquirers suggested that they did not wish to differentiate between children of different achievement levels and therefore avoided grouping. Individual monitors claimed that children were at such different levels of achievement that they had to be taught separately. Teachers using groups of similar achivement level did so in order to save time.

Further insights were revealed by the ORACLE teachers (Tann, 1979) as to why groupwork was not often used. The problems identified related to fears about how to manage peer groups in terms of possible noise and distraction, what size groups to use and what tasks were suitable. Also, doubts were expressed about what the supposed benefits of groupwork really were and therefore what the children might be learning. Finally, there were reservations about how groupwork could be monitored.

3 Aspects of groupwork

TASK FACTORS

A very obvious but nevertheless important aspect to consider is the suitability of a particular task for a groupwork context. Each context has its own demands and the particular skills, attitudes and knowledge required all play an important part in developing the children's repertoire of learning approaches. Clearly, there are many activities, which take place in any classroom, which are equally well or better done by individual children on their own, or by a whole class together. There are, however, many types of activities which can benefit from a variety of approaches, depending on the special needs of the children concerned.

Before discussing and choosing activities it is important that a teacher should identify the general task type and analyse the task demands as well as the children's needs, so that an appropriate match can be made.

A recent study based on observations in primary classrooms (Bennett *et al*, 1984) found considerable mismatch between the teachers' intended task purpose and the child's task response. The range of purposes identified were:

a *incremental* – step-by-step advancement
b *restructuring* – requiring the child to invent a solution
c *enrichment* – requiring the child to apply skill
d *practice* – consolidation of learnt skill
e *revision* – further reinforcement of known skill

Bennett's study found that 60% of tasks were intended as practice, across the whole ability range. It reported a considerable amount of mismatch between the level of cognitive demand which the teacher intended to be made of the child and the actual demand made. This mismatch was greater for the high-ability child than for the low-ability child. However, these tasks were in an individual context and did not include the demands inherent in the social context of group-work which could further stretch the children and allow members' other skills to be evidenced.

At present very much less research seems to have been under-taken in the area of task analysis and its effects on group processes, than in the area of discussion analysis and its contribution to group processes.

One common classification of activities is in terms of 'closed' and 'open'. A closed task is one in which the children complete the activity in a pre-defined way to meet pre-set goals. An open task allows for interpretation of the boundaries and outcomes and also experimentation in the processes of achieving the chosen outcome.

These terms refer to the degree of structure that a task has and how much room is left for children to contribute. Reitman (1965) suggests distinguishing between tasks in terms of the type of structure and the consequent demands made:

a *transformation*: where the initial and terminal states are known but the intermediate processes are not (eg children are given materials and told to make a space model, but left to find their own way of doing it)
b *creation*: where the terminal state is unknown (eg children are given some artifacts and asked to suggest purposes for which they could be used)
c *causality*: where the initial and intermediate states are unknown (eg children are given rods which they are told will span a specific width and they are asked to try to build an appropriate bridge)

The differences here are not so much in terms of different degrees of structure but of different types of structure. This may have implications for different types and timing of guidance which might be needed, in order to support children with special needs.

Another aspect of task which could be considered is the type of resources and reference points which could be involved, either in the process of exploring the task or for presenting the outcomes. For example:

- manipulable materials
- visual and graphic resources
- oral and aural resources
- written resources
- own recalled experiences
- own imagination and ideas

Clearly, each of these resources makes different demands of the children. Hence, it is important to balance the kinds of resources, particularly in mixed-ability groups, so that the context of the task allows each child to contribute in some way. By carefully preparing a task a teacher can ensure that it is so structured that it provides an opportunity for each child to draw upon at least one of the range of resources at each stage of the task, so that the participation of each child is sustained.

An alternative task typology, offered more recently by Phillips (1985) focuses on the dynamics of the discussion strategies needed by both the contributors and respondents:

a *operational*: where children are engaged in some kind of practical activity, such as making a model, rehearsing a play. The children will probably use many imperatives (give commands and directions) and use a lot of reporting and describing, containing a high density of pronouns (this, those, here, and there). The context will make the meaning clear and there will be little need for great precision and explicit elaboration. The contributions may well be acknowledged non-verbally and acted upon to show acceptance. Verbal responses may be limited to agreements, asking for repetition or clarification, or met by a counter-suggestion which may require negotiation. The discussion may also make use of any or all of the following discussion 'types'.

b *experiential*: where children draw upon their own experiences. Children will probably use recall and employ reporting and describing strategies to recount their anecdotes. Responses may be limited to agreements, asking for clarification or elaboration, and initiating related, contrary or unique anecdotes.

c *expositional*: where children provide information and explanations, often in response to questions. This is commonly a typical teacher style of talk and does not feature often or for long in children's discussions!

d *hypothetical*: where children are trying out ideas, often tentatively. Typical strategies used will include questions beginning with 'how about' or 'what about', and suggestions marked by 'might' or 'if'. Contributions may well include original and creative suggestions, or integration and application of ideas. This mode often quickly merges with the following one.

e *argumentational*: where children signal an invitation for members to confirm, modify or counter, by using tags such as 'don't they?', 'isn't it?', 'will it?' Responses may be signalled by 'yes, but', 'yes, well', 'yes, and'. Responses will probably be more varied in this mode and may include accepting, asking for clarification or elaboration, counter-suggestions and modifications, negotiation and evaluation, or rejection.

Such distinctions may also provide a possibly useful basis for analysing the task demands for mixed-ability groupwork, within a well-established framework.

Although the last typology focused on discussion strategies, the emphasis was on the possible cognitive, task-orientated functions. It is now time to include the social aspects of discussion strategies.

DISCUSSION STRATEGIES

The unique context of small-group discussions results in considerable demands being made of the participants, not only in terms of the task content, but also the communication and social skills needed. It may appear somewhat academic to make fine distinctions between discussion skills, for often contributions which participants make may well serve many functions simultaneously. However, it can be useful as a framework for analysing discussion processes and to help to make us more aware of what in fact is being demanded of children with different competencies in language.

In terms of verbal communication skills, for example, children need to be able and willing to express themselves so that they can engage in reporting, describing, imagining, reasoning, hypothesising, empathising, evaluating. Because this occurs within a social context, children also need to exchange ideas and information, which means the ability to listen and respond, rather than 'talk at' other participants. This entails being willing and able to enquire, accept, modify, extend, query, reject.

In terms of social skills, children need to be able and willing to establish and sustain supportive relationships, to encourage members to participate, to take turns, monitor the progress of the task and the feelings of the group, and to handle conflict. A tall order in the integrated classroom! None the less, they are important skills for children of all abilities to acquire and thereby become more sensitive and supportive group members.

Argyle suggests a 'social skills model' as being a useful way of understanding the nature of group processes. This includes:

a *role-taking*: this includes the importance of participants being able to put themselves 'in someone else's shoes'. Experiments have shown that even nursery-aged childen are able to do this, in a supportive environment (Dickson, 1982). Nevertheless, this often remains difficult to achieve in the 'cut and thrust' of discussion.
b *reciprocity*: this closely related aspect refers to the participants' ability to be aware of, respond AND adjust to others' needs. It has been suggested that this skill depends on the 'social intelligence' of the participants (Burley, 1976).
c *rules and conventions*: this includes a number of social skills such as self-presentation and attention to non-verbal communication (effecting group relationships), synchronising participation (relating to turn-taking and 'bidding' skills (Willes, 1983)).

In the context of an integrated classroom, it is important to remember that group work provides an opportunity for taking alternative roles and for demonstrating and developing additional skills to those which may be deployed in a whole-class situation (Tann, 1981). For example, it allows children who may not be able to contribute very successfully in academic terms to play a positive role socially – social sensitivity is not the prerogative of the academic high-flyer. Conversely, it may provide a 'safer' context for the shy child to join in, or for more reflective children to have time to express their ideas. It also provides a further challenge to socially adjusted children to try to help those who are less well-adjusted, in situations where peers can often be of more influence than teachers.

4 Implications for teacher and children

MODELLING

An important technique for developing positive discussion skills is for the teacher to model these, in both whole-class and group situations. Opportunities arise naturally in class discussions, whether during 'news-time' or follow-up work after a TV programme or visit, or during end-of-the-day report-back sessions. A teacher can identify and reward positive task strategies that were used successfully, eg 'That was a very clear *explanation*', or identify, ask for and thus reinforce a particular strategy, eg 'Can you *describe* that for us very carefully?' A teacher can encourage interactive response (social) strategies, for example, by asking a child to *comment* on a previous contribution, eg by modifying, extending, querying, countering.

MOTIVATING

A crucial component of a successful discussion is that the children are clear as to its purposes – in terms of the 'substantive task' and the expected 'outcomes', as well as the 'discussion processes'. The importance of attitudes towards groupwork is of concern here. This includes attitudes towards discussions and towards the group.

Initially, many children (and also parents and teachers) appear to regard discussions as 'not work', because 'talking is fun'. If children's conception of learning is one of writing down facts, then oral discussion of ideas and opinions will not count as 'work'. In addition, some children perceive 'work' as an individual and essentially competitive activity. Hence, working collaboratively in a group is perceived as 'people pinching my ideas', 'copying', or 'letting others do it all for you'. Nevertheless, children also appreciate aspects of group work. For example, they like the fact that they can 'learn to work together', 'to combine ideas', 'to listen to others', 'to organise things ourselves', 'get more confident', 'makes you think hard', and 'you have to say things clearly'. However, none of these benefits was identified as relating to learning.

It would seem, therefore, to be important that children are aware of the processes and are encouraged to become responsible for those processes and for their learning within the group context. To help in this development, children need a language to be able to discuss their discussions – a meta-language by which they can identify the strategies and goals and monitor their progress.

Clearly, the attitudes of the members of the group are also very important. 'Good' discussions have been found in groups which are able to provide both support and challenge (Smith, 1976). The composition of groups, therefore, is most important. Friendship groups can, in fact, be insufficiently challenging – if the group members are more concerned with maintaining 'friendship' than tackling the challenge of a task which may divide the group. Conversely, an antagonistic group may be more concerned with scoring 'points' at each other's expense than with meeting the challenge of the task.

MANAGING

Size and composition Selecting the members of a group is of fundamental importance to the success of the group – and one of the hardest set of choices to make. A teacher, very obviously, needs to know her children as individuals, but also to be able to hypothesise about how they will combine as a group. The group itself, once formed, often takes on a character of its own, which is frequently difficult to predict. Webb's review of such factors (1982) draws attention to individual characteristics, group norms, reward structures, and the nature of the interaction – and teacher intervention – that takes place, which all contribute to the success of the discussion processes and to the group's sense of satisfaction with the outcome.

The typical variables which are usually considered include whether the group should be chosen by the children or allocated by the teacher. If the latter is decided, the options may range from same- or mixed-sex groups, similar- or mixed-ability groups, similar- or mixed-personality groups, and possibly similar or mixed age groups. The important point is that there is no evidence that any of these criteria are more or less effective. The important consideration is to ensure that the composition – and size – of the groups is suited to the purpose of the particular task.

Many teachers would recommend organic groups, or those which emerge naturally through a desire to share an activity in which there is mutual interest. Even these may experience problems when clashes of interest develop – but then part of the purpose of group-work is learning to cope with such conflicts.

Other alternatives have been developed, mostly in America, which adopt a more structured approach to the problem of encouraging all members to participate. These include the many variations of the 'teams-games-tournaments' where mixed-ability participants pool individual scores to form a team total (as in 'quiz events'), or the 'jigsaw' approach where each participant has a unique set of information and therefore a needed contribution, so that the whole group – not just the 'brighter' members – can solve a particular problem; or, the more flexible 'group investigation' approach, where a group is set a common task to investigate and report on (Sharan, 1980). Such activities are said to be successful in building group cohesiveness and interdependence, as a prerequisite to more organic, collaborative groupwork in the mainstream classroom.

Stages of group discussions A further aspect with which it is useful to become familiar is the 'life-cycle' of group work. Tuckman (1965) suggested that four stages can often be identified: *forming* (when the group is establishing who's who and establishing relationships in order to 'get started'), *storming* (when groups often experience confusion and conflict during the 'get settled' process), *norming* (where group conventions develop and the group begins to 'get going') and *performing* (where the substantive task is tackled and the group 'get on with it').

Having begun to 'get on with it', there are still further stages for the group to pass through. For example, the group may begin at an 'initial stage' by exploring the task, then go on to a 'development stage' by exchanging ideas, elaborating, evaluating and following through, and finish with a 'concluding and reviewing stage'.

The group may experience difficulties at any stage, and the teacher will need to offer particular intervention strategies to support the group. These may include 'opening up' the discussion, by offering ideas and eliciting issues for consideration, 'sharing' the discussion, by encouraging participants to comment and respond to each other's comments, 'enriching' the discussion, by asking for clarification and extension, 'weighing' the discussion, by suggesting criteria for making judgments and ways of assessing the pros and cons, 'focusing' the discussion, by helping the children choose one of the alternatives offered, and 'concluding' the discussion, by helping the children to review their success (see Tough, 1981, and Brown and Edmondson, 1984).

Using groupwork Children can come together in groups for specific and short-term purposes, perhaps only for a few minutes, as well as for more prolonged and elaborate tasks which may extend over a number of weeks.

Short-term groupings may be used for 'buzz-group' sessions, to generate as many different ideas as possible in, say, a three-minute period. The openness of this kind of group may be helpful for shyer children. The group could be quite large – perhaps eight to twelve, so that plenty of ideas can be collected, which can later be sorted and considered in a more leisurely manner in a smaller group, if appropriate. Groups can also be used for more specific practical 'problem-solving', which could be of a mathematical or scientific nature. A group of more than perhaps four to six may become difficult to manage; it may be hard to ensure that suitable roles are allocated for each of the participants. Groups of this size can also be used as a 'forum' for sharing thoughts and feelings, for example, in response to a story or poem, or to provide critical support for each other's writings. A further way of using groups may be to undertake an 'investigatory project', which could involve a number of different related activities and which would require a high level of sophistication from the children in deciding the component tasks and the contributory part each could play.

In each instance, the 'end-product' could be different, which would thus allow children to develop a range of skills suited to their own needs. Alternatives could cover many different media for communicating the outcomes:

- *oral*: informal feedback; taped presentation
- *visual*: table of ideas or findings; chart or flow diagram to show the group's work; poster/picture/collage, (paper or fabric) model
- *dramatic*: mime; play (eg with puppets)
- *written*: story; poem; factual report

School support An important feature of developing groupwork is the acceptance that, because it incorporates so many skills – language for cognitive and affective purposes, social, possibly practical – it therefore takes a long time for children to come to understand all that is being demanded of them in the many different situations where groupwork can be employed. A vital prerequisite, therefore, is that a consistent school policy is developed which can support and sustain the efforts of teachers and children during their time in school. A great advantage in supporting such a policy would, of course, be if its aims were understood by parents and that they also were involved in supporting staff in the classroom as well as at home. The value of extra help in the classroom is detailed in Chapter 8 where suggestions are made on how to incorporate and manage such additional resources.

MONITORING GROUPWORK

A key factor here is that of raising the awareness of both teachers (and helpers) and the children about the purposes and processes of groupwork. Developing a policy on groupwork and identifying roles for classroom helpers would contribute towards this goal. In devising such a policy, the participants themselves would have had to work as a group and would therefore have had a chance to examine their own processes and become aware of the skills, attitudes and knowledge needed. This framework of understanding could be used to form the basis of a checklist or profile of children's achievements, in different kinds of contexts, for different kinds of tasks.

A further important aspect of raising awareness is to include the children themselves in the process of monitoring their own responses to groupwork and their own progress. It is important to create time to allow the children to discuss their discussions, to identify difficulties they experienced and to suggest strategies which they believe would help to overcome them.

This opportunity can be very valuable for the teacher and the children, but, it takes time to establish as a regular practice of review. Children as young as seven have been found to be remarkably perceptive and practical in the analysis of their own group sessions (Tann and Armitage, 1987). Children of this age devised their own list of guidelines for their discussions:

• *critical listening*: say two nice things; then ask a question; then offer suggestions

- *constructive talk*: explain well – speak clearly, choose words carefully, put things in order; take turns – listen to others, wait till they've finished; ask questions if you don't understand; don't upset other people, or be bossy; give lots of suggestions; sort out the ideas; choose an idea, test it, do it.

These suggestions are remarkably close to many of the key discussion skills which researchers have identified. By identifying them for themselves in language which they understood, these children were able to become highly aware of their own progress (and problems) and to take responsibility for their own development.

A final aspect relating to monitoring groupwork is suggested by Ghaye (1986). He reports a successful experiment with 11 to 12 year-olds who were asked to record their 'inner experiences' through the use of logs or diaries. These could then be compared to the 'outer experiences' as recorded on video. The two sources of data together provided considerable insights into how children respond to and interpret their situation.

Conclusions

Collaborative groupwork can, as has been indicated above, provide a valuable context for learning, in addition to whole-class and individual learning situations. It makes very specific kinds of demands of the group members in terms of language skills, social skills and often problem-solving skills. Research has indicated that because of the distinctiveness of the context it can encourage children to take on new roles and greater responsibility for their learning.

It has been suggested that groupwork can be a valuable way of incorporating children of all levels of ability and thus of maximising learning opportunities to all children in an integrated classroom. However, such benefits do not come easily and may only come at all if individual teachers become aware of and act upon the many variables involved in such a learning context and if teachers within a school work together to develop a consistent programme of support for each other and for the children. Such a whole-school programme would need to bring together the knowledge which staff have of individual children and their needs. Together with these, the programme would need to bring: a method of analysing the demands of the tasks and the types of resources required; ways in which discussion strategies can be modelled; alternative ideas for motivating and managing groups; and techniques for monitoring the processes and outcomes of groupwork by the children themselves as well as by the teacher.

References

Argyle, M. (1983) *The Psychology of Interpersonal Behaviour* (4th ed) Harmondsworth: Penguin.
Barnes, D. (1975) *From Communication to Curriculum* Harmondsworth: Penguin.
Barnes, D. and Todd, F. (1977) *Communication and Learning in Small Groups* London: Routledge and Kegan Paul.
Barnes, D., Britton, J. and Torbe, M. (1986) *Language, the Learner and the School* (3rd ed) Harmondsworth: Penguin.
Bennett, N., Desforges, C., Cockburn, A. and Wilkinson, B. (1984) *The Quality of Pupil Learning Experiences* London: Lawrence Erlbaum Associates.
Brown, G. and Edmondson, R. (1984) 'Asking questions' in T. Wragg (ed) *Classroom Teaching Skills* London: Croom Helm.
Burley, P. M. (1976) The role of social intelligence in helping behaviour DPhil (unpublished), University of Oxford.
CACE (1967) *Children and their Primary Schools* (Plowden Report).
DES (1976) *A Language for Life* (Bullock Report).
DES (1978) *Primary Education in England and Wales* London: HMSO.
Dickson, W. P. (1981) *Children's Oral Communication Skills* New York: Academic Press.
Feldman, R. S., Devin-Sheela, L. and Allen, V. (1976) 'Children tutoring children: a critical review of research' in V. Allen (ed) *Children as Teachers* New York: Academic Press.
Galton, M., Simon, B. and Croll, P. (1980) *Inside the Primary Classroom* London: Routledge and Kegan Paul.
Ghaye, A. (1986) 'Outer appearances and inner experiences: towards a more holistic view of group work' in *Educational Review*, 38, 1, 45.
Johnson, D. W. *et al* (1983) Interdependence and interpersonal attraction among heterogeneous and homogeneous groups' in *Review of Educational Research*, 53, 1, 5–54.
Peterson, P. L., Janicki, T. and Swing, S. R. (1981) 'Ability and treatment interaction effects on children's learning' in *American Educational Research Journal*, 18, 4, 453.
Phillips, T. (1985) 'Beyond lip-service: discourse development after the age

of nine' in G. Wells and J. Nicholls, *Language and Learning* London: Falmer Press.

Reitman, W. R. (1965) *Cognition and Thought* Chichester: Wiley.

Roberts, A. (1984) 'Group methods? Primary teachers; differentiation policies in mathematics' in *Educational Research*, 36, 3, 241.

Sharan, S. (1980) 'Co-operative learning in small groups' in *Review of Educational Research*, 50, 2, 241–71.

Smith, P. B. (1976) *Group Processes and Personal Change* London: Harper and Row.

Swing, S. R. and Peterson, P. L. (1982) 'The relationship of student ability and small group interaction to student achievement' in *American Educational Research Journal*, 19, 2, 259–274.

Tann, C. S. (1979) 'A study of groupwork' in *Forum*, 21, 3, 91–95.

Tann, C. S. (1981) 'Grouping and Groupwork' in B. Simon and J. Willcocks (eds) *Research and Practice in the Primary Classroom* London: Routledge and Kegan Paul.

Tann, C. S. and Armitage, M. (1987) 'Children discussing discussions' in *The Times Educational Supplement*, October.

Tough, J. (1981) *A Place for Talk: Children with Moderate Learning Difficulties* London: Ward Lock.

Tuckman, B. (1965) 'Developmental sequences in small groups' in *Psychological Bulletin*, 63, 6.

Webb, N. B. (1982) 'Student interaction and learning in small groups' in *Review of Educational Research*, 52, 3, 421–445.

Willes, M. J. (1983) *Children into Pupils* London: Routledge and Kegan Paul.

10 The forgotten A in behaviour analysis: the importance of ecological variables in classroom management with particular reference to seating arrangements

Kevin Wheldall

When I first started school in the early 1950s I sat with my peers in one of several rows of double desks facing the blackboard and the teacher's desk. (I must also have been one of the last to be issued with a slate and chalk, but that is another story!) When my son, Robin, started school in the 1970s he was seated in a table group with seven other pupils. When we went on to secondary school, however, we both found ourselves, from the first day, seated in rows.

What had happened in the years between my son's and my own primary education to cause this change in primary classroom seating arrangements? The answer, of course, is the Plowden Report of 1967. This extremely influential government report on *Children and their Primary Schools* had a rapid and massive impact on primary-school practice in the UK. It did much to promote the concept of 'child-centred' education, already beginning to be practised in so-called 'progressive' schools. Without referring to any supporting empirical evidence, the Plowden Report urged the replacement of rows with table groups since the received wisdom was that effective learning could only take place under conditions of continued peer interaction.

The Plowden Report argued that children should be seated in groups to help in the socialisation process. Apparently, as a result, the slower members of the group would be helped, through inter-action with the more able. 'Apathetic' children would be 'infected by the enthusiasm of the group' and interaction would also benefit more able children through the 'cut and counterthrust of conversation' and the 'opportunities to teach as well as to learn' (para 757). So potent was the heady brew distilled by Plowden that the educational establishment became a little drunk on the spirit of idealism. 'Discovery learning' was on almost every primary teacher's lips and table groups displaced rows in the vast majority of classrooms.

Boydell (1974, 1975), however, has suggested that it might be more difficult than is generally supposed to set up group working conditions as envisaged in the Plowden Report. Plowden argued that seating in groups would help children to learn to get along together, enable them to help one another and help them realise their own strengths and weaknesses, but the results of Boydell's research suggested that sustained conversations in which children explain and develop their ideas and suggestions may be relatively unknown. Only half the conversations concerned children's work and most were of less than twenty-five seconds' duration. She suggested that children were more likely to be work-orientated when they were not interacting than when they were. More recently, the research of Galton, Simon and Croll (1980) has shown that while the tables formation is the commonest in junior schools, individual, non-collaborative work is the norm in these schools. It is hardly surprising then that Boydell and, also, Bennett, Desforges, Cockburn and Wilkinson (1984) have found that most of the social interaction observed in table groups is non-work related.

In this chapter I would like to consider classroom seating arrangements as an example of behavioural ecology and to draw attention to the continuing neglect of the role of antecedent variables in behaviour analysis in education in the UK.

Antecedent control and behavioural ecology

Behavioural practice in British schools has increased in recent years but it has yet to achieve the subtlety and sophistication which a thorough-going implementation of applied behaviour analysis would permit. Current behavioural methods employed in British schools (both special and mainstream) are often typically characterised by crude consequence management strategies which are both intrusive and also less likely to bring about generalisation of learned behaviour to control by the natural environment. The work of Risley (in the United States), Glynn (in New Zealand) and the present author (in the UK), among others, has sought to demonstrate the power of antecedent control (Risley, 1977; Glynn, 1982, 1983; Wheldall, 1981).

Contemporary applied behavioural research has rightly focused on antecedents, the A in the ABC, three term analysis for behaviour, thereby helping to correct, in part, the previous preoccupation with and over-emphasis on consequence management strategies. In earlier papers (Wheldall, 1981, 1982) I have linked my concern over the dangers of 'behavioural overkill' with a plea for a greater consideration of the behavioural ecology of the classroom.

The heading of antecedent conditions encompasses a variety of features of the environment which may potentially influence behaviour. These range from specific actions by another person, to the more global aspects of the environment; from what the teacher last said, to the temperature or lighting level in the classroom, for example. In this context, researchers have talked, sometimes rather loosely, of antecedent conditions (or stimuli or events), setting events and ecological variables alongside more established concepts such as the discriminative stimulus. To my knowledge, however, no adequate conceptualisation of the relationships and differences between the multiplicity of environmental variables preceding and/ or accompanying behaviour, has yet been proposed, although Wahler and Fox (1981) have provided a useful 'conceptual and methodological expansion' of the term setting event, following up Bijou and Baer's original formulations (Bijou and Baer, 1978). The following is a very simple model of antecedent control.

It is not sufficient to attempt to analyse behaviour simply in terms of behaviours and reinforcers. As well as considering what happens after a behaviour occurs (the consequence) we must also consider what happened before it occurred. We must examine events which precede as well as events which follow behaviour. Events which precede behaviour or settings in which behaviours occur are known generally as antecedent stimuli or conditions. Many school situations provide such settings. The cookery or woodwork rooms provide special settings in which the number of children permitted is small, where there is a lot of special apparatus of a practical nature and where the expected activities allow more physical freedom than in most other classrooms. If a teacher of French, say, is obliged to use such a practical room s/he will encounter special difficulties not only from the unsuitability and insufficiency of the furniture and its layout but also because of the way children are accustomed to respond in this special setting. Being in the cookery room has become associated with a different form of behaviour, involving more movement about the room, perhaps.

Sometimes the settings themselves constrain and limit responses. If the temperature is too low one cannot concentrate on the task; if the lighting is too dim or too bright one cannot see. If the classroom is experienced as a cold place, there will tend to be a scramble for places near the radiator. Similarly, crowding may influence children's behaviour. For example, it has been shown that nursery children pay more attention at story-time when they have plenty of space than when they are allowed to crowd around their teacher (Krantz and Risley, 1977).

We can take another example which highlights how other antecedent events may also influence behaviour. The teacher asks a child a question in class (the antecedent stimulus), the child gives a silly answer (the behaviour) and his classmates laugh (the consequence). If this consequence is positively reinforcing, we may expect the child to produce silly answers upon subsequent similar occasions. He will probably be less likely to do so, however, when his classmates are not there. In other words, the presence of his peers has become a discriminative stimulus for his behaviour. This gives some idea of the need to consider the context in which behaviours occur, the relationships between A, the antecedent conditions, B, the behaviours and C, the consequences.

Antecedent events can also serve to prompt a certain behaviour. Take the example of when a teacher leaves the room and his class is left alone. For some classes this occurrence will have become a cue for noisy, disruptive behaviour since there is no one around to reprimand the children. Some classes even post a look-out to give a warning of when the teacher is returning! When he does return the noisy, disruptive behaviour will cease. We can see here that this specific antecedent condition has control over this particular behaviour. This control is derived from its association with certain consequences.

It may be seen from the above examples that antecedents may influence behaviour in at least two basic ways. First, there are those antecedent conditions which provide physical constraints or opportunities for behaviours. At its simplest, the physical presence of a football allows ball-kicking (behaviour) to take place. Similarly, overcrowding invites pushing and jostling. Second, there are antecedent conditions which have acquired power over behaviour by association with rewarding or punishing consequences. Being in Softy Simpson's room may rapidly become the stimulus for unruly behaviour, for example, whilst few would dare even to breathe loudly in Biffer Barnes's classroom. From the practical point of view, these distinctions need not necessarily concern us greatly, but theoretically their present obfuscation is a serious handicap to our conceptual progress in applied behaviour analysis. The current rag-bag, catch-all label of antecedent stimuli is conceptually confusing, hinders communication and probably blunts our analyses.

Changing children's behaviour by changing from tables to rows

The literature concerning classroom seating arrangements and its effects on children's learning and classroom behaviour, goes back over fifty years (see Wheldall, Morris, Vaughan and Ng, 1981, for a thorough review). Studies were carried out by Griffith in 1921 and Dawe in 1934 on the relationship between seating position and academic performance. More recent studies on class seating arrangements include those by Axelrod, Hall and Tams (1979) and my own research. In this chapter I will be reviewing these studies as an extended example of the power ecological factors exert over children's and teachers' classroom behaviour.

Axelrod *et al* (1979) compared the effects of two seating arrangements, tables versus rows, on the on-task and disruptive behaviour of second-grade children in the United States. The mean study level for the class of an inner-city elementary school increased by 20% when the children were moved from groups to rows seating and, similarly, in a second class, disruptive 'talk-outs' decreased markedly during rows seating. The researchers suggest that this manipulation of antecedent or setting events is an effective and powerful means of classroom management.

My students, Marion Morris and Pamela Vaughan, and I subsequently carried out two parallel studies comparing 'tables' and 'rows' seating arrangements in two state junior schools in the West Midlands (Wheldall, Morris, Vaughan and Ng, 1981). In both schools a fourth-year class of 10 to 11-year-old children was chosen. One class consisted of 28 mixed sex and ability children attending a school in an urban residential area whereas the other class consisted of 25 similar children from a school on a council housing estate. In both classes the children normally sat round tables in groups of four, five and six. The design, procedure and, indeed, results of the two studies were very similar.

The children were initially observed for two weeks (ten days) in their normal seating arrangements round tables. An observation schedule using a time sampling procedure was employed to obtain estimates of on-task behaviour. This was defined, by the teachers, as doing what the teacher instructed, ie looking at and listening to her when she was talking to them, looking at their books or work cards when they were required to complete set work, being out of seats only with the teacher's permission, etc. In the first study observations were made only during purely academic lessons when the children had been given specific work to complete but in the second study observations were carried out at different times including all lessons except PE, Art and Music. Calling out, talking to neighbours, interrupting, etc, were regarded as off-task by the teachers in both studies.

The observation schedule required each child to be observed twice per lesson in random order for 30 seconds. This was broken down into six five-second periods. If the child was on-task for the whole five seconds he scored one point; if off-task for any of the five seconds he did not score. This yielded a score out of six for each thirty-second period and a score out of twelve for the two observation periods per child per lesson combined, which was subsequently converted to a percentage. This gave us an estimate of percentage on-task behaviour for each child for each lesson which, when averaged, gave an estimate of on-task behaviour for the whole class.

After observing the class for two weeks sitting round tables (baseline data), the desks/tables were moved into rows without comment from the teacher and the children were observed for a further two weeks (eight days in the first study, ten days in the second study), using the same procedure. Finally, the desks were moved back to their original positions, again without comment, for a further two weeks of observation (seven days in the first study; ten days in the second study). This time there were a few complaints from the children since they preferred sitting in rows.

In short, in both classes on-task behaviour rose by around 15% overall, from around 70% to about 85%, when the children were placed in rows and fell by nearly as much when they returned to tables. Looking at individual children, the most marked improvements in on-task behaviour occurred within those children whose on-task behaviour was previously very low. As we might expect, the effect was lessened in the case of children with high initial on-task behaviour. One or two children in each study showed higher on-task behaviour in groups; especially one child in the second study, the noisy ringleader of an anti-school group, who spent most of his time in rows trying to regain contact with his group!

Josephine Ng (Lam) and I then went on to carry out a more detailed study on seating arrangements in a special school for ESN (M) children with behaviour problems (Wheldall and Lam, 1987). In this study we also included observations of disruptive behaviour and teacher behaviours. A huge amount of data was collected in this study, of which only a brief report can be presented here.

Three classes were observed for four phases of ten observations, each spread over approximately two-week intervals. Again, seating was normally arranged round tables. In the first phase, observation was carried out in the usual (tables) conditions to provide baseline data, followed by Phase 2, in which the class was moved into rows. Phase 3 constituted a return to the tables seating arrangement, followed by Phase 4, in which seating was again arranged in rows. All lessons took place in the same room and were maths lessons given by the same teacher to all three classes: a junior class of 11 children, a middle class of 11 children and a senior class of 12 children. The results dramatically confirmed and extended our previous findings. For every class on-task behaviour doubled during rows, from around 35% to about 70%, and fell back during tables conditions. Similarly, rate of disruptions trebled during tables and fell during rows. We also observed changes in teacher behaviour. Positive comments consistently went up during rows conditions whilst negative comments decreased. The teacher apparently found it easier to praise and to refrain from disapproval when the children were seated in rows.

Several, more recent (as yet unpublished) studies have also been completed with my students, Sue Rendall, John Fielder and Anne Croft, which attempt to answer some of the possible objections to the earlier studies. These studies have shown that the results are not due to a novelty effect (on-task behaviour remains at higher levels after many weeks of sitting in rows) and that the quantity and quality of work produced is also appreciably greater during rows conditions. Bennett and Blundell (1983), following up our work, also studied the effects of tables and rows on the quantity and quality of work produced in reading, language and mathematics by two classes of 10 to 11-year-old children. Their results suggested that quantity of work completed generally increased when the children were seated in rows. No increase in quality is reported, although the researchers claim that it was maintained.

Before commenting on the conclusions to be drawn from our studies we must attempt to answer the question, 'Why does seating round tables lead to more disruption, less on-task behaviour and less desirable teacher behaviour?' The answer is quite simple. A table arrangement is geared towards enhancing social interaction. It facilitates eye contact, a prime means of initiating a social encounter, and provides a setting for increased participation in such encounters by involving the whole group. After all, we engineer such seating arrangements in precisely this way when we wish to encourage social interaction, in committees or when playing bridge, for example. Moreover, tables provide ideal cover for covert aggression or teasing, by means of kicking or pinching under the table, thereby increasing disruption. Rows formations, on the other hand, minimise either form of social contact, allowing fewer occasions for the teacher to comment adversely and more instances of desirable behaviour for him or her to comment upon favourably. In short, it could be argued that it amounts to little short of cruelty to place children in manifestly social contexts and then to expect them to work independently. I must immediately emphasise, however, that I am certainly *not* advocating a return to rows for all work. It is one possible strategy to encourage academic work which requires the child to concentrate on the specific task in hand without distractions. Rows would be totally inappropriate, for example, for small-group discussions or group topic work, where table arrangements might prove more effective.

The effects of mixed and same-sex classroom seating arrangements

Few studies have been reported which consider both sex differences and seating arrangements. Our earlier studies suggested that both boys' and girls' on-task behaviour increases when they are seated in rows but that boys make higher gains when moved to the rows condition and higher losses when moved back into groups. As far as it is possible to ascertain, the effects of location of boys and girls in the classroom, whether seated in rows or groups, does not appear to have been investigated. An isolated case is that of Burdett, Egner and McKenzie (1970), who found that some children worked for longer periods when boys were seated next to girls and less hard when boys were seated by other boys. Frazier and Sadler (1973), however, describing a strategy for the elimination of sexism in primary schools, advocate that boys should not be 'punished' (*sic*) by being forced to sit next to girls.

Most teachers would advocate that, ideally, children within their classes should be given as much choice as possible as to where they sit and with whom. In those classrooms arranged in table groups this almost inevitably leads to girls and boys being seated round separate tables. Similarly, in rows classes it is almost always found that children of the same sex prefer to sit together. Teachers often claim, however, that one of the most effective ways of curbing the disruptive behaviour of children, particularly boys, is to sit them next to a member of the opposite sex. The aim of the following studies was to determine whether mixed-sex seating did, in fact, demonstrate such advantages, in terms of improved on-task behaviour.

The first of these studies, carried out with one of my Masters students, David Olds, was completed in a three-form entry junior school in an inner-city area of Birmingham. Two classes in the school were involved in the study. The third-year class consisted of 31 mixed-ability children (16 boys, 15 girls) aged nine to ten years. The fourth-year class consisted of 25 academically mixed ten to eleven-year-old children (13 boys and 12 girls). Both classteachers were female.

In the third-year class, hereafter referred to as the Groups Class, the children were seated round six groups of tables. Three of the groups of tables were occupied solely by girls, the other three by boys. During the intervention phase of the study, the boys and girls were mixed so that boys and girls were now sitting next to each other. In the fourth-year class (hereafter referred to as the Rows Class) the children were seated at conventional double desks, not tables. The desks were arranged in three rows and, with the exception of one boy who sat on his own, all of the other children normally sat next to a member of the opposite sex. During the intervention period, girls and boys in each row changed places so that they were now sitting by a member of the same sex.

A version of the OPTIC schedule, developed by my colleage Frank Merrett and myself, was used to record teacher behaviour, pupil disruptive behaviour and pupil on-task behaviour. Since the schedule is described in detail in Merrett and Wheldall (1986) it will only be summarised here. The schedule is divided into three sections, each section requiring three minutes to complete, which is repeated three times in sequence. Section A is concerned with the teacher's use of approval and disapproval responses addressed to the academic and social behaviours of the pupils. Section B deals with pupil disruptive behaviour, those behaviours which interrupt the normal working behaviour of the class. Section C records class on/off-task behaviour. For a pupil to be recorded as on-task he/she should have been attending to the teacher or the assigned task, according to the teacher's instructions. In this study the schedule was amended to differentiate between boys and girls in the various behaviour categories.

An ABA or reversal design was employed. Data were collected over a two-week baseline period, followed by a two-week intervention phase, then a reversal allowing the collection of two more weeks of baseline data. The alteration of seating arrangements for boys and girls in both classes took place during Phase 2. All observations, both in the rows and in the groups classrooms, were taken during mathematics and English lessons throughout the three phases of study.

Data collection took place over a two-month period. The total of 30 observation days, when data collection took place, was divided into three 10-day phases. Each of the baseline and intervention periods of the study was introduced to the two classes simultaneously. Between the first baseline and intervention period there was a week when no observer was present or data collected. Similarly, there was also a one-week break in data collection between the intervention phase and the second baseline phase. This enabled the children and teachers to become accustomed to their changed seating positions. Except for the fact that observers were present in the classrooms and seating arrangements for boys and girls varied, normal school routine was followed on all observation days. In both classes teacher responses to pupils' academic and social behaviours were minimal throughout the three experimental phases and hence will not be detailed here.

During the baseline phase mean on-task behaviour was 75% for the group class. When a mixed-sex seating arrangement was employed, the mean on-task level rose to 92%. The return to single-sex seating resulted in a lower mean on-task study level of 67%. Comparison of pupil on-task behaviour for the boys and the girls separately showed clearly that both sexes were similarly affected by changes in seating arrangement. The figures showed that boys were marginally more on-task during the first two experimental phases and clearly more on-task during the last ten sessions of the return to baseline phase. The figures for pupils' disruptive behaviour also showed movements in the expected direction over the three phases. During the baseline phase the mean number of disruptions was 22, during intervention the figure was 11 and for the return to baseline phase, 41. Similarly, both boys' and girls' disruptive behaviours were affected by the changes of seating arrangement. Over all three experimental phases the boys were observed to be more disruptive than the girls.

The results for on-task behaviour in the rows class showed that during the baseline phase when a mixed-sex seating arrangement was in force the mean on-task level was 90%. During the intervention phase when the children changed to a single-sex seating arrangement the mean on-task level fell to 76%. The return to baseline with normal mixed-sex seating arrangements resulted in a mean on-task level of 89%. The results for mean on-task levels for boys and girls separetly in the rows class over the three experimental phases again showed clear similarity of effect. The girls were slightly more on-task for the two baseline phases and marginally less on-task than the boys during the intervention phase. The means for pupil disruption were 10 during baseline, 19 during intervention and for the return to baseline phase, 8. Thus, over the three phases the movement was in the expected direction. In general, disruption levels were low for both boys and girls in this class. The results show that girls were less disruptive than the boys over all three experimental phases.

These results clearly show that on-task behaviour in the rows class decreased when the children of the same sex sat together whereas in the groups class on-task behaviour increased when the normal same-sex seating was changed in favour of mixed-sex grouping. Thus in these two classes with differing furniture configurations the conclusion to be drawn is that mixed-sex seating produces the highest pupil on-task levels. Similarly, disruptive behaviour in both classes was at its lowest when boys and girls sat together. What also emerged clearly from the results was that the children with the lowest on-task study levels were the most positively affected by the change from mixed to same-sex seating, although all children in the class were observed to be substantially more on-task when a mixed-sex seating arrangement was employed. This study is reported fully in Wheldall and Olds (1987).

Studies of pupil interaction by Boydell (1975) and Galton, Simon and Croll (1980) have reported that up to 80% of pupil interaction in junior classrooms was between children of the same sex. It could be suggested, therefore, that in order to discourage interaction in lessons requiring the individual pupils to work on their own it is only necessary to mix the sexes. Whether this is desirable on other grounds is a matter for the teacher to decide.

These results support the finding of Burdett *et al* (1970) who also found that some children worked for longer periods when boys were seated next to girls and less hard when boys were seated by other boys. What the results of this study do not show is whether the rises in on-task levels were accompanied by increases in the quantity and quality of academic work produced. Some tentative evidence is provided, however, by another of my masters students, Stephen Wigley, who demonstrated similar effects with a class of older, secondary-aged pupils.

This second study was carried out in a large comprehensive school in the West Midlands. Subjects comprised a below-average third-year class of 27 pupils who were generally regarded as troublesome. Observations were completed during history lessons, which were taught by a male history graduate of five years' experience. He commented that the pupils were 'not bad' but that he was 'always ready for an outbreak of trouble'.

The class was normally seated in rows of same-sex pairs. They were observed on three separate occasions during baseline over a two-week period. During the intervention pupils were instructed not to sit next to a member of the same sex and they were again observed on three occasions. Finally, in the return to baseline phase pupils were permitted to resume same-sex seating and were observed three more times.

During each observation lesson each child was observed in

random order at least twice for thirty seconds. Percentage on-task estimates were calculated for each individual pupil and for the whole class. On-task behaviour was defined as attention to the relevant materials or to the teacher when he was speaking, carrying out the teacher's instructions and staying in-seat. An attempt was also made to collect product (output) data. During the lessons in each phase, the pupils were asked to underline the last word they had written after twelve minutes of writing time had elapsed. The number of words written by each individual in this time was counted and a class average was also calculated.

Mean on-task behaviour during baseline (same-sex seating) was 76% and rose to 91% during the mixed-sex seating intervention. During the return to baseline phase mean on-task behaviour fell back to 83%. The results for boys and girls were very similar. Marginally more words were produced during mixed seating than during the (same-sex) baseline condition and there was evidence for a bigger drop in production during the return to baseline phase. As might be expected, the effect was more pronounced for boys than for girls. The teacher's subjective judgment was that the work produced during the intervention was of a higher quality.

The results of this small-scale study clearly replicate the earlier study with older, secondary-aged pupils. Both boys and girls spent more time attending to their work when seated next to a member of the opposite sex than when seated next to a person of the same sex. Whether this would be true for pupils older than 13 to 14 years remains an empirical question. There is some evidence to suggest that the resulting on-task behaviour is accompanied by greater work output. Subsequent discussion with the pupils revealed that, in general, they felt that they concentrated less when seated next to friends and that they felt that they had worked harder during the intervention phase.

The results of these two studies provide further evidence that studies of the behavioural ecology of classrooms can be used to help determine management strategies. They can act as pointers to those strategies which, in certain circumstances, appear to be most effective. Certainly, the findings from this series of studies should cause us to doubt our current preoccupation with fixed classroom seating arrangements and to encourage us to experiment with seating so as to optimise the appropriate behaviour for the task in hand and to discourage inappropriate behaviours.

References

Axelrod, D., Hall, R. V. and Tams, A. (1979) 'Comparison of two common classroom seating arrangements' in *Academic Therapy*, 15, 29–36.
Bennett, N. and Blundell, D. (1983) 'Quantity and quality of work in rows and classroom groups' in *Educational Psychology*, 3, 93–105.
Bennett, N. S., Desforges, C. W., Cockburn, A. D. and Wilkinson, B. (1984) *The Quality of Pupil Learning Experience* London: Lawrence Erlbaum Associates.
Bijou, S. W. and Baer, D. M. (1978) *Behaviour Analysis of Child Development* New Jersey: Prentice Hall.
Boydell, D. (1974) 'Teacher-pupil contact in junior classrooms' in *British Journal of Educational Psychology*, 44, 313–318.
Boydell, D. (1975) 'Pupil behaviour in junior classrooms' in *British Journal of Educational Psychology*, 45, 122–129.
Burdett, C., Egner, A. and McKenzie, H. (1970) *Report of the Consulting Teacher Program*, Vol 2 Vermont: University of Nebraska Press.
Dawe, H. C. (1934) 'The influence of size of kindergarten group upon performance, in *Child Development*, 5, 295–303.
Department of Education and Science (1967) *Children and their Primary Schools* London: HMSO. (Plowden Report)
Frazier, N. and Sadler, M. (1973) *Sexism in School and Society* London: Harper and Row.
Galton, M., Simon, B. and Croll, P. (1980) *Inside the Primary School* London: Routledge and Kegan Paul.
Glynn, T. (1982) 'Antecedent control of behaviour in education contexts' in *Educational Physchology*, 2, 215–229.
Glynn, T. (1983) 'Building an effective teaching environment' in Wheldall, K. and Riding, R. J. (eds) *Psychological Aspects of Learning and Teaching* London: Croom Helm.
Griffith, C. R. (1921) 'A comment upon psychology of the audience' in *Psychology Monographs*, 30, 36–47.
Krantz, P. J. and Risley, T. R. (1977) 'Behavioral ecology in the classroom' in K. D. O'Leary and S. F. O'Leary (eds) *Classroom Management: The successful use of behavior modification* (second edition) New York: Pergamon.
Merrett, F. and Wheldall, K. (1986) 'Observing Pupils and Teachers In Classrooms (OPTIC): a behaviour observation schedule for use in schools in *Educational Psychology*, 6, 57–70.
Risley, T. R. (1977) 'The ecology of applied behavior analysis' in A. Rogers-Warren and S. F. Rogers-Warren (eds) *Ecological Perspectives in Behaviour Analysis* Baltimore: University Park Press.
Wahler, R. G. and Fox, J. J. (1981) 'Setting events in applied behavior analysis: towards a conceptual and methodological expansion' in *Journal of Applied Behavior Analysis*, 14, 327–338.

Wheldall, K. (1981) 'A before C or the use of behavioural ecology in classroom management' in P. Gurney (ed) *Behaviour Modification in Education-Perspectives No. 5* Exeter: School of Education, University of Exeter. (Also in N. Entwistle (ed) *New Directions in Educational Psychology*, Vol 1: *Learning and Teaching* London: Falmer Press (1985).)

Wheldall, K. (1982) 'Behavioural pedagogy or behavioural overkill?' in *Educational Psychology*, 2, 181–184.

Wheldall, K. and Lam, J. (1987) Rows versus tables II: the effects of two classroom seating arrangements on classroom disruption rate, on-task behaviour and teacher behaviour in three special school classes. Centre for Child Study, University of Birmingham (for publication).

Wheldall, K., Morris, M., Vaughan, P. and Ng, Y. Y. (1981) 'Rows versus tables: an example of the use of behavioural ecology in two classes of eleven year old children' in *Educational Psychology*, 1, 171–189.

Whedall, K. and Olds, D. (1987) 'Of sex and seating: the effects of mixed and same-sex seating arrangements in junior classrooms' in *New Zealand Journal of Educational Studies*, 22, 71–85.

11 Systematic assessment and teaching – in context

Jonathan Solity

Introduction

In recent years many books have been published in the area of special education. Whilst many texts have focused on its philosophy, psychology and sociology, far fewer have been devoted to teaching methods and instructional techniques. Educational psychology has addressed this topic to some extent, through developing methods to teach the mentally handicapped. However, considerably less information is available to inform classroom practice as far as teaching children who have difficulties in mainstream education is concerned.

Much of the current interest in teaching children with special needs tends to focus on the themes of integration, curriculum development, assessment and the effective utilisation of Local Education Authority (LEA) resources. So, whilst there is frequent discussion on the most suitable provision to meet children's needs, the subject of specific teaching methods has on the whole received far less attention.

This chapter will look at specific approaches to teaching children presenting difficulties in the context of:

assessing children's educational needs
everyday classroom practice
the overall aims of teaching
the stage of learning reached by children, and being developed by
    teachers

Initially, therefore, the discussion will relate particular teaching methods and patterns of classroom organisation to a comprehensive framework for identifying children's educational needs and the most suitable provision to meet those needs. The importance of careful and systematic selection of teaching procedures will be highlighted within this process.

Second, it must be remembered that teaching children experiencing difficulties does not happen in a vacuum. It invariably takes place in an environment alive with children engaged in a range of activities and interactions. If the aim of fully integrating children with special needs into mainstream education is to be achieved, teaching children requiring extra help needs to become a part of everyday classroom practice. It must itself become an integrated part of a typical school day (if there is such a thing!) and take its place alongside all the other daily classroom activities.

Third, it is important to know why efforts are directed towards teaching children presenting problems in mainstream. It would appear reasonable to suggest that *how* we are going to teach is going to be influenced directly by *why* teaching is taking place. It is unlikely that any form of provision will be fully appreciated or maximally effective unless its purpose is clearly recognised.

Finally, the choice of teaching methods and approaches to organising the classroom will be considered in the light of the stage of learning reached by a child when acquiring new skills and concepts. It is suggested that these will vary according to the level of learning being developed by the teacher.

Background

When staffroom conversation moves towards children experiencing difficulties in school, through a perceived learning or behaviour problem, it is invariably not long before attention focuses on the extra demands they create. Their presence and the manifestation of their difficulties can be disquieting, unnerving and disheartening.

The initial concern is usually one of time. 'How can enough teaching time be found during a busy school day to give the child with difficulties the required level of attention?' This is coupled with worries about whether the rest of the children will be getting the help they need. Can giving additional support to one pupil with difficulties, even when the need for it is apparent and the spirit willing, be justified in the light of the competing demands of other pupils?

Underlying these thoughts is a more immediate and personal threat, challenging the professional competence of the classroom teacher. How can we help a child experiencing difficulties when the starting position for teaching is that 'these children have not made progress despite our most determined efforts?' We begin with the knowledge that the approaches that worked for all the other children in the class have failed with the small number of pupils presenting problems.

It is almost inevitable, therefore, that, when all but a couple of children make progress, we assume that these children not making progress have a difficulty. This is the explanation that often finds favour, simply because the alternative is likely to cause a certain amount of unease. If the situation is examined from a different perspective, it would be possible to suggest that, instead of looking at 'children with learning difficulties', perhaps the teacher should become the focus of attention.

Children who fail to fulfil expectations, either in terms of their behaviour or learning, present teachers with a challenge to their professional expertise and teaching skills. It is invariably when difficulties arise in the classroom that these qualities are most seriously threatened.

Behind the statement that a 'child has a learning difficulty' are a number of assumptions. We assume that the opportunities for learning of all children has been the same. We assume that a child's attendance and exposure to the same teaching during his school life as his peers', ensures they have shared the same learning experiences. We also assume that everything possible has been done at a local authority, school and classroom level to ensure that a child has been provided with the best possible environment in which to learn.

Tomlinson (1982) challenges these assumptions directly, questioning the conventional views about the development of special education and its purpose within the education system. Through retaining a healthy scepticism about much that has happened in the area of 'special education' in the past, it could be reasonably concluded and argued that there have been only two things wrong with it; one, that it isn't 'special' and, two, that it isn't 'education'.

Approaches to assessment

Through the association and influence of the medical profession within the field of education, the starting point for investigating why a pupil is failing to learn or is misbehaving is 'the child'. Which aspects of the child's level of functioning have been 'faulty' and so resulted in a difficulty in learning? The difficulty is diagnosed and then treated accordingly through programmes of remediation. The pattern of assessment associated with this way of thinking, that of trying to identify the nature of a child's disability, has been described by Howell, Kaplan and O'Connell (1979, Figure 11.1). This approach to assessment sets out to locate the area of difficulty

Figure 11.1 *A possible sequence for testing to identify the nature of a pupil's disability*

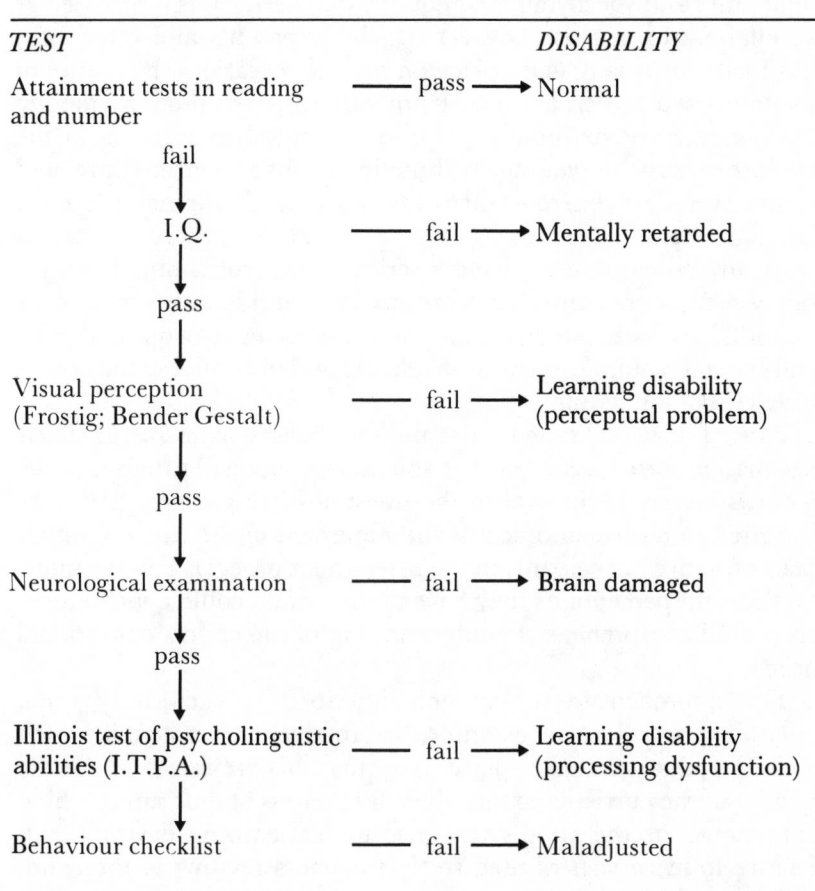

TEST		DISABILITY
Attainment tests in reading and number	—— pass ——	Normal
fail ↓		
I.Q.	—— fail ——	Mentally retarded
pass ↓		
Visual perception (Frostig; Bender Gestalt)	—— fail ——	Learning disability (perceptual problem)
pass ↓		
Neurological examination	—— fail ——	Brain damaged
pass ↓		
Illinois test of psycholinguistic abilities (I.T.P.A.)	—— fail ——	Learning disability (processing dysfunction)
↓		
Behaviour checklist	—— fail ——	Maladjusted

and attributes the child's problems to it. A pupil thus becomes categorised, classified and labelled according to a specific handicap.

This view of assessment is also characterised by a number of other features. The main responsibility placed on schools and teachers is primarily to liaise with parents and call upon the help of one of the LEA support services, usually the remedial reading department or schools' psychological service. These services, the recognised 'experts', are then expected to 'assess the child' and offer an explanation which accounts for the difficulties experienced by the pupil.

The assessment takes place outside the classroom, and is carried out by those who are regarded as having a considerably greater expertise than teachers in identifying and diagnosing children's difficulties and specifying their educational needs. It is rarely seen as a collaborative activity between teachers, parents and other professionals. It usually takes place on a single occasion, the nature of the tests used preventing their being administered more frequently than once every six months. The tests themselves, apart from the attainment tests in reading, arithmetic, language, etc, are unrelated to the everyday classroom activities with which the child is most familiar.

An unknown person, giving a series of tests containing exercises rarely seen or encountered before, creates considerable pressure for a child. S/he is expected and assumed to perform at an optimal level, and the test results are viewed as reliable and indicative of the child's true level of functioning.

Parents play a limited role in their child's assessment. Their permission for an assessment is sought but thereafter their involvement is largely peripheral to the questions being asked. They are expected to receive and accept the judgment of the experts, rather than be active participants in the assessment process. Yet, the information and perceptions they have of their child could contribute to an overall comprehensive understanding of the child's educational needs.

The approach to assessment described is exclusively pupil orientated, and does not examine the broader environment in which a child's education takes place. No questions are raised about the quality of the curricula in use, the effectiveness of different teaching approaches or the child's response to his learning environment. Failure to learn is attributed solely to factors relating to the child, which to a large extent promulgates and maintains the notion that the school, the local authority and education system at large are all right, and efficiently organised.

However, in recent years there has been a discernible shift in emphasis from trying to identify a child's handicap to identifying his educational needs, irrespective of a pupil's specific disability. This has arisen, in part, through acknowledging that children's needs often differ, even though they may be seen to be experiencing identical 'handicapping' conditions.

Within the context of teaching in the United Kingdom, this change in orientation has been represented in the 1981 Education Act (DES, 1981) and in particular in the guideline for implementing the Act proposed in Circular 1/83 (DES, 1983). Here assessment is seen as a continuous process, taking place over a period of time rather than being a one-off event. The focus of attention is the way the child interacts with his environment, with a view to finding out the pupil's educational needs and the most appropriate provision to meet those needs. This is achieved in two ways. First of all, the assessment is 'experimental' in the sense of different teaching approaches being implemented, with their resulting effects on children's learning being carefully monitored and evaluated. An important consequence of adopting such an approach is the need to develop a record-keeping system which can be used easily and relates children's learning outcomes to how they have been taught. This point is emphasised in Circular 1/83.

Second, assessment should be related to education. Whilst this statement is not clarified at any length in Circular 1/83, it is perhaps most constructively seen as a desire to make the assessment of a child's educational needs more closely related to the teaching that forms a part of everyday classroom practice. The curricula, teaching methods and patterns of classroom organisation which comprise the 'normal' classroom environment should also be at the heart of the process of assessment. The assessment should not be grafted on to existing classroom procedures and organisation. On the contrary, it should develop naturally from everyday teaching.

Such an approach to assessment takes as its starting point a child's existing classroom. It is the suitability of this environment and the child's interaction with it that is being evaluated, not the child. The process of assessment which encapsulates these aims is Curriculum Based Assessment (CBA) and has been referred to elsewhere as assessment-through-teaching (Raybould, 1984; Pearson and

Tweddle, 1984). However, it is important to note that the terms are synonymous and can be used interchangeably, as they describe exactly the same process.

CBA has been defined by Blankenship and Lilly (1981) as, 'the practice of obtaining direct and frequent measures of a student's performance on a series of sequentially arranged objectives derived from the curriculum used in the classroom' (p. 81). Figure 11.2 shows the approach to this kind of assessment proposed by Glaser (1962).

Figure 11.2: *Curriculum based assessment*

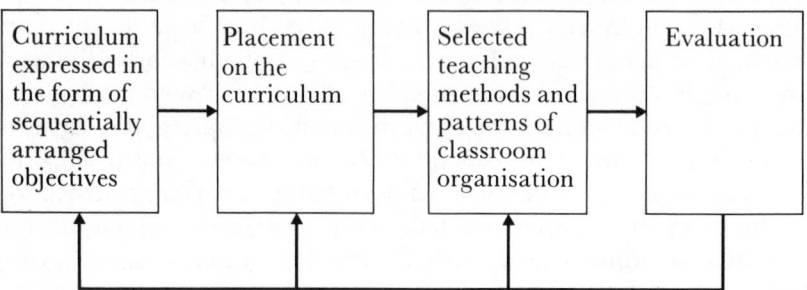

Curriculum based assessment, its assumptions, principles and practical classroom implications have been described comprehensively by Solity and Bull (1987). However, its essential features can be summarised as follows. The first stage requires that a curriculum be designed and expressed in terms of tasks children have to undertake to show that learning has taken place. When relating this to children with special needs, a number of important considerations should be acknowledged to ensure the curriculum facilitates successful learning experiences for the children.

Initially, children might be seen to have a difficulty in learning because systematic observation and evaluation of their progress indicates they are falling behind their peers in learning important basic academic skills, eg in the areas of literacy and numeracy. An important subsequent aim in teaching these children, is to enable them to 'bridge the gap' in attainment levels that exists, so that within a short period of time their performance is commensurate with that of peers.

In order to achieve this, their progress must be accelerated in some way; their learning must be enhanced. One way of accomplishing this goal is to design a curriculum which enables children to learn through being taught problem-solving strategies and generalisable skills and concepts. Children will therefore be shown how to apply their knowledge in a variety of contexts, rather than having to learn everything by rote. Through combining the principles of Direct Instruction and Task Analysis (Carnine and Becker, 1982; Englemann, 1980; Englemann and Carnine, 1982; Solity and Bull, 1987) at the curriculum development stage, curricula can be prepared which achieve the aim of accelerating and enhancing children's learning, by showing them how to generalise and apply their knowledge and skills.

The second stage in curriculum-based assessment involves placing children on the curriculum. The skills they have already learned need to be identified, as do those skills which need to be taught next. By pin-pointing precisely where a child is on the curriculum, it should then be possible to set future work for children which is at an appropriate level of difficulty. It is important that children have successful learning experiences immediately, so that they can begin to feel confident.

The third stage directs attention to the classroom environment, in its broadest sense, and the way it is organised to facilitate and develop children's learning. The selection of suitable teaching methods, materials and patterns of classroom organisation is determined by a number of factors, which must be referenced to other activities taking place in the classroom.

The final stage in CBA-evaluation relates children's learning to the three earlier stages: selected teaching methods and patterns of classroom organisation, placement on the curriculum and curriculum design itself. The aim of CBA is to find out how these different components of the child's classroom environment affect his learning outcomes. They are all within a teacher's immediate sphere of influence and can be changed or amended in the light of what children learn. CBA should therefore be seen as a procedure which creates a scenario whereby the relationship between various teaching approaches and pupil progress is established.

The classroom environment

The remainder of this chapter will focus on the third stage in CBA, patterns of classroom organisation and selection of teaching methods. They are areas discussed in considerable detail in Bull and Solity (1987).

The classroom can be seen as comprising three components: physical, social and educational. The teacher, through separating them, can organise and manage each area, so that the overall effect is to secure successful learning experiences for children in the class-room.

THE PHYSICAL COMPONENT

This refers to the actual environment in which both teachers and children find themselves. For the most part this will be the surroundings in the classroom itself, ranging from the 'old-fashioned' schoolroom of the later part of the nineteenth century to the more up-to-date design of the open-plan classrooms of more recent times. Every classroom has its own assortment of furniture, materials and equipment which can be arranged judiciously according to the activities about to be undertaken. Of course, not all teaching takes place in the classroom, as certain curricular activities require different settings and the use of specialised equipment. However, the principles governing the organisation of the physical environment apply wherever teaching occurs. Research studies (Glynn, 1982) have highlighted some of the significant ways in which the physical surroundings directly influence children and others working within the classroom.

THE SOCIAL COMPONENT

This part of the environment relates to the nature of the interactions taking place in the classroom at any one time. A social component exists whenever differing combinations of children and teachers come together in an educational setting. A teacher will work with various groupings of children during the course of the school day. These may be large or small, mixed ability or 'sets' or specific individuals within these groups. Equally, there will be times, particularly in an open-plan setting, where teachers may work as a team, sharing responsibility for the teaching of an entire year group within the school. Whatever the size of the group or the activity in which it is engaged, it comprises a collection of individuals who bring different experiences and expectations to the situation. The likelihood is therefore that these group situations will never be the same and will differ in some significant way. Nevertheless, there are general principles which can be applied to a group context, which, when effectively managed, lead to the whole group interrelating cohesively.

THE EDUCATIONAL COMPONENT

This is based on the school's curricula, and the skills, concepts and information children are taught at various stages in their learning. The activities on which they are engaged at any given time, their organisation and presentation and the way they are sequenced across the school day, are all key features of the educational component.

The aim when teaching children with special educational needs

As well as placing the teaching of children with special needs in the appropriate context, it is equally important to have a clear purpose underlying their education. How they are taught is directly related to why they are being taught.

Englemann and Carnine (1982) have looked carefully at the criteria that would need to be satisfied before it could be stated confidently that an individual had a difficulty in learning. After carefully studying the relationship between the environment and the learner, they argued it would only be reasonable to reach this conclusion once it had been demonstrated that the educational environment had been organised in such a way that nothing more could have been done to improve the quality of teaching offered. Thus, given existing knowledge about how to teach, every attempt should be made to ensure that the most effective curricula, patterns of classroom organisation and teaching approaches are adopted to teach children who appear to have a difficulty.

They have argued for the need to develop principles about how the classroom environment influences the teaching process and children's learning. Three areas are identified as being of specific relevance;

1 how the environment operates to influence learning outcomes;
2 how the information taught to children can be organised to ensure optimal learning;
3 how the teacher communicates skills and knowledge most effectively to pupils, so that what is learned is remembered over time and can be generalised and applied in other educational settings.

Englemann and Carnine (1982) are suggesting a shift in emphasis from the question 'How do children learn?' to 'What is the most effective way of teaching?' The former is often considered without taking into account the teaching arrangements that have contributed to children's learning. Reformulating the question in the manner advocated requires that these factors are noted and then related to children's learning outcomes.

The starting point for teaching is optimistic, since it is assumed that the reason some pupils fail to perform certain tasks satisfactorily is because they have never been taught the necessary skills. It is felt that children's learning depends on their being in the right place at the right time, getting the appropriate help from both school and home to meet their specific educational needs. Although, clearly, alternative explanations for children's failure to learn in the past are possible, they are invariably of only limited value when taking decisions about how to teach in the future. At worst they offer explanations for failure which lead to children being given potentially harmful labels (ie educationally subnormal, maladjusted). Instead, it is seen as preferable to find out what children can do, and use this as the platform from which to plan and implement future teaching strategies. Through concentrating on the question 'How can we teach effectively?' rather than pondering on why children have failed to learn in the past, it is anticipated that children can be given positive and successful learning experiences in the future. The key to achieving this is focusing on those aspects of the classroom environment which can be influenced by the teacher.

The instructional hierarchy

Having set the scene for CBA through emphasising its integral role in the teaching process and briefly discussed the aims when teaching children with difficulties, it is time to concentrate on the specific procedures which can help systematise teaching. This corresponds directly to the third stage in CBA, selecting teaching methods, materials and patterns of classroom organisation.

This choice is determined by the stage of teaching reached in Haring and Eaton's (1978) instructional hierarchy (Figure 11.3), which outlines five stages in children's learning. Teaching methods vary for each stage, depending on the specific aspect of a skill being developed.

Figure 11.3 *The instructional hierarchy*

Acquisition	Children are shown how to use a skill for the first time and learn to perform it accurately.
Fluency	Children learn to perform the new skill with fluency as well as accuracy.
Maintenance	Children are still able to perform the skill accurately and fluently even after a period of time when no teaching takes place.
Generalisation	Children are shown how to use the skill in different contexts.
Adaptation	Children are set problems which require them to use their newly acquired knowledge in novel ways.

ACQUISITION

At this initial level children are introduced to a new task for the first time and so are likely to make errors. However, over time their performance should improve, leading to corresponding increases in accuracy. As children are being introduced to a new skill, teaching will require a high level of pupil-teacher interaction. The following are some of the teaching methods most strongly advocated for this stage. They can be divided into procedures which describe how tasks are presented (model, lead, imitation, instructions, test); those which help the child complete the task once it has been started (cues, prompts, fading, shaping, chaining); and, finally, how to respond once the task has been completed (feedback, rewards, diagnosing and correcting errors).

Model On the first occasion a new skill is introduced the teacher models it for the child. The teacher would start by getting the child's attention, perhaps by saying, 'It's my turn, watch me. Are you ready?' and then proceed to complete a task while the child watched.

Lead The next step is for the pupil to complete each step of the task at the same time as the teacher. When leading, the teacher might say, 'Let's do this together. Are you ready?' The teacher then starts and the pupil joins in, copying exactly what the teacher does.

Imitation When the child imitates her teacher, the teacher performs the whole of the task first and only when it has been finished does the child have a turn. It is therefore different from leading, where teacher and pupil perform the task together.

Instructions These are verbal directions from the teacher, which will enable the child to complete the task successfully. Vocabulary and sentence structure should be within the child's range of competence and should also be the same from one day to the next to minimise confusion.

Often what might seem like a small change in an instruction leads to a sigificant change in the nature of the task. For example, when teaching sight vocabulary to children with the aid of flash cards, the cards are often laid out in front of the pupil. Typically, the teacher will point to each card in turn and ask 'What does this word say?' This is a recall task where the child tries to remember what the word says. If the question is changed to 'Point to the word which says ------', the task becomes one of recognition rather than recall. Here the word is given to the child, who then has to scan the array and point to the correct one, which is easier than actually reading the word, as was required with the previous instruction.

Test Once the task can be completed accurately via leading and imitating, the teacher will want to see whether it can be performed following an instruction only. The teacher might therefore say to the pupil, 'Now it's your turn. Are you ready?' An instruction is given and the child then tries to finish the activity without any further teacher assistance.

Cues These are usually visual features of the materials being used, which help a child succeed in a task. It could be a dot on a sheet of paper to indicate where to start writing from, or an arrow, to indicate the direction of pencil movement required to form a letter during a handwriting lesson.

Prompts This is help given by the teacher to a child while the task is being completed and can be one of three types, physical, gestural or verbal. Physical prompts are used most frequently when teaching motor skills such as handwriting. A teacher could place a child's hand in the correct starting position to form a letter and then perhaps slowly guide the pupil's hand in forming the letter.

No physical contact is made with the pupil when using a gestural prompt. The teacher uses gestures alone, maybe through nodding, directing gaze or making appropriate hand movements to help the pupil complete the task. A verbal prompt takes the form of a brief statement to guide a child through a task. The three types of prompts can be used on their own or in combination. Once they have helped the pupil complete the task successfully, they are gradually withdrawn so the pupil works with less teacher assistance.

Fading The above strategy of gradually withdrawing prompts applies to cues as well: it is known as fading.

Shaping This occurs where a teacher accepts a response on a task, even though it is not initially 100% correct. Subsequently, small improvements in performance are praised, until eventually, the desired learning outcome is achieved. It is used most frequently when teaching language or handwriting skills. For example, if a child was experiencing difficulties in pronouncing certain words, the teacher would initially accept the pupil's best attempt and then encourage successive improvements towards the correct pronunciation.

Chaining This is the name used to refer to teaching a series of skills which have already been learned separately and are now to be taught in a specific temporal sequence. Each individual activity making up the chain, contributes to a more complex task being completed. For example, 'some of the separate skills learned which are required in order to add to them might be:

- equation reading
- naming numerals (0–10)
- writing numerals (0–10)
- constructing sets
- counting (from 1–10)

These and other skills, when taught in the appropriate order, would enable a child to add numerals where the answer did not exceed ten.

Feedback To be most effective, this should be both positive and frequent. A particularly powerful form of feedback is to give children knowledge of results. This enables them to see whether they are improving and helps them appreciate which aspects of the task are being performed correctly and which have resulted in errors and need further practice.

Rewards These play an important role in improving children's learning, particularly at this stage in the hierarchy. It can take several forms, which are summarised in Figure 11.4 (taken from Bull and Solity, 1987).

DIAGNOSING AND CORRECTING ERRORS

Inevitably children will make errors on a task while being tested. At such times the teacher has to think and react quickly. The cause of the error has to be diagnosed and corrected so that children do not fall into the position of practising their own mistakes.

Carnine and Silbert (1979) describe an effective correction procedure involving five steps (model, lead, test, alternative test and delayed test) which can be used on an individual or group basis. It is highly positive, since the teacher does not criticise the pupil for making an error, but adopts an approach which emphasises the correct way of completing the task.

FLUENCY

Once tasks can be performed accurately, teaching concentrates on developing fluency. Children would be expected to work independently and are provided with numerous opportunities for practice.

Figure 11.4 *Types of reward and some classroom examples*

Type	Main features	Examples	Comments
Social rewards	involve pleasant interactions with other people	praise, applause, the opportunity to sit with friends or show good work to favourite teacher. Touch, hugs (young children). Smiles. A written note to parents about good progress or behaviour	They are determined by the behaviour of others. Often the natural consequence of social behaviour
Activity rewards	involve opportunities for enjoyable activities	any preferred activity: play as individual or group; games; read to the teacher; clean board; work on topic of interest; free choice of activity, etc.	The activity offered must be the child's preferred activity. It is best to avoid curricular activities. May also involve social reinforcers, e.g. playing a group game with friends
Token rewards	visual, tangible signs of approval or progress	stars, points, grades, ticks, badges, merit cards, certificates	These can be used alone or exchanged for activity of material rewards later: they are easier to arrange immediately
Material rewards	tangible/usable/ edible items	sweets, playthings, trinkets and prizes, presents of all kinds	These are generally reserved for use as a back-up only with very young children or when all other types are ineffective. Always pair these with other types of rewards to strengthen the effectiveness of the new reward

Unfortunately, many of the activities which increase fluency are repetitive and not as interesting or enjoyable as might be desired. As a result it is important children are given regular feedback and reward for their progress, to keep their motivation high during this essential stage of learning.

The need to teach skills to high levels of fluency cannot be emphasised enough, as it can make all the difference between children learning or continuing to experience difficulties. Using criteria based on accuracy alone could be misleading when transferring a child from one task to the next.

The following are the three teaching procedures which are most helpful in encouraging fluency.

Practice Skills need to be practised once accuracy has been achieved so that they can then also be completed fluently. Haring (1978) described a particular form of practice as 'the opportunity to perform a task repeatedly until the quality and fluency of performance increases to a specified level' (p 14). Practice can therefore be seen as giving a pupil as many opportunities as possible to perform the task.

During acquisition a high level of pupil-teacher interaction is required in order to monitor the responses of students carefully, to ensure the task is being completed accurately. This is not necessary for fluency-building, where the emphasis is on children working on their own, with as few distractions as possible.

Feedback There is always a risk that some children will lose motivation and interest when given repeated opportunities for practice because of the repetitive nature of the activities involved in developing fluency. However, this essential stage in learning cannot be omitted simply because it will not always be appealing. The vast majority of children will establish fluency within a short period of teaching and will not require much time to practise. For those pupils who do not become fluent at the new skills so quickly, the teacher faces an uncomfortable dilemma: how to keep a child involved and sustain interest during the periods of practice. It is essential that a pupil appreciates why a task is being practised so regularly. If an activity has a clear purpose which can be understood, a child is more likely to try to improve through practice. A significant consideration is the effects on interest and motivation that can be realised when feedback is given in the form of knowledge of results. Under these circumstances feedback can be based on the improved performance levels reached in using the new skill and, if presented and displayed visually, can be extremely motivating and encouraging for the learner.

Rewards Feedback is often coupled with rewards, the two procedures combining to sustain the child's enthusiasm for work. The most likely combination of rewards is social with token rewards (points, stars, tokens, etc), since they can be given immediately, which makes them particularly effective when building fluency.

MAINTENANCE

Teachers cannot afford the time to let children forget what they have learned and to keep going back and re-teaching skills. Over time it becomes imperative that children maintain their levels of performance without any further teaching taking place. However, reaching this point cannot happen by chance, so this stage of the hierarcy aims to teach children to reach this position.

At the end of the maintenance stage children should be able to use a new skill on their own with accuracy and fluency, without receiving any help whatsoever from their teacher. It should be regarded as a period where 'overlearning' can occur. Pupils should be involved in the same type of activities that were used to develop fluency, but with any rewards being gradually withdrawn. The overall aim is for children to continue using a skill and to derive intrinsic satisfaction, rather than being motivated by the teacher and her use of rewards. Maintenance represents a change in role for the teacher from the active involvement of acquisition and fluency, to the more passive position of facilitator, creating time during the school day for children to work on activities so that they reach a point where no further practice is required.

GENERALISATION

Acquisition, fluency-building and maintenance, the first three stages in the hierarchy, focus on *skill-getting*, whereas generalisation and adaptation represent a move towards *skill-using*. Prior to generalisation, children will have been working on a single task. Once they reach this stage, they are presented with two or more tasks (which have been taught to maintenance) and have to respond appropriately to each task. The critical features of the separate tasks would be identified and children shown how to apply their skills and knowledge to the new activities.

The teacher takes an active role in teaching children how to generalise skills. Several teaching procedures can be adopted which might include the use of modelling, instructions, cueing, testing, practising, feedback, reward and a correction procedure. However, in all probability it is likely that instructions alone will be sufficient for the majority of pupils with just the occasional prompt or reliance on cues.

Initally, it is important that pupils receive quick feedbacks so that they can see the generalisations made were correct, thus increasing their levels of confidence. Feedback can subsequently be withdrawn as children become more competent at generalising their skills.

The aim of this stage in the hierarchy is to show children how to generalise the skills, knowledge and concepts they have been learning. Through demonstrating how this is done, rather than hoping they will learn to do so on their own, it is anticipated that their overall rate of learning can be accelerated and the gap in attainment levels that exists with their peers narrowed.

ADAPTATION

During adaptation children apply the skills they have learned on a much wider basis than has hitherto been the case. They are required to extend their learning to problems which involve their making novel responses to the presented tasks. The teacher takes very much a back seat during adaptation, there being no specific instructional procedures to follow, and the way children work being viewed as offering 'creative' solutions to set questions.

Changes occur in both teacher involvement and the teaching approach, in several ways, as skills are taught at different stages in the hierarchy. Initially, pupil-teacher interactions are high as teachers introduce new skills and concepts to children. However, teachers gradually assume the role of facilitator, providing the appropriate learning environment in which a pupil's skill development can flourish. This change is mirrored in the nature of the teaching process, which gradually becomes less structured, as it moves from being teacher-directed to one which is more child-directed.

These developments are accompanied by similar changes in the source of children's motivation. In the early stages the teacher's role is central in capturing children's interest and making learning meaningful and relevant. This is achieved in part by creating a learning environment in which children make progress and can appreciate that they are improving. In time, though, it is hoped that children will become self-motivating as they experience success in areas of the curriculum which had previously baffled them. These changes are shown in Figure 11.5 (taken from Solity and Bull, 1987).

Teaching in small groups

As stated earlier, a frequent concern when planning to teach children experiencing difficulties is that much of the teaching will have to be carried out on a one-to-one, pupil-teacher basis. The stages of learning highlighted in the instructional hierarchy indicate that, in fact, this is a requirement only during the acquisition and generalisation stages. Nevertheless, it could pose a problem during the course of the school day, since it may not always be possible to give the desired level of individual help just when it is needed. One way of tackling this issue is, where appropriate, to teach children as a group rather than individually. Gathering up to seven or eight children together and teaching them as a group for half an hour a day could prove more effective and be more economical of time than teaching children on their own for the same period.

Small-group teaching is common practice in many primary classrooms. Desks and tables are arranged together so that children can work with each other on tasks. The role of the teacher is to help children, monitor their progress and give appropriate feedback. Group work run along these lines typically involves children completing activities at their own pace and in a style that suits them.

There is one major drawback to this pattern of classroom organisation in relation to children experiencing difficulties. Unfortunately, they may not be concentrating to the anticipated level all the time they are supposed to be working. They might chat to friends or be distracted by other events in the classroom.

Such a scenario highlights the distinction made between *scheduled teaching time* and *academic engaged time*. The former refers to the amount of time set aside for different activities during the day and

Figure 11.5   *The instructional hierarchy and its implications for appropriate teaching procedures*

	Acquisition	Fluency	Maintenance	Generalisation	Adaptation
Nature of task presented to pupil	All tasks require use of skill drawn from the same skill area (eg addition to 10)	All tasks require use of skill drawn from the same skill area	All tasks require use of skill drawn from the same skill area	Tasks require use of skills drawn from two or more skill areas	Task set which requires use of skills drawn from several skill areas
Response	Single response required	Single response required	Single response required	Two or more different responses required	Range of different responses required
Emphasis of instruction	Teaching skills through specific techniques which in general are presented prior to the task being completed	Child builds fluency through practice	Child maintains skills through practice	Pupil taught to make correct response through making appropriate discriminations and differentiations	Instructions given. Teacher acts as a facilitator
Feedback and rewards	Feedback and natural rewards	Feedback together with natural and artificial rewards is important to sustain interest	Artificial rewards withdrawn	Feedback on success of performance (either correct or incorrect) is essential	Some feedback may occur and it is to be hoped pupils will derive intrinsic reinforcement
Pupil/teacher contact time	High	Low	Low	High	Low

refers to the time children are *expected* to work on specific activities. Academic engaged time, however, refers to the time children *actually spend working*.

Inevitably children do not spend all the available scheduled teaching time actively engaged on work. Clearly, when trying to accelerate progress, it is important that scheduled teaching time is not just optimistic planning and timetabling but becomes academic engaged time.

It is with the specific concept of academic engaged time in mind, that a particular type of small-group instruction has been evolved within the approach to teaching children with difficulties, known as direct instruction. It has a number of clearly identifiable features designed to ensure that small groups of children are taught together with high levels of academic engaged time. Space precludes a description of the procedures here, but details of their rationale, organisation and implementation can be found in Carnine and Silbert (1979) and Solity and Bull (1987).

This chapter has concentrated on teaching methods which may be adopted when helping children with difficulties in the ordinary school. They have been discussed in relation to the aim of accelerating pupils' progress, so that children can catch up with their peers.

It has also been stressed that teaching needs to be placed in the appropriate contexts; that it should be related to the process of assessment aimed at identifying children's educational needs and also that it should form an integral part of everyday classroom practice.

Finally, the specific procedures described have been related to an instructional hierarchy, which advocates that children should be involved in a range of activities depending on the stage of learning being developed.

References

Blankenship, C. and Lilly, M. S. (1981) *Mainstreaming Students with Learning and Behaviour Problems* New York: Holt, Rinehart and Winston.

Bull, S. L. and Solity, J. E. (1987) *Classroom Management: Principles to Practice* London: Croom Helm.

Carnine, D. W. and Becker, W. (1982) 'Theory of instruction: generalisation issues' in *Educational Psychology*, 2, 3–4, 249–262.

Carnine, D. W. and Silbert, J. (1979) *Direct Instruction Reading* Ohio: Charles E. Merrill.

Department of Education and Science (1981) *Education Act* London: HMSO.

Department of Education and Science (1983) *Assessment and Statements of Special Educational Needs* Circular 1/83.

Englemann, S. (1980) 'Towards the design of faultless instruction: the theoretical basis for concept analysis' in *Educational Technology*, 20, 519–523.

Englemann, S. and Carnine, D. W. (1982) *Theory of Instruction: Principles and Practice* New York: Irvington.

Glaser, R. (1962) *Training Research and Education* Pittsburg: University of Pittsburg Press.

Glynn, T. (1982) 'Antecedent control of behaviour in educational contexts' in *Educational Psychology*, 2, 3–4, 215–229.

Haring, N. G. and Eaton, M. D. (1978) 'Systematic instructional procedures – an instructional hierarchy' in N. G. Haring *et al The Fourth R – Research in the Classroom* Ohio: Charles E. Merrill.

Howell, K. W., Kaplan, J. S. and O'Connell, C. Y. (1979) *Evaluating Exceptional Children: A Task Analytic Approach* Ohio, New York: Charles E. Merrill.

Pearson, L. and Tweddle, D. A. (1984) 'The formulation and use of behavioural objectives' in D. Fontana (ed) *Behaviourism and Learning Theory in Education, British Journal of Educational Psychology Monograph Series*, No 1, 75–92. Scottish Academic Press.

Raybould, E. C. (1984) 'Precision teaching and pupils with learning difficulties and perspectives, principles and practice' in D. Fontana (ed) *Behaviourism and Learning Theory in Education, British Journal of Educational Psychology Monograph Series*, No 1, 43–74. Scottish Academic Press.

Solity, J. E. and Bull, S. J. (1987) *Special Needs: Bridging the Curriculum Gap* Milton Keynes: Open University Press.

Tomlinson, S. (1982) *A Sociology of Special Education* London: Routledge and Kegan Paul.

12 Parents in the classroom

Sheila Wolfendale

Introduction

Recent developments in the relationship between teachers and parents have been chronicled, and models have been proposed to enhance home-school links, based on evolving good practice (Wolfendale, 1983; Long, 1986). The many initiatives that currently abound reflect the multiplicity of ways in which teachers and parents can and do work together. Accounts in the literature describe cooperative ventures at the 'macro', whole-school level, one instance of which is the representation of parents by parent governors on schools' governing bodies (Kogan, 1985). The earlier chapters in this book by Ingrid Lunt and Geof Sewell provide the broader school context to the participation by parents in classroom as well as in home-based learning.

The demonstration in recent years of successful collaboration between school and home has provided the spur to recent calls for the adoption of school and LEA policy with regard to the involvement of parents in education. The National Confederation of Parent-Teacher Associations (1986) urges LEAs to accept responsibility for promoting parental interest by producing a policy paper on home–school links. It calls upon LEAs to appoint advisory officers with a brief for a 'closer partnership'. At the school level, the NCPTA acknowledges the importance of parental involvement by suggesting that time be made available to staff to carry out a range of home–school activities, some of which are specified in the report. In *Primary Schools and Special Needs* (1987) I outline a number of areas with which a school's policy on involving parents could be concerned. A framework for the expression of collective responsibility towards all children provides the broader perspective. Parents play their part as 'team members' whose active participation is invoked at any agreed time.

These ideas are compatible with the ecological perspectives with which this book is concerned, wherein children's learning and other needs are appraised in relation to their whole circumstances, and within which adults significant in a child's life are considered as having a part to play at all times and actively at certain times.

Much of the earlier American work on compensatory education and early intervention routinely incorporated parents in early learning programmes (Bronfenbrenner, 1979) and thus paved the way for later 'ecologically valid' enterprises in the United Kingdom (see Wolfendale, 1983, Chapter 5, for a summary; also Widlake, 1986). These encompass mainstream education – for example, the involvement of parents in their children's reading (Topping and Wolfendale, 1985, and see later in this chapter) – and, within the realm of special needs, parent-professional programmes such as Portage (Copley *et al* 1986; Cameron, 1986).

The rationale on which this work has been based can be summed up in the succinct words of the Plowden Report (1967): 'by involving parents, the children may be helped' (para 114). Or, in the later, somewhat more sophisticated sentiments of Bloom (1983), who says that, on the basis of evidence, it is clear that when home and school have 'congruent learning emphases' and shared aspirations, the child has little difficulty in later school learning.

This is applicable to all children, though the Warnock Report (1978) went on to relate this principle explicitly to children with special needs in order to make some forceful points about the proven effectiveness of involving parents directly in their children's learning and development. Later, the Circular to LEAs No 1/83, which accompanied the 1981 Education Act, echoed these views, making it clear that an integral part of special needs policy and provision in mainstream or special school is the active involvement of parents.

Involving parents in children's learning – the concept of the open classroom

Parents, acting in their time-honoured role as educators (Topping, 1986) can enact this part anywhere and at any time, from birth onwards. Professional educators, that is, teachers in schools, educational psychologists and education advisers with a brief to foster conducive learning environments, are now formally acknowledging this perennial role of parents, and are maximising their commitment and the unique contribution that parents can make to their children's upbringing.

The title to this chapter is an indication of one aspect of the working relationship between teacher and parent(s). It serves to emphasise the centrality of the teacher's position regarding curriculum planning and the organisation of children's learning experiences.

However, contemporary classrooms are opening up to include other adults (see Chapter 8) and, at times, children from other classes and year groups, as for example in peer and cross-age tutoring (Paired Reading Bulletin, 1985, 1986; Wheldall and Mettem, 1985). It is antithetical to an ecological perspective that perceives school, home and the community as the learning environments of all children, that classrooms should remain closed to others, unreceptive and unaffected by 'outside' influences and happenings in the wider world. The community school is part of the educational scene in a small but growing number of local educational authorities (Rennie, 1985), and the idea of 'schools without walls' has been floated on both sides of the Atlantic (see Wolfendale, 1983, Ch. 5).

The term 'the open classroom' is used in this chapter to convey the extent of children's formal and incidental education within and outside school, and thus to provide the context for the specific ways in which teachers and parents can work together to enhance children's learning. A number of current initiatives, and the issues that are inevitably associated with these innovations, will be described that span parental involvement in learning at school and at home.

Parents in schools: an evolving relationship

The parental presence in schools can be visible within the classroom itself and within school generally. Substantial evidence now exists, via survey (Cyster *et al*, 1979), HMI reports (DES, 1978), accounts of school provision that routinely includes parents (Stierer, 1985), project reports (Griffiths and Edmonds, 1987), that parents are contributing to school life and school-based learning in a number of ways.

The signs are that parental input into schools is increasing and the evolving reciprocal relationship is acknowledged in tangible terms. For example, a fair number of schools now have a parents' room, analogous to the teachers' staffroom, which can be used as a retreat, a base, a place in which to hold discussions, workshops, prepare materials, hold displays.

For children it is no longer novel, especially in primary schools, to see parents moving around the school engaged in a number of activities. Perhaps we are moving towards a stance whereby we will all take for granted the legitimacy of this new, open interface between school and home.

From the general premise specific practice evolves whereby teachers and parents work together to promote children's learning and to ensure their well-being. Several examples of such practices are briefly described or referred to in the following section. Together they exemplify evolving educational practice. Separately, each 'area' is at a differing stage of evolution, with some areas (eg involving parents in assessment) at an earlier, embryonic stage of development compared with the involvement of parents in reading. Even where such ventures are routinely a part of school's provision, there is, in many cases, an evident dynamic, a momentum, that propels the participants into maintaining the initiative.

It is intended that reference to work involving parents in the classroom will demonstrate the applicability of these approaches for all children. An integral part of the rationale, however, is that their structure and organisation facilitates adoption of specific, short or long-term programmes or interventions for children with special educational needs. Overall, children's needs are not differentiated in terms of their universality; but the methodology as well as the underlying principles are conducive to individualising the content.

Opening classrooms to parents: complementary perspectives

It would be unrealistic to believe that one could introduce educational innovation into one discrete area without there being a spin-off or generalisation to other areas. So it would be inevitable that participation in the classroom would be accompanied by commensurate home-based parental involvement in school-initiated learning.

Many instances of classroom-focused involvement report upon this reciprocal link. The area of reading is to date the best documented example of this complementary exercise, whereby parents can work at home in tandem with the class-based reading programme. This dovetailing presupposes parents' awareness of the method and stages adopted by the teacher. Some schools at the outset of a parental involvement in reading scheme include 'pre-training' and awareness sessions for parents along these lines (Branston and Provis, 1986; Griffiths and Hamilton, 1984).

There are encouraging signs that the generalisation could effectively work in reverse. That is to say, where the effectiveness of home-based intervention has been demonstrated, as in the case of Portage (Sturmey and Crisp, 1986), the applicability of its methodology is being explored in classrooms, using parents or other adults as key agents.

Reference to these two examples briefly mentioned, reading and Portage, will, it is hoped, serve to make the point that, by incorporating the skills of other adults, but particularly of parents, into learning and skill-acquisition activities, it is possible to individualise learning. Within an integrated classroom there can co-exist literacy programmes for the whole class that involve parents as well as more directed learning programmes for children with special educational needs, such as a child who learns at a slower pace, or children with sensory or physical handicaps. The precise, sequenced instruction and assistance such children need, as of right, which may necessitate the use of aids, can be provided by their own or other parents working under the direction of the classteacher or advisory teacher.

Involving parents in children's reading

Mostly the correspondence has been 1:1 – that is, parents have been involved solely with their own children. However, earlier work characterised by parents coming into school to 'help' has provided the foundation for diversification.

As befits its ecological underpinnings, parental involvement in reading (PIR) as a discernible 'movement' has had twin thrusts from the outset. One major strand, exemplified by seminal work in

Haringey, and later at Belfield School in Rochdale and PACT in Hackney has been home-focused. In these programmes (see accounts in Topping and Wolfendale, 1985) parents listen to their children reading for a pre-agreed length of time daily or several times a week and prompt, correct or praise their children as pre-instructed. Paired reading at home, as a quite specific technique with its own instructional ground rules based on a set of principles (Morgan, 1986), continues the tradition. These techniques are routinely part of many schools' home-focused PIR programmes.

The other major strand has been for parents to come into school, into classrooms to work with teachers in a number of ways, along-side them, in adjacent rooms, with small groups or individual children. Smith and Marsh (*The Fox Hill Reading Project* in Topping and Wolfendale, 1985) describe reading workshops with middle infants and their parents which, after initial success, extend to language. Long (1986) shows, via a chart, a model for parent reading workshops with classroom and home-linked activities.

In a handbook designed to accompany in-service courses on PIR, Wolfendale and Gregory (1985) give an account of follow-up work in several primary and secondary schools in East London. A main feature was the arrangement for parents to come into school regularly to work with their own or other children, and to discuss reading progress with an advisory teacher (Gregory).

Williams (also in Wolfendale and Gregory) describes a spelling project in one of these secondary schools, the primary objective of which was to raise the spelling attainment of children by enabling parents to become educators. The children all had identifiable spelling difficulties. Williams adopted features of the precision teaching model (Raybould and Solity, 1985). The mothers contracted to spend ten minutes daily for five days a week with their child on the spelling programme and to come into school once a week to review progress and to plan the following week's work. They were briefed as to the rationale behind the spelling approach ('Look, Cover, Write, Check' – see Peters, 1985) and participated in making materials. The outcomes reported by Williams were positive in terms of gain in spelling ages and notable decrease in errors. The essential corollary to the home-based work was the weekly parents' session held at school.

A postal questionnaire to primary schools administered by Stierer (1985) confirmed the still-growing trend for unpaid helpers, mostly parents (and usually mothers) to assist with the teaching of reading on the school premises on a regular, voluntary basis. The average length of such input is two hours a week; however, many work for longer hours. Typically, the helpers hear children read, and whilst they tend to work mostly with the 'better' readers, nevertheless a significant proportion of them do work with children with reading difficulties. Stierer identifies a number of issues associated with the notion of unpaid volunteer help with reading (see later in this chapter).

There has been a certain implicit consensus about the skills which parents as educators bring to their participation in reading programmes. However, the instructions and pre-training themselves identify the particular response strategies parents are expected to use, ranging from being passive listeners to actively responding, giving direct 1:1 attention, correction, and reinforcement as instructed. Some of the training procedures are based explicitly on the view that parents are capable of developing considerable expertise as 'tutors' (Glynn and Winter in Topping and Wolfendale, 1985) and can become competent in handling behavioural approaches (cf PAIRS described by Solity and Reeve in the same volume).

Now that the first wave of demonstrably successful pioneering in PIR is passing, second-stage, more focused research can take place into the unique contribution of parents as educators. An example of a potentially fruitful line of enquiry which could relate the pedagogical expertise of teachers with the particular skills of parents in the teaching of reading is the research of Hannon and his colleagues (Hannon *et al*, 1986) into parents' and teachers' strategies in hearing young children read. The identification of a number of different strategies (the authors identify 21 'categories of moves') could lead to a matching between the relative contribution made by each 'significant adult' to learning at school and at home.

Kemp conceived of parental participation in reading as validly occurring at home and in school. He describes an approach that brings home and school together in literacy teaching (Kemp, 1985). His model incorporates readiness/preparation for learning to read (termed a preventive role); surveillance of progress through reading; and the corrective role that responds to children's difficulties in learning to read and write. The programme included parent training and work in classrooms as well as at home.

PIR remains the predominant vehicle for parent-teacher co-operation as an end in itself and as a means whereby home-school links generally are facilitated. On the whole, teachers who have experienced working alongside parents in the classroom have been comfortable in opening up their own practice to this sort of public scrutiny, and have been reassured that they remain in charge and in control of deploying their 'aides'.

Parental involvement in other curriculum areas: progress and possibilities

The above account of PIR provides a brief overview of parental involvement in school and at home in one of the major areas of the curriculum. This section looks at some promising lines of development in other curriculum areas. As is likely to continue to be the case, parental involvement is variously angled: home-based, directly within the classroom or located elsewhere within the school.

Maths It is not uncommon for schools to hold sessions on maths for parents to acquaint them of current developments in the teaching of numeracy. Increasing now is the direct participation of parents in workshops, to learn ways in which they can assist their children's progress.

In some areas, for example Kirklees and parts of the Inner London Education Authority, this approach extends to a scheme involving a number of schools and parents. In an exploratory study, Woolgar (1986) devised an objectives curriculum for a home-based parental involvement in maths project for first-year junior age children who were experiencing difficulties in number work. The results were encouraging in terms of attainment gains and also because of the enthusiasm that was generated by the children and their parents.

Evidence of parents coming into school and into the classroom to help with maths is far less solid and more anecdotal to date than with PIR. However, it would be relatively safe to predict that parental involvement in maths will grow for several reasons, amongst which are:

i that PIR models, which have worked, are transferable to maths;
ii that parents are reassured, via workshops and pre-training, that

they do have the requisite competence to assist and work with their children.

By involving parents and demonstrating the relevance of the various levels of numeracy to everyday life, it is hoped that maths teaching and learning can be demystified.

Note Dr Alan Graham at the Centre for Mathematics Education at the Open University co-ordinates PRISM (Parent Resource in Support of Maths) which is a loose network of parents, teachers, researchers, and psychologists interested in making use of what parents have to offer.

Language development and communication skills In the UK after the first flurry of EPA projects involving parents in the early 1970s, a number of which incorporated language programmes, little attention had been paid to the potential of matching teachers' and parents' expertise in the area of developng children's language. In some PIR schemes, language, 'talking' exercises, form part of the general reading activity, but sustained study and research into this area is scarce.

On the face of it, there is considerable potential in devising language intervention at various levels and for different purposes, eg for concept and vocabulary development, expressive skills, grammatical precision and so on. A suitable rationale exists for children in mainstream schools, based on the researchers of Wells (1984) and Tizard and Hughes (1984) amongst others. It is a question of making effective use of the child's discourse with adults in a favourable ratio of 1:1 or 1:2, as is the case with parents at home, and capitalising upon this by bringing parents into the formalised curriculum. Parents coming into the classroom for language work could be an effective concomitant of dialogues and discourse at home, and could impart a naturalistic dimension to school learning.

There are very few accounts which attest to the potential in this area (see Widlake and McLeod, 1984). Wolfendale and Bryans (1986) compiled a booklet comprising a large variety of language activities for young children and their parents. This is essentially for parents, teachers, or nursery staff to use as a basis for putting together language programmes which could run simultaneously in school and at home. Steps in setting up, maintaining and reviewing a language programme are outlined and sample record-keeping illustrates how the programme could be run over a number of weeks or months. The authors provide 'keynotes', described as features of the adult's behaviour in the adult–child discourse which enhance the child's language development. Essentially the keynotes are 'teaching pointers' for the adult involved with the child.

Getting ready for school One first school in Surrey is aiming to increase parent-teacher communication and cooperation in preparing children for school by offering suggestions for carefully structured activities and experiences aimed at reducing discontinuities between pre-school and school (Cleave, Jowett and Bate, 1982). These suggestions are offered in pack form (comprising books, games and tapes) which parents borrow to use with their child in the term before admission to school. The activities cover language, social/independence and classroom (including fine motor) skills. Two-way communication between parents and teachers is built into the scheme by the inclusion of a parent comment sheet in each pack.

Parents are introduced to the scheme at an evening meeting at which they are shown a two-part video. The first part pin-points the areas of discontinuity between pre-school and school, even for those children who have attended some form of nursery provision, thus enabling parents to acquire a situationally specific understanding of the challenges that will confront their child on admission to school. The second part shows a parent and child carrying out some of the activities and suggestions in the pack, thus providing a model for positive parent-child interaction. The scheme has been developed by the head and reception class teachers in collaboration with the school's educational psychologist, and, although it is in its early stages, initial response from parents and teachers has been enthusiastic and encouraging.

Note For further information contact Sonya Hinton, educational psychologist, via County Psychological Service, Surrey Education Department, County Hall, Kingston-upon-Thames.

There are implications in these and other budding developments to do with roles and deployment of personnel involved, particularly the parents. How are such collaborative schemes managed and maintained? How does the increasing oppenness, which is a corollary of such moves, relate to public accountability? For example, some LEAs, such as the London Borough of Croydon, have recently published primary age curriculum guidelines for parents, which enable them to ask specific questions of their children's teachers. Likewise the duties towards the curriculum, which are part of school governors' overall remit, empower parent governors to ask pertinent questions and to insist upon some guarantees and safeguards. An instance could be (and this is based on personal experience) that the governing body of a junior school, spearheaded by a parent governor, asks the school to produce a reading policy where none had previously existed. Curriculum and curriculum policy are then on the way to being public property, more open and accessible to parents than hitherto.

Involving parents positively in learning and behavoiur management: children with special needs

It is hoped that this sketch of the current and developing scene in teacher-parent co-operation has conveyed the general applicability of the principles and operations. The point was made earlier that under this umbrella the needs of all children could be met in part through the legitimate participation of parents in children's learning.

Within the area of special education and special needs a substantial number of examples have accumulated of effective collaboration between parents and professionals (Pugh, 1981). Some of these initiatives provide precedents to pursue, within integrated classrooms, ways in which parents can assist their children's learning.

Thomas, in this volume and elsewhere (Thomas, 1986) has described the deployment of other adults in the classroom. The area of severe learning difficulties has been a pace-setter in demonstrating the effectiveness of 'room management' (RM) techniques through the provision of other staff in the classroom, each of whom has an explicit job for an agreed period of time during a day. During this 'activity' period, specific roles are allotted, such as 'individual helper', 'activity manager', 'mover'. The EDY programme exemplified RM in action (Farrell, 1985). Thomas (1986) considers how these principles and practices could be applied within mainstream schools, using parents as the additional personnel.

In a chapter on 'Organisation of classroom and school' Wolfendale (1987) lists a number of 'pedagogic advantges' in extending RM to mainstream schools. In terms of the specific contribution that parents in the classroom could make, it would be part of collective responsibility and teamwork to negotiate with parents as to what they could offer, such as:

1 working with groups on reading, language, maths, other curriculum workshops;
2 acting as an identified 'helper' as in the RM model;
3 providing one-to-one assistance on an individual teaching programme for a child whose statement of needs prescribes clear teaching and learning objectives.

Behavioural programmes and instructional techniques (Jewell and Feiler, 1985), by virtue of the clarity of task analysis and other specifications within the methodology, lend themselves to the inclusion of parents. The collection of baseline data from observation can be undertaken by them in class and/or at home, utilising the various recording formats that are available (Westmacott and Cameron, 1981; Newson and Hipgrave, 1982).

Parents' assessment of their child at home could complement school-based assessment and would be in keeping with the Warnock Report model of stages of assessment which specifies their involvement. This model incorporates continuous record-keeping, a process in which parents play a part by virtue of their own periodic written assessments, for instance, the production of 'parental profiles' using broad or more structured guidelines (Wolfendale, 1986a).

With particular reference to behaviour difficulties and behaviour management, the parental presence in schools has been conspicuously absent, except in crisis situations, often at the point of suspension or exclusion of a particular child. Although there has been considerable research and intervention into home-based behaviour management in which parents have been supported by professionals (for a review see Topping, 1986, Ch 8), there is far less reported work on parents and teachers working together on school and/or home-focused programmes.

Utilising a positive rather than a negative set of premises, Wolfendale (1986b) proposed a whole-school approach to involving parents in behaviour management. Adoption of this 'systems' model, within which four levels are postulated, would allow for the evolution of parent-teacher collaboration in the way of discussion, in-service training, skills analysis, the design and implementation of behaviour-change programmes in school and/or at home. Integral features of this joint approach to intervening, which rests on a 'simple' rationale of parental rights to be involved with their children's education and their responsibilities for their well-being, are: sharing and listing concerns; assessment at school and at home; agreement as to 'who will do what, when, where, how'; and review. The view is put forward that a pre-requisite for an effective policy on parental involvement in behaviour management is for a school to have an existing, active, overall policy on parental involvement.

Emphasis in this section has been on the techniques and means by which parents can be involved. Within the concept of the 'open classroom', schools would need to develop the appropriate forums at which teachers, parents, support staff can exchange information, plan, review progress and evaluate outcomes. The traditional parents' open evening is being reviewed in some quarters, as its limitations are acknowledged. The Hargreaves Report (1984) suggests that a tutor group might be an effective alternative. Other organisational frameworks could be class meetings for primary schools and parent conferences (Lombana, 1983).

The open classroom: promise and pitfalls in involving parents

The initiatives described in this chapter are a reflection of profound changes in British education. Many more teachers are expressing positive views about working with parents, as periodic surveys on in-service courses carried out by Wolfendale since 1983 have attested. An increasing number of parents have demonstrated their desire for closer home-school links by their voluntary and willing participation. The rationale for these ventures ranges from the purely pragmatic and expedient, to the political, the ecological and social, and the pedagogic. 'Parent power' has been taken up enthusiastically in various quarters, including politicians of all parties, who see their promises to give parents more say in education as a potential vote winner. The teaching unions have given parental participation in education qualified endorsement, though they have reservations over the use of parents in the classroom as 'aides'.

As the potential and the parameters are explored, so a number of issues are uncovered, some of which can be resolved, since the nature of innovation is defined in part by problems and their attempted resolution. Other issues, that is to say, limitations upon extensive parental involvement may be endemic to the nature of systems and power-holding and may be less amenable to resolution.

In general terms, a number of legitimate charges could be made which need to be seriously considered by even the most ardently committed exponent of parental involvement. Within an area which is quite novel in British education, that is, direct face-to-face communication between teachers and parents on a regular basis, there are bound to be some unexpected, unforeseen concomitants of this dialogue, that challenge existing perceptions of role, power, professionalism, even the nature of democracy itself. Some of these are listed below in the form of assertions:

i to expect participation by parents amounts to an imposition upon their time;
ii parental involvement in curriculum and school activities amounts to an erosion of paid professional duties;
iii parental involvement leads to diffusion and confusion over role;
iv parental involvement could create a momentum that cannot be realistically sustained by all parties;
v we cannot be certain that programme outcomes can be ascribed to the involvement of parents;
vi 'meddling' with family life is intrusive and unethical.

(Wolfendale, 1985)

Some of these issues relate specifically to the broader context of home-school links, whilst others have direct relevance to the presence of parents in the classroom. These headings provide a summary of what ought to be fundamental considerations in setting up and maintaining parental participation programmes.

Home-school links

The question of involvement versus partnership is often raised. The phrase 'parents as partners' has frequently been used more as a slogan than as a basic premise which defines a working relationship between parents and professionals. The nature of 'partnership' as an ideal, an aspiration, rather than a state which can be attained, still remains an academic issue rather than one that has been actively pursued in practice. Partnership with parents has been presented as a model which is seen to be workable in practice, provided a number of prerequisites and caveats are acknowledged (Wolfendale, 1983; Lombana, 1983). There are implications in partnership, as well as in involvement models, for the re-definition and re-alignment of the power base. There is a need to reconcile the realities of human power-play and vested, institutionalised power with the abstract niceties of democratically opening up the educational process to parents and other citizens. Beattie (1985) tackles these issues within broad considerations of political and social change. He raises questions about the dichotomy between the role of government and the devolution of decision-making to local groups whose rights to participate in these processes they regard as unassailable.

Parents' rights to access into education are seen by some writers to extend legitimately into all aspects of service delivery and child services. Gliedman and Roth (1981) assert that parents should oversee, even orchestrate, the services that professionals provide for their children. This would make for an accountability far more direct than having lay citizens as councillors on local education, health, or social services committees. McConkey (1986) expresses the view that the active and central involvement of parents in problem definition and decision-making provides a surer foundation for effective service provision. Elsewhere he pursues these ideals (McConkey, 1985) and translates them into practical suggestions for effective co-operative working.

Parents in the classroom

A number of other contributors to this volume provide a blueprint for involving parents in classrooms. By examining some of the conditions and requisites for effective grouping, management, classroom arrangements, curriculum applications, deployment of personnel, they are also setting out the pre-conditions for successfully involving parents.

There are, however, a number of planning considerations which are unique to the involvement of parents. The careful incorporation of these into a set of ground rules ought to do much to maximise parental participation, whilst at the same time reducing misunderstanding and role conflict (for examples, see the specifications put forward in 'Topping and Wolfendale, 1985, and Topping, 1986).

Irrespective of the focus of the particular initiative – classroom, home or both – a number of features need to be explored, resolved, agreed, such as

- the terms and conditions of the parental input;
- the nature of the skills and expertise offered by parents in a complementary match with those of teachers;
- the amount of time that parents can realistically offer and the amount of time teachers likewise need to invest;
- what form reviews will take.

Initial planning will include negotiating along these lines and discussion as to the methods of programme maintenance that are likely to prove most effective in the given circumstances. In particular, clarification of role and skills matching are seen as fundamental to these operations.

The notion of parents as 'aides' or 'para-professionals' generates emotion in some quarters. Fears are expressed of the likely erosion of teachers' professionalism, the possible reduction of their sacrosanct position in the classroom, the threat to their conditions of service and so on. Fears from a parental perspective may be to do with being used just to provide an extra pair of hands, as a dogsbody (see Chapter 1).

There are wider political implications in the deployment of volunteer parents in class and in schools at a time of economic retraction and resource reduction. Stierer found from his survey (1985) that practical considerations had governed the increasing use of parent volunteers – yet many teachers discovered that considerable educational benefits derived from the practice. Just as well, some would argue. Fortunately the rationales for involving parents are robust and proven enough to silence the cynics on this point.

Another finding by Stierer accords with another piece of evidence about the use of para-professionals. McKenzie and Hook (1986) reported that 23 resource teachers who worked with para-professionals favoured expanding the skills of the para-professionals to enable them to conduct more specialised and complex tasks. The teachers in Stierer's survey expressed the need for more training for themselves to help them deal effectively with parent helpers and to have more time to co-ordinate and supervise this work.

The introductory chapter to this book sketches out the components of the 'organic classroom'. It is terrain characterised by openness to the community, accessible by parents. The co-editors say intervention should be based in the natural contexts in which we expect learning to occur. We can more confidently define the classroom as a natural context for learning if we fully acknowledge the centrality of the parents' role as educators at home and its valid extension into school.

Unlike those of us whose schooldays are long past, perhaps the children of the future will accept it as natural for home and school to be aligned and working co-operatively on their behalf.

References

Beattie, N. (1985) *Professional Parents* Lewes: Falmer Press.
Berger, E. (1983) *Beyond the classroom, parents as partners in education* London: C. V. Mosby Co.
Bloom, B. (1983) *All our Children Learning* New York: McGraw Hill.
Branston, P. and Provis, M. (1986) *Children and Parents Enjoy Reading* London: Hodder and Stoughton.
Bronfenbrenner, U. (1979) *The Ecology of Human Development: Experiments by Nature and Design* Camb, Mass: Harvard University Press.
Cameron, R. J. (ed) (1986) *Portage parents and professionals: helping families with special needs* Windsor: NFER/Nelson.
Cleave, S., Jowett, S. and Bate, M. (1982) *And so to school: a study of continuity from pre-school to infant school* Windsor: NFER/Nelson.
Copley, M., Bishop, M. and Porter, J. (eds) (1986) *Portage: more than a teaching programme* Windsor: NFER/Nelson.
Cyster, R., Clift, P. S. and Battle, S. (1979) *Parental involvement in primary schools* Windsor: NFER/Nelson.
DES (1967) *Children and their Primary Schools* London: HMSO (The Plowden Report).
DES (1978) *Primary Education in England* HMI Report, London: HMSO.
DES (1978) *Special Educational Needs* London: HMSO (The Warnock Report).
Farrell, P. (ed) (1985) *EDY: its impact on staff training in mental handicap* Manchester: Manchester University Press.
Gliedman, J. and Roth, W. (1981) 'Parents and professionals' in W. Swann (ed) *The Practice of Special Education* Oxford: Basil Blackwell and Open University Press.
Griffiths, A. and Hamilton, D. (1984) *Parent, teacher, child* London: Methuen.

Griffiths, A. and Edmonds, T. (1987) *Report on the Calderdale preschool parent book project* Calderdale Education Department, School Psychological Service.

Hannon, P., Jackson, A. and Weinberger, J. (1986) 'Parents' and teachers' strategies in hearing young children read' in *Research Papers in Education*, 1, March.

ILEA (1984) *Improving Secondary Schools* London: ILEA (The Hargreaves Report).

Jewell, T. and Feiler, A. (1985) 'A review of behaviourist teaching approaches in the UK' in *Early Child Development and Care*, 20, 1.

Kemp, M. (1985) 'Parents as teachers of literacy' in M. Clark (ed) *New Directions in the Study of Reading* Lewes: Falmer Press.

Kogan, M. (1985) 'Parents and school governing bodies' in C. Cullingford (ed) *Parents, Teachers and Schools* London: Robert Royce.

Lombana, J. (1983) *Home-school partnership: guidelines and strategies for educators* London: Grune and Stratton.

Long, R. (1986) *Developing parental involvement in primary schools* Basingstoke: Macmillan Education.

McConkey, R. (1985) *Working with parents: a practical guide for teachers and therapists* London: Croom Helm.

McConkey, R. (1986) 'Service based research' in J. Harris (ed) *Child Psychology in action, linking research and practice* London: Croom Helm.

McKenzie, R. and Hook, C. (1986) 'Use of paraprofessionals in the resource room' in *Exceptional Children* 53, 1, 41–45.

Newson, E. and Hipgrave, T. (1982) *Getting through to your handicapped child* Cambridge: Cambridge University Press.

National Confederation of Parent-Teacher Associations (1986) *Parents – partners in a shared task of education, a report* 43 Stonebridge Road, Northfleet, Gravesend, DA11 9DS, October.

Paired Reading Project *Paired Reading Bulletin* No 1, Spring; No 2, Spring 1986. Kirklees Psychological Service, Oldgate House, Huddersfield, West Yorkshire, HD1 6QW.

Peters, M. (1985) *Spelling Caught or Taught: a new look* London: Routledge and Kegan Paul.

Pugh, G. (1981) *Parents as partners* London: National Children's Bureau.

Raybould, E. and Solity, J. (1985) 'Teaching with precision' in C. Smith (ed) *New Directions in Remedial Education* Lewes: Falmer Press and The National Association for Remedial Education.

Rennie, J. (ed) (1985) *British Community Primary Schools* Lewes: Falmer Press.

Stierer, B. (1985) 'School reading volunteers: results of a postal survey of primary school headteachers in England' in *Journal Research in Reading* 3, 1, 21–31.

Sturmey, P. and Crisp, A. G. (1986) 'Portage guide to early education: a review of research' in *Educational Psychology* 6, 2, 139–157.

Thomas, G. (1985) 'Room management in mainstream education' in *Educational Research* 27, 3, 186–193.

Thomas, G. (1986) 'Integrating personnel in order to integrate children' in *Support for Learning* 1, 1, 19–26.

Tizard, B. and Hughes, M. (1984) *Young Children Learning* London: Fontana.

Topping, K. and Wolfendale, S. (eds) (1985) *Parental involvement in children's reading* London: Croom Helm.

Topping, K. (1986) *Parents as Educators* London: Croom Helm.

Wells, G. (1984) *Language Development in the Preschool Years* Cambridge: Cambridge University Press.

Westmacott, E. V. S. and Cameron, R. J. (1981) *Behaviour Can Change* Basingstoke: Globe.

Wheldall, K. and Mettem, R. (1985) 'Behavioural peer tutoring: training 16-year-old tutors to employ the "pause, prompt, and praise" method with 12-year-old remedial readers' in *Educational Psychology* 5, 1.

Widlake, P. and McCleod, F. (1984) *Raising Standards* Coventry Community Development Centre.

Widlake, P. (1986) *Reducing educational disadvantage* Milton Keynes: Open University Press.

Wolfendale, S. (1983) *Parental Participation in Children's Development and Education* London: Gordon and Breach Science Publishers.

Wolfendale, S. (1985) 'Parental involvement in children's development and education: an overview' in *Educational and Child Psychology* 2, 1.

Wolfendale, S. and Gregory, E. (1985) *Involving parents in reading, a guide for in-service training* Reading and Language Development Centre, Nene College, Northampton.

Wolfendale, S. (1986a) 'Parental contribution to Section 5 (Education Act 1981) assessment procedures' in *Early Child Development and Care* 24, 219–293.

Wolfendale, S. (1986b) 'Involving parents in behaviour management: a whole-school approach' in *Support for Learning*, 1, 4, November.

Wolfendale, S. and Bryans, T. (1986) *Word Play* Stafford: National Association for Remedial Education.

Wolfendale, S. (1987) *Primary Schools and Special Needs: Policy, planning and provision* London: Cassell.

Woolgar, J. (1986) 'Learning how to "count us in" ' in *Special Education* 13, 4, December.

13 The social context of special needs in classrooms

Andrew Pollard

In this chapter I attempt to analyse some of the social properties of the classrooms and schools in which teachers work with children who are deemed to have special educational needs. The chapter is particularly concerned with the ways in which the concept of 'special educational needs' is constituted and enacted through 'ordinary' classroom life in primary schools.

Introduction

Critics of policy, provision and practice in special education often point out that it is a far more problematic area than is often supposed. One aspect of this is the question of definition, which work that derives insights from sociological studies of deviance, power, knowledge and social structures has done much to highlight. For instance, Squibb (1981) suggested that periodic changes in the numbers of children officially categorised as handicapped reflect the diagnostic and remedial provision which is available, rather than any absolute changes in need. Further, when considering the high incidence of special needs among children from less advantaged circumstances – backgrounds of poverty, unemployment, over-crowding or family instability – he concluded that 'the concept of the special child can be seen in terms of low status within the educational hierarchy'. Further, he suggested the existence of an 'ideology which legitimates the hierarchy' and which contains 'knowledge, beliefs and values which "explain" the position of those at the bottom' (Squibb, 1981, 50).

Bogdan and Kugelmass (1984) have argued that important elements of this explanatory ideology are contained within the 'unconscious assumptions of the field's practitioners'. These can be expressed as follows:

- special educational needs are produced by the problems and conditions of individuals;
- special educational needs can be identified objectively;
- special educational provision can be improved by the development of more efficient assessment and intervention procedures.

Such unconscious assumptions have been greatly influenced by medical and psychological orthodoxies and are well established. As Tomlinson (1982) implies, this confidence may be justified in the case of normative categories of handicap – such as deafness, blindness, speech defects and physical and mental disability – but one is on far weaker ground in the case of non-normative categories such as 'slow-learning', 'disruptive' or 'maladjusted'. In such cases, the application of medical/psychological orthodoxies produces a clinical concept of 'special educational needs' rather than recognising the social factors which influence the definition of categories. In other words, they underplay both the extent to which individual actions are a response to circumstances and the ways in which perceptions and knowledge, for instance, of 'need', 'normality' and 'deficiency', reflect wider social ideologies. Compounding this, they gloss the problems in the assessment of 'need' which lead to policies, adopted relatively unproblematically, for improving the technical operation of the system of remediation.[1]

The ecological approach advocated in this volume represents an important development in the analysis of special educational needs in that it provides a direct challenge to the individualisation of the medical and psychological paradigms. However, I have some reservations about some varieties of the approach (and I will return to these towards the end of the chapter). For this reason the approach to classroom analysis on which I want to draw in this chapter is not strictly 'ecological'. In fact, it has been developed in the context of the sociological debate about macro/micro relations and is based on symbolic interactionism. It derives from work on the concept of 'coping strategy' (Woods, 1977; Hargreaves, 1978), the idea that individuals act meaningfully in situations on the basis of their personal perspectives and perceptions of the situations they face. The concept thus embraces both ideas of individual autonomy and more deterministic ideas concerning the constraints of material circumstances and social structures. In so doing it explores the possibility of bridging micro and macro issues (Pollard, 1982).

Children with special educational needs in ordinary classrooms

In the Warnock Report it was established that one in five children had special educational needs at some point in their school careers. Junior school teachers' concern about this proportion of children has been documented in a survey by Croll and Moses (1985), which is important because of its empirical grounding.[2]

The teachers in the Croll and Moses' study described the nature of the special educational needs which they ascribed to the children in their classes. About four-fifths were identified as having 'learning difficulties', of which the most common were concerned with reading. Children with 'behaviour problems' were the next largest category (two-fifths), and many of these children also had learning difficulties. This was also the case for the smaller proportion of children who were identified as having medical problems. Such findings are consistent with the judgments made in the Warnock Report and convey, very clearly, the pervasiveness of the conception of children with special educational needs in ordinary schools. We can note, however, that the vast majority of children deemed to have special needs are categorised in non-normative ways (they have 'learning difficulties' or 'behaviour problems'). The rather more 'objective' normative categories which are associated with mental/physical disability were applied to only 4.4% of children.

Where a policy of integration is implemented children with special needs find themselves in classrooms with large numbers of other children (DES statistics indicate a mean class-size in primary schools of 25.2 for January, 1985). However, in the Croll and Moses study it was shown that, in terms of the ways in which activities were organised in class and in terms of the basic curriculum content which was offered, children identified as having special educational needs were treated in much the same ways as other children. To their credit, teachers did manage to spend rather more individual time with children who were felt to have special needs, although, because of overall class-sizes, this remained a very small part of each individual child's experience. The most distinctive feature of the activity of children with special educational needs concerned the extent of their distraction from work and, in particular, distraction which did not involve interaction with other children. Croll and

Moses thus suggest that there is a distinctive set of behavioural characteristics among children with learning difficulties. As they put it:

> This involves lower levels of engagement in work, particularly work directly on a curriculum task, high levels of fidgeting and much more time than other children spent on their own, distracted from work.
>
> (Croll and Moses, 1985, 133)

Croll and Moses also identified considerable variation between teachers in the extent to which they perceived special educational needs. This variation was partly attributed to differences in the characteristics of the children but it was also related to 'differences in the way that different teachers regard special educational needs'. In other words, an important part of the variation was attributable to the non-normative nature of many significant categories of special educational need and, thus, to the possibility of situational differences in perception.

This brings us to the main concerns of the chapter. How do classroom contexts relate to special educational needs? What affects the initial process whereby children are identified as having special educational needs? What lies behind Squibb's (1981, 48) observation that identification starts in 'normal schools where teachers, for a variety of reasons, have sought to have the child diagnosed as special and removed from the class'?

We must start by analysing the 'normal' conditions of classrooms and, since teachers are particularly important in this process, I will do this through discussion of what I take to be three major teacher concerns – relationships, classroom order and learning.

Classroom relationships

An immediate question which might be asked is, 'Why are the relationships which are developed between teachers and the children in their classes so often regarded by teachers as being of paramount importance?' There are many possible reasons for this.

First, relationships are a central component in the dominant child-centred ideology of primary schooling. This set of perspectives lays great store by the mutual respect of teacher and child and the positive supportive working environment which it is hoped will result. Second, relationships are important because it is suggested that children learn best when they feel secure, when they trust their teacher and when they both understand and accept the class 'rules' and the 'standards' which are expected of them. In such circumstances, it is thought, children are more likely to be open, receptive and well-motivated. A third reason for teachers' believing relationships to be important is that the development of close relationships in class can provide a sense of personal fulfilment and pleasure. A good relationship rewards both the teacher's and the children's sense of self. Fourth comes the issue of class control, for there is little doubt that, even for experienced teachers, control and discipline are issues which every teacher must bear in mind at all times. Classroom relationships are thus very important both for those who teach and for those who learn in primary schools.

My own work on the analysis of relationships began by describing the subjective perceptions of teachers and children regarding their classroom interaction (Pollard, 1985). The ways in which they defined classroom situations and their particular concerns and interests-at-hand in classrooms were considered. It was proposed that the most important interest for both teachers and children is their 'self' – with various facets of it being prominent, such as maintaining self-esteem, controlling workloads, avoiding stress and obtaining enjoyment. It was further suggested that children and teachers have the power to make coping with classroom life very difficult for one another. The teacher has a great deal of formal power to initiate events and to evaluate the children, but, on the other hand the children easily outnumber the teacher and can, if they so wish, pose considerable discipline problems.

In fact, conflict in primary-school classrooms is rare and this draws attention to the extensive processes of negotiation which take place between teachers and children. At the start of each school year, or, during an initial period with a new teacher or student-teacher, both teachers and children usually approach each other with considerable care. There is a 'process of establishment' (Ball, 1980) in which they interpret and learn more about the aims, needs, moods, expectations and abilities of each other. This normally results in the negotiation of what can be called a 'working consensus', that is, a mutual acceptance of the ways in which the class will operate and of the parameters of normal and 'acceptable' behaviour. It is an agreement in which the children recognise the legitimacy of the teacher's power when it is used 'fairly'. Bearing in mind the teacher's and children's concern with 'self', the essence of the working consensus can also be seen as a mutual exchange of dignity and it is this, I would argue, which is the central factor leading to the establishment of a positive classroom climate and a 'good relationship'. In simple terms, a working consensus can arise only when there is a level of empathic understanding by teachers and children of the needs of one another. It represents a tacit agreement by each to co-operate in the teaching and learning processes and not to threaten the interests of the other.

A working consensus has considerable consequences because of the understandings, rules, parameters and routines about behaviour, standards of work, noise levels, inter-personal relations, etc, which follow from it. By legitimising certain types of teacher and child action and by defining others as being outside the bounds of shared understanding, a working consensus can be seen as providing a type of social morality for a classroom. It yields a type of classroom culture which is fully understood only by those who are 'members'. Other very important products of this process are the definitions of 'normality' which are socially constructed.

However, various types and degrees of membership in classroom culture and participation in negotiation about understandings are possible – as can be illustrated in the case of classroom order and discipline.

Classroom order, children's perspectives and strategies

In the preceding discussion I have treated 'children' as if they are a homogeneous group. Such an assumption is unjustified and the degree to which individual children indentify with and participate in classroom culture is likely to vary considerably. At the same time, it is possible to identify some patterns in interaction which are associated with peer-group cultures and with the children's own, informal social structures and relationships.

In a case study of eighty eleven year-olds and their relationships and perspectives I suggested that, for analytical purposes, three types of group could be identified – 'goodies', 'jokers' and 'gangs' (Pollard, 1984).

Goodies tend to be conformist and to be concerned to avoid any risk of stress and threat to their dignity. Many of these children seem relatively quiet and withdrawn in classroom interaction. They tend to be passive – for instance, having a laugh only when it is 'safe' because a teacher has initiated it. Many teachers find such children a little dull and other children are also typically somewhat deprecating.

'Joker' children are much more active. Typically, they are able and articulate children who seem to have much more self-confidence than goodies. Such children may be relatively successful academically and be highly involved in extra-curricular activities. The 'jokers' whom I studied were more socially competent than most other children and could interpret a classroom situation rapidly and accurately. For instance, their awareness of the importance of teacher mood and of the indicators by which it could be inferred from moment to moment were particularly impressive. In my study I found that such children comprised the majority of each class and that they were well regarded by teachers and by most other children. Teachers enjoyed teaching them because they could trust and relate to them in three important ways. First, joker children were able to provide a high quality of work in terms of educational products. Such capacities could offer teachers confirmation that their professional efforts were worthwhile. Second, such children were good company for a teacher. They could participate intelligently in a discussion, 'get' a joke, and generally acted as 'consociates' for teachers – and thus as a medium of personal involvement and as a source of personal fulfilment. Finally, such children could be trusted behaviourally because, although they liked to 'have a bit of fun' they 'knew the limits'. Such children were particularly active in the negotiation of a working consensus and, because of this commitment and their social competence, they were able to make accurate judgments about the appropriateness of behaviour.

Gang group members were less favourably disposed towards school. They had lower levels of academic achievement and were more disposed to engage in deviant behaviour of the sort that would challenge teachers and threaten their interests. In fact, on occasions such 'winding up the teacher' was engaged in consciously and actively. Most gang group members were concerned to be seen to be 'tough' and able to stand up for themselves. They tended to come from working-class families and to have less favourable attitudes to the value of education than most other children. Overall, children in gang groups could be seen as developing a degree of independence through alternative value systems which explicitly devalued the school life in which many of them were deemed relative failures.

If one can risk generalising from this analysis, it is apparent that, from the point of view of teachers' vital concerns with classroom order and with discipline, whilst good group children tend to pose few problems and joker group children are generally amenable to negotiation and request, gang group children are likely to present more significant difficulties. A working consensus and the quality of relationships which are regarded as being so important in classrooms cannot thus be entirely taken for granted. They have to be maintained and sustained against the ever-present threat of a breakdown in classroom order. I would suggest that this is a central concern of 'normal' classroom life, both for teachers, in assessing and acting to maintain structured and ordered activities, and for children, in monitoring such efforts, working within them, but also in 'having a laugh' when appropriate.

Learning

Learning is a third major concern of teachers and children in most classrooms and, again, considering the way it is promoted and experienced may help in analysing the nature and social construction of 'special educational needs' in ordinary schools.

Learning is of enormous consequence for teachers and children. Teachers' effectiveness in developing the children's knowledge, concepts, skills and attitudes is taken as an index of their competence. Expectations impinge on teachers from parents, the media, colleagues, advisers, HMI and, increasingly, from the government. The teacher's role and the accountability of individual teachers to that role are becoming contractually defined and open to appraisal. That children should learn is thus a source of pressure on teachers. However, for a great number of teachers it is also a deeply internalised commitment, without which little fulfilment from the job could be derived. It is thus doubly significant. For children, also, the curriculum defines learning tasks and sets targets against which they can expect to be assessed. Of course, assessment of one sort or another has always been an ever-present aspect of school life for pupils and the curriculum represents the official terrain over which they must develop and demonstrate their competence. If they are successful, they are likely to derive considerable personal satisfaction and develop a positive self-image.

Potentially, then, there is no difficulty. Each major party to the interaction can succeed by facilitating the success of the other – the idealistic aspiration which has inspired many teachers. Unfortunately, there is a growing body of evidence which suggests that 'normal' classroom life is somewhat different. Class sizes ensure that teachers are working with what Jackson (1968) graphically described as 'crowds', and resources of space, materials and personnel are strictly limited. Such difficulties may also be aggravated by the degree of individualisation which is employed in the organisation of some primary classrooms. In such circumstances the commitment to maximise the quality of the learning experiences of each child can easily and understandably become subverted by a concern to 'cope' with the class more pragmatically. The result seems to be a dependence on the 'basic' curriculum of reading, writing and mathematics, taught with a heavy reliance on routine activities. Among the sources of evidence which support this type of analysis are HMI's Primary Survey (DES, 1978), Bassey's questionnaire survey of 900 teachers (1978), Barker-Lunn's study of junior school classes (1984), and the Oracle study based on the systematic observation of 58 classes (Galton, Simon and Croll, 1980). This last is significant, too, in documenting the rare appearance of questions with a high level of intellectual challenge. This finding can be set alongside that of Bennett *et al* (1984), who, in a study of carefully selected 'good' infant classes, found that a large number of tasks in mathematics and language work were still poorly matched to the existing level of the children's understanding.

The overall impression from such work is that the curriculum is much narrower than might be expected, that there is a considerable amount of routine work in primary classrooms and that the children work and gain their classroom experience, for the most part, under tight forms of teacher control. To state this is not, in any way, to decry the efforts of the teachers but these issues have to be faced if we are to understand some very important features of many 'normal' primary school classrooms.

The responses of children will obviously vary, but I have suggested that two common strategies are 'evasion' and 'drifting'

(Pollard, 1985). Two examples of eleven-year-olds will illustrate these strategies. First, Robert explains with considerable clarity the basic limits to evasion:

If we have to, I do it – that's if we *have* to. If we don't have to, we don't have to, and I don't. It's as simple as that.

Second, Jonathan explains his perspective:

Well, I don't mind doing the work, that's if I can, but mostly it's all right. Like, I like doing maths 'n that because we use cards and once you've got the hang of them you can do them easy. I just do what the teacher wants really. Writing stories is OK 'cos all you've got to do is a few lines.

In my experience it is not at all uncommon to find children who report feeling 'bored' in school. However, the meaning of 'being bored' is by no means clear and requires further study. It can relate to the experience of work that is difficult or too easy. More importantly, it may relate to motivation and to the suitability of the curriculum. In any event, for many children the experience of what they term 'getting bored' is commonplace in school. In my study of children's perspectives I found that this was a particular concern of 'gang' group children. For instance, here is Patrick:

You sort of give up because you know you can't do it – you just sit there getting bored stiff – you try to do it, get about halfway and then just sit there . . . you just sit there and you feel right sorry for yourself.

Even more graphic was Andrew's comment:

Being bored is being unhappy; you get miserable like when Mrs Linford's talking and you start fidgeting and you get bored and start throwing things about and then you get into trouble. They just stand talking. They talk too much.

Here, quite clearly in my view, we find the children who were described by Croll and Moses (1986) as having a distinctive behaviour set – fidgeting, distracted, disengaged from work activities – children who are often characterised as having 'special needs'.

'Normal' classrooms and special educational needs

I have described three important features of what I take to be normal life in primary school classrooms – establishing relationships, maintaining classroom order and learning. These are worthy and necessary priorities for teachers. However, a problem may arise if one considers the way different children fare in terms of such issues. I would suggest that whilst 'good' children are seen as a mixed blessing by many teachers – reliable but not very stimulating to work with, 'joker' children are seen as almost unqualified assets. Typically, they are at the centre of the development of good relationships, they know and 'keep within the limits' regarding behaviour and they can produce high-quality work. 'Gang' group children are, unfortunately, viewed less positively in each dimension. They are often 'difficult' to relate to, they often 'push things too far' and their work is typically not of a high standard.

However, most teachers are caring people, and, while fully aware that the risk of labelling and stereotyping exists, many seek to do their very best for the children for whom they are responsible. This may well include identifying children who have 'special educational needs', of whom several may reasonably be expected in any class of thirty – if Warnock estimates are accepted. From the work of Croll and Moses we know that large numbers of such children are seen as having learning and/or behavioural difficulties. We know furthermore that, since the 1981 Act, the newly institutionalised and legally enshrined system of assessment for special educational needs will enable the exact nature of such common individual problems to be 'identified' so that action can be taken on behalf of the child.

But what is happening here? Some children – the deaf, blind, physically or mentally handicapped – have needs that may well require particular forms of diagnosis and provision, but the fact remains that the very large number of children who are at present diagnosed as having special educational needs may tell us more about the consistent failure of normal classroom life to provide for the dignity and fulfilment of each child than about the individuals themselves. Indeed, in some circumstances it may be an understandable, a 'normal', reaction to act in ways which render one 'special'.

To explain such problems we have to return, initially, to analyses of the everyday conditions of classroom life and to the struggles of

teachers and children to cope with them. We could do this through a
more direct focus on 'ecological' models.

The social context of 'ecology'

Following the thrust of my argument above, the increasing interest
in ecological analyses of classrooms is important and, in some ways,
complements symbolic interactionist studies. As an example we can
take the work of Doyle (1977, 1978, 1979, 1980), which is often cited
as the most detailed attempt to apply ecological analysis to classrooms.

For Doyle, classrooms are far more complex than analyses have
hitherto suggested. They are seen as information-processing
environments in which teachers and children, each with limited
capacities for processing such information, must act and adapt.
Doyle has thus identified strategies which enable teachers to reduce
the complexity of the classroom environment (Doyle, 1977) and has
focused on 'understanding the situationally defined task of teaching
and the character of the environment in which that task is accomplished [which] enables a teacher to select activities, interpret events,
anticipate consequences, and monitor a complex system with
maximum efficiency' (Doyle, 1979, 30). 'Students' too, are seen to
'manage behaviour and academic task structures' in ways which
must be considered, if their motivation is to be understood (Doyle,
1978).

In drawing attention to the complexity of classroom situations in
innovative ways, Doyle's analysis is a valuable contribution to the
field. However, from the point of view of recent developments in
sociology, it can be criticised on at least two major counts.

First, it fails to take account of the wider social context within which
classrooms and schools are located. For instance, the existence of
structural constraint and pressure in the form of policies, resources
and procedures for accountability is not discussed; nor is the key influence of culture, history and ideology in the formation of teacher's
interpretive knowledge considered. Thus, the advance over psychological and medical models of special educational need, which ecological analyses provide in terms of appreciating the effects of
immediate classroom contexts, is not complemented by a further
attempt at contextualisation in societal terms (Barton and Tomlinson,

1981 and 1984). This omission from the analysis brings with it the risk that 'expert explanation' might simply move from a focus on the individual to a focus on the classroom and the characteristics of teachers. If this happened, it is possible that one deficit model would simply be replaced by another. This is a particular danger at a time when teachers are so often the subject of public criticism.

The second area in which sociologists might criticise ecological work and be able to contribute towards greater understanding in this area concerns the way individuals are conceptualised. There are several complementary developments here. For instance, there are new approaches to child development in terms of recognition of the importance of interpretive activity (see, for example, Desforges *et al*, 1984) and through 'constructionist' approaches to the psychology of learning. However, such approaches do not always recognise the 'socialness' of the individual – the fact that each person has a biography, and draws on particular cultural resources, knowledge and perspectives which are applied to interpret their actions and the actions of others in social situations. Interpretation, in other words, cannot simply be seen in situational terms. We also need to consider the biographical career of individuals over time in socio-economic, cultural and experiential terms. The recent work of sociologists such as Sikes, Measor and Woods (1985), Nias (forthcoming) and Ball and Goodson (1985) is very helpful here in considering the careers and biography of teachers. Substantial research on children remains to be done.

This brief consideration of the importance, but also the limits, of ecological approaches to classroom life brings me back to the symbolic interactionist concept of coping strategy and the question of links between micro and macro levels of analysis. In simple terms, it can be suggested that structural factors ultimately determine what has to be coped with: class sizes, the curriculum, resources, legal requirements. But only individuals can express what 'to cope' means to them – what types and levels of satisfaction, of self interests and concerns are acceptable.

A full analysis of special educational needs in ordinary classrooms would have to cast its net wide. To some extent the conceptualisation of the 'special needs' of a child can be seen as a way for a teacher to cope with that child in the particular situation, just as the behaviour of each child can be seen as a way of coping with those same ecological circumstances. But this is not enough. We also need to contextualise the situation by highlighting the wider, macro factors which structure it, and to develop a deeper understanding of teachers and children as individuals. 'Special educational needs' cannot be seen as an objective term. It is a product of its era, of its circumstances and of the people who enact it together. Nevertheless, to trace its constitution in classrooms is an important and necessary beginning.

Notes

I would like to thank the editors and Alvin Jeffs of Bristol Polytechnic for their constructive comments on this chapter.

1 With such arguments in mind, Barton and Tomlinson (1984) suggest that a sociological analysis of the social interests which lie behind the history of legislation and current practice in provision for special educational needs could help to de-mystify the issues and reveal links between macro and micro levels of social analysis. If this could be done, the emphasis on individual deficits and on individual pathologies could be contested and perhaps replaced by an understanding of the role of power, interests and ideologies in influencing taken-for-granted knowledge and social practices. My argument is sympathetic to this position, although the analysis here is more directly concerned with social contexts at the classroom level.

2 Croll and Moses provided quantitative descriptions derived from the systematic observation of 34 classrooms and from interviews with 428 teachers.

References

Ball, S. J. (1980) 'Initial encounters in the classroom and the process of establishment' in P. Woods (ed) *Pupil Strategies* London: Croom Helm.

Ball, S. J. and Goodson, I. (1985) *Teacher's Lives and Careers* Lewes: Falmer Press.

Barker-Lunn, J. (1984) 'Junior school teachers: their methods and practices' in *Educational Research*, 27, 3, 178–188.

Barton, L. and Tomlinson, S. (eds) (1981) *Special Education: Policy: Practices and Social Issues* London: Harper and Row.

Barton, L. and Tomlinson, S. (eds) (1984) *Special Education and Social Interests* London: Croom Helm.

Bassey, M. (1978) *900 Primary Teachers* Slough: NFER.

Bennett, N., Desforges, C., Cockburn, A. and Wilkinson, B. (1984) *The Quality of Pupil Learning Experiences* London: Lawrence Erlbaum.

Bogdan and Kugelmass (1984) 'Case studies of mainstreaming: a symbolic interactionist approach to special schooling' in L. Barton and S. Tomlinson (eds) *Special Education and Social Interests* London: Croom Helm.

Croll, P. and Moses, D. (1985) *One in Five* London: Routledge and Kegan Paul.

Department of Education and Science (1978) *Primary Education in England* London: HMSO.

Department of Education and Science (1978) *Special Educational Needs* London: HMSO. (The Warnock Report)

Desforges, C. *et al* (1984) 'Understanding classroom learning: an ecological approach' in C. Richards (ed) *The Study of Primary Education* Lewes: Falmer Press.

Doyle, W. (1977) 'Learning the classroom environment: an ecological analysis' in *Journal of Teacher Education*, 28, 6, 51–55.

Doyle, W. (1978) 'Student management of task structures in classrooms', paper given at the conference on Teacher and Pupil Strategies, St Hilda's College, Oxford.

Doyle, W. (1979) 'Making managerial decisions in the classroom' in D. L. Duke (ed) *Classroom Management* Chicago: University of Chicago.

Doyle, W. (1980) 'Student mediation responses in teacher effectiveness' North Texas State University, Texas: Denton.

Galton, M., Simon, B. and Croll, P. (1980) *Inside the Primary Classroom* London: Routledge and Kegan Paul.

Hargreaves, A. (1978) 'The significance of classroom coping strategies' in L. Barton and R. Meighan (eds) *Sociological Interpretations of Schooling and Classrooms* Driffield: Nafferton.

Nias, J. *Being and Becoming a Teacher* London: Methuen (forthcoming).

Pollard, A. (1982) 'A model of coping strategies' in *British Journal of Sociology of Education*, 3, 1, 19–37.

Pollard, A. (1984) 'Goodies, jokers and gangs' in M. Hammersley and P. Woods (eds) *Life in School* Milton Keyenes: Open University Press.

Pollard, A. (1985) *The Social World of the Primary School* London: Holt, Rinehart and Winston.

Sikes, P., Measor, L. and Woods, P. (1985) *Teachers' Careers* Lewes: Falmer Press.

Squibb, P. (1981) 'A theoretical structuralist approach to special education' in L. Barton and S. Tomlinson (eds) *Special Education Policy, Practices and Social Issues* London: Harper and Row.

Tomlinson, S. (1982) *A Sociology of Special Education* London: Routledge and Kegan Paul.

Woods, P. (1977) 'Teaching for survival' in P. Woods and M. Hammersley (eds) *School Experience* London: Croom Helm.

Conclusion

Probably at no time in this century has education for children who are experiencing difficulty taken a sharper turn. In contrast to the orientation of preceding decades, when the emphasis was on the separate education of those who couldn't or wouldn't fit, today's orientation is towards meeting all children's needs in mainstream classes.

Yet this change in orientation has not been matched by any concerted reappraisal of the methods of either the special sector or the mainstream. The message of this book is that a host of previously unformulated questions have to be addressed in taking the new orientation. Those questions are about the way in which the school as a whole, and the classteacher in particular, adapt practices and methods to accommodate and incorporate all children. Until now those practices and methods could evolve with scant regard for the education of those who were less successful; those children were assessed by experts, taught by specialists, or possibly removed altogether to be taught in a special school.

The new questions have to be answered at the level of the school: how might the school's policies affect the way in which all children are helped to be active participants and contributors to school life? How might parents play a fuller part in their children's education? And they have to be answered at classroom level. How are support services going to be incorporated into the classroom? How might grouping practices be adapted to encourage the meaningful participation of all children?

These new questions are not about the failings of individual children. Teaching strategies which depended on the assessment of such individual weaknesses have been shown to be ineffective. But, equally important, such strategies are simply not workable within the framework of the busy mainstream class. The new questions *are* about assimilating an entirely new attitude to learning and adjustment difficulties.

Special education must sometimes seem like a battlefield to observers: integrationists versus non-integrationists; behaviourists versus anti-behaviourists . . . Though we have touched on one or two of these issues we have tried to steer clear of rehearsing the arguments (important though they undoubtedly are) here. Uniting the varied contributions which comprise this book is a view of the child operating within a set of systems which are open to change. Sometimes this involves opening up areas which have for years been neglected – such as parental involvement; sometimes it involves reappraising classroom traditions, and sometimes it involves re-evaluating and reformulating ideas on wider whole-school issues, like the curriculum or the work of the support department.

A successful education for *all* children must be the keynote of our deliberations now. Our belief is that such a goal may be realised only through taking excursions into areas which have until recently been almost unexplored by those of us in 'special needs'.

Contributors

Anthony Feiler
Fieldwork Tutor
Department of Psychology
University College London

Ingrid Lunt
Course Tutor
Professional Training in Educational
Psychology
University of London Institute of
Education

Andrew Pollard
Reader in Primary Education
Department of Education
Bristol Polytechnic

Geof Sewell
Senior Teacher
Thirsk Comprehensive, North
Yorkshire

Jonathan Solity
Lecturer
Department of Education
University of Warwick

Gordon Stobart
Research Officer
University of London School
Examinations Board

Will Swann
Lecturer
School of Education
The Open University

Sarah Tann
Senior Lecturer
School of Education
Oxford Polytechnic

Gary Thomas
Senior Educational Psychologist and
Staff Tutor
London Boroughs of Enfield and
Barnet and University College
London

Geoff Trickey
Test Development Adviser
Psychological Corporation, Sidcup

Jane Weightman
Principal Researcher
Management and Organisation of
Secondary Schools Project
Department of Management
Sciences, UMIST

Sheila Wolfendale
Course Tutor to MSc in Educational
Psychology
Department of Psychology
North East London Polytechnic

Kevin Wheldall
Director
Centre for Child Study
University of Birmingham

Name index

Subject index